SOUTH AFRICAN FROGS

SOUTH AFRICAN
FROGS

N. I. PASSMORE Ph.D.
and
V. C. CARRUTHERS

WITWATERSRAND UNIVERSITY PRESS
JOHANNESBURG
1979

1 Jan Smuts Avenue, 2001 Johannesburg
South Africa

ISBN 0 85494 525 3

Printed by Cape & Transvaal Printers (Pty) Ltd, Cape Town
BD7862

TO JANE AND ALISON

CONTENTS

FOREWORD

Neville Passmore, zoologist, and Vincent Carruthers, naturalist and photographer, constitute a remarkable team. To me it is not surprising that their collaboration has resulted in this fine work. Both are true enthusiasts — the sort of people, always in short supply, who show the rest of us what can be done. The calls, the photographs and the observations which, together, make up this book, have been attained under the most difficult conditions and with the greatest of care.

Having worked with them in the field, I have come to realize that there is a fascination to 'frogging' which makes one quite forget any discomfort, and which makes every outing an adventure. This is why I welcome this book. It will, I hope, be the way to a fuller life for many. It will guide the newcomer gently into the specialized world of frogs, and show him beauty he would never expect. It will also guide him to the work still to be done — work to which the keen amateur can contribute.

Frog studies in South Africa are still very incomplete, but now we have a practical guide for all which should stimulate fresh enthusiasm for this fascinating group of animals which have been on earth so much longer than man. Elsewhere, frog studies have contributed much to our knowledge of species and speciation, to animal behaviour and to ecology. I shall be surprised indeed if this book does not initiate a tide of such studies in South Africa.

H. E. H. Paterson
Professor and Head, Department of Zoology
University of the Witwatersrand
Johannesburg

ACKNOWLEDGEMENTS

We are grateful to the many people who, with willing and generous assistance, have contributed to the completion of this book.

Special thanks are due to Mr H. H. Braack of the National Parks Board, and Mr J. Culverwell of Mbabane who gave us considerable assistance in the field and spared no effort to provide us with information and specimens for photography. We also wish to thank the following people for their help in the acquisition of material: Dr A. Channing, Mr J. Clarke, Dr D. Dodds, Mr F. L. Farquharson, Mr J. C. Greig, Mr M. Picker, Dr J. C. Poynton, Mr G. Ranger, Mr B. Rose, Dr D. E. van Dijk, Mr J. Visser, Mr P. Watson and Mrs M. Winkens. We are grateful to the Transvaal Museum, and in particular to Mr W. Haacke, the Natal Museum and the South African Museum for the loan of preserved specimens.

Several people kindly gave up their time in order to assist us in the field. We wish to thank Mr J. Andrews, Mr O. Borquin, Mr R. Boycott, Dr A. Channing, Mr C. H. Fey, Mr P. C. Fleischack, Dr C. Gow, Dr J. Loveridge, Mr L. R. Minter, Mr M. Picker, Mr K. Thomson, Mr R. Veale and Mr B. Washington for so generously making their time available to us.

We are grateful to Mr H. H. Braack for permission to use calls from his excellent library of amphibian recordings, and to Mr R. Boycott, Dr A. Channing, Mr G. Craye, Mr J. C. Greig, Mr L. R. Minter, Mr M. Picker, Dr J. C. Poynton and Mr S. R. Telford for providing voice recordings of several species.

We acknowledge with thanks the assistance given by Dr J. C. Poynton of the University of Natal, and Dr J-L. Perret, of the Muséum d'Histoire Naturelle, Geneva, on questions of nomenclature.

We have enjoyed the help and hospitality of many institutions and private property owners in the course of our field studies. In particular, we wish to tender our special thanks to Dr U. de V. Pienaar, Director Nature Conservation, National Parks Board, the Board itself, and the Department of Forestry, Zululand region, for the enthusiastic manner in which they encouraged us to work in the areas under their jurisdiction. Thanks are also due to the Transvaal Nature Conservation Division, the Cape Department of Nature and Environmental Conservation, and the Inanda Game Park for permission to work in their reserves. The hospitality of Mr E. A. Galpin and Mr R. Galpin of Mosdene Private Nature Reserve, Mr I. Garland of Twinstreams, Mr and Mrs L. McGregor of Canowie, and Mr G. Ranger of Glennifer is gratefully acknowledged.

We thank the Council for Scientific and Industrial Research for its financial contribution towards the cost of conducting this study, and the Senate Research Committee of the

University of the Witwatersrand, Johannesburg for providing funds towards the purchase of sound recording equipment.

We wish to thank Dr D. E. van Dijk of the University of Natal for providing photographs of the limbs of *Leptopelis xenodactylus*, page 223, Ms C. O'G. Deane for the illustration of call sites on page 13, Mr R. Boycott for the photograph of *Breviceps adspersus pentheri*, page 102, and Mr J. Thompson and Mr P. Hudson of the University of the Witwatersrand for printing the black and white photographs.

Johannesburg 1979

N. I. Passmore
V. C. Carruthers

We wish to thank the copyright holders for permission to quote from and reproduce illustrations from the following publications:

CHANNING, A. Life histories of frogs in the Namib desert. *Zoologica Africana* 11, 1976. Zoological Society of Southern Africa. CHANNING, A. and VAN DIJK, D. E. *A Guide to the Frogs of South West Africa.* Illus. Librarian, University of Durban-Westville Press. CARRUTHERS, V. C. *A Guide to the Identification of the Frogs of the Witwatersrand.* Illus. Conservation Press, Johannesburg. CARRUTHERS, V. C. The Sandveld Pyxie — a new species of frog from the Kruger National Park. Illus. *Custos,* June 1976. National Parks Board of Trustees, Pretoria. CARRUTHERS, V. C. and ROBINSON, G. A. Notes on amphibia in the Tsitsikama National Parks. Illus. *Koedoe,* 20, 1977. National Parks Board of Trustees, Pretoria. HART, SUE. In the wild. *Rand Daily Mail*, 1 July, 1975. South African Associated Newspapers. LAURENT, R. *Traite de Zoologie* — Amphibian Systematics. Illus. Professor P-P. Grassé. PASSMORE, N. I. Mating calls and other vocalizations of five species of *Ptychadena* (Anura: Ranidae). Illus. *South African Journal of Science* 73 (7), July 1977. Editor. PASSMORE, N. I. Vocalizations and breeding behaviour of *Ptychadena taenioscelis* (Anura: Ranidae). *Zoologica Africana* 11, 1976. Fig. 2. Zoological Society of Southern Africa. POYNTON, J. C. *The Amphibia of Southern Africa: a faunal study. Annals of the Natal Museum* 17, 1964. Director of the Natal Museum, Pietermaritzburg. POYNTON, J. C. and PRITCHARD, S. Notes on the biology of *Breviceps*. (Anura: Microhylidae). *Zoologica Africana* 11 (2), 1976. Zoological Society of Southern Africa. ROSE, W. *The Reptiles and Amphibians of Southern Africa.* Maskew Miller, Cape Town. We also include quotations reprinted from *Amphibians of Malawi* by M. M. Stewart by permission of the State University of New York Press.

Witwatersrand University Press

INTRODUCTION

This book is essentially a field guide intended to help amateur naturalists and professional biologists working on the ecology, behaviour or evolution of frogs. In spite of their abundance in South Africa, frogs in their natural state seem to have attracted less investigation than other vertebrates, and our knowledge of their ecology remains extremely limited. Since the validity of field work depends on reliable identification of animals, it is to this end that the book is chiefly directed.

A work of this nature only becomes possible after a comprehensive treatment of the systematics of the group. In South Africa this was provided in 1964 with the publication of a monographic revision of *The Amphibia of Southern Africa* by Poynton. We have also had the benefit of the ecological and life-cycle studies published by Rose, *The Reptiles and Amphibians of Southern Africa*, Wager, *The Frogs of South Africa*, and other authors. These pioneering works have done much to stimulate interest and it is hoped that this field guide will add momentum to that trend.

Unavoidably the coverage has been restricted largely to the area within the boundaries of South Africa. Nevertheless, the frog fauna of this region is appreciable, and there is a high percentage of endemism so the employment here of political rather than ecological boundaries is, we hope, excusable.

Being a guide to identification, the emphasis is on species and the ways in which they can be reliably distinguished from one another. Since many of the established species criteria have a morphological basis, and since the external form of an animal is immediately apparent, considerable attention is given throughout the book to structure. The description and characterization of frog species in purely verbal terms is seldom adequate and sometimes impossible. Extensive use has therefore been made of photographs to avoid lengthy and often ineffective descriptions. In addition, the over-all *look* of an animal is frequently an important basis for identification. This often defies verbal description, but is at once evident in a photograph.

Despite the obvious emphasis on external form, it is always inadvisable to completely divorce structure from *function*, and attempts are made to relate the two wherever possible. The initial part of the book explains some aspects of function with which many readers may not be familiar, and which may make field observations more interesting and rewarding.

At the time of going to press, the authors were aware of several yet undescribed species and subspecies which occur in the region covered by this book. These have been excluded from the present treatment as formal descriptions have not as yet been published.

Photographs

A colour photograph is provided for each species. The backgrounds in these photographs are authentic, and generally indicate the type of environment in which the species might be found. Most aspects of morphology are variable within species, and for this reason, no single photograph can ever be entirely typical of all individuals. Only specimens with commonly encountered coloration have, however, been photographed. Where variation in colour and pattern is substantial, this is indicated in the description and, wherever possible, examples of some of the major differences have been illustrated.

Black and white photographs have been used to illustrate details. A dorso-lateral view reproduced to actual size has been included in each species treatment. This indicates, not the maximum size, but the *usual* adult size. In the species descriptions, attention is drawn only to those characters which differentiate a species from *others in the same genus*. Generic differences are pointed out in the illustrations accompanying the generic descriptions.

In view of the variations which might arise between populations of a species in different regions, the locality of the specimen is given below each illustration. The photographer's name also appears below any photograph which was not taken by V. C. Carruthers. A few of the photographs have been published previously by the authors.*

Sound Recordings

Considerable emphasis is given in this book to frog sounds. It has long been recognized that the voice is the *most diagnostic* feature of any frog species. Furthermore, it is more usual to hear a frog than to see it distinctly. Verbal descriptions of voices convey little to anyone who has not previously heard the call and the use of a gramophone record has been preferred, with brief verbal 'reminders' in the text. In cases where calls have been described in the literature, but where a recording has not been available, the written description has usually been quoted.

The species occur in the same sequence in both the text and the record. Each voice is preceded by an identification of the species. A list of the species is provided on the record cover.

Sonagrams

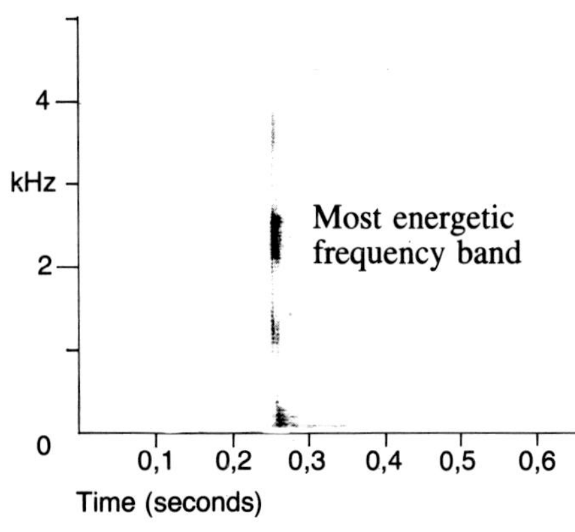

For all recorded calls, a wide-band (300 Hz) *sonagram* of one and occasionally two calls is provided in the text. These are located on the first page of each species section. All sonagrams are directly comparable with one another, and the same scale has been used throughout.

There is no mystique attached to sonagrams and basic interpretation is easier than reading music. Sonagraphic analysis has recently become a standard technique in the study of animal sounds.

**Custos*, June 1976; *Koedoe*, 20, 1977; *A Guide to the Identification of the Frogs of the Witwatersrand*, Johannesburg, Conservation Press, 1976; *South African Journal of Science*, Vol. 73, No. 7, July 1977.

It provides a simple pictorial representation of a sound using combinations of two co-ordinates. In this work these co-ordinates are *time* on the horizontal axis and *frequency* on the vertical axis. In addition, the darkness of the pattern of the sonagrams indicates the amplitude of the sound. The following examples illustrate how commonplace sounds are portrayed sonagraphically:

Example 1. Frequency

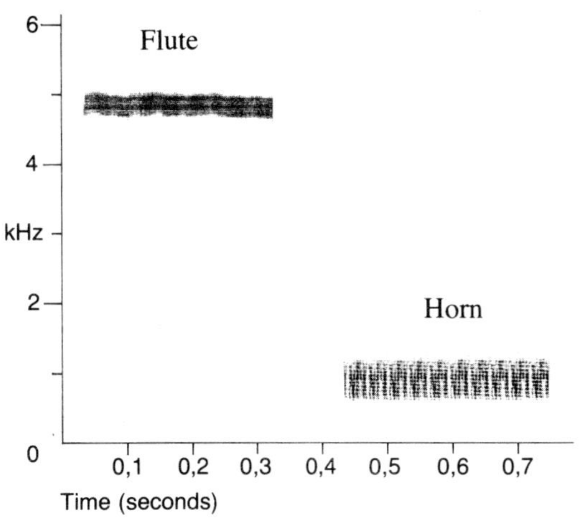

The high pitched sound of a note played on a flute is high on the frequency axis when compared with the low pitched sound of a ship's horn.

Example 2. Duration

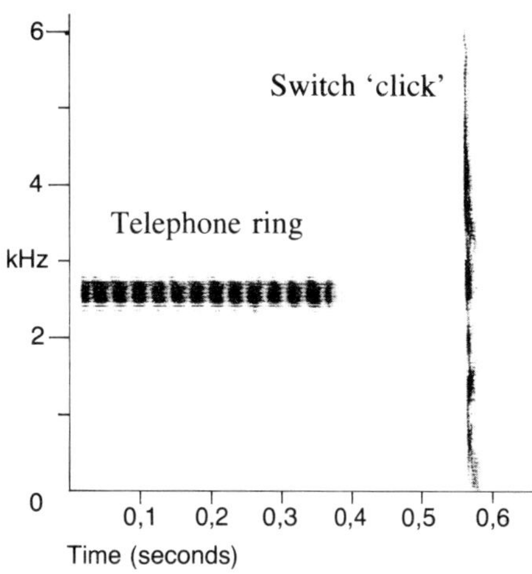

The single ring of a 'cricket' telephone spans a considerable distance along the time axis compared with the short sound produced by throwing a light switch.

Example 3. Pulse

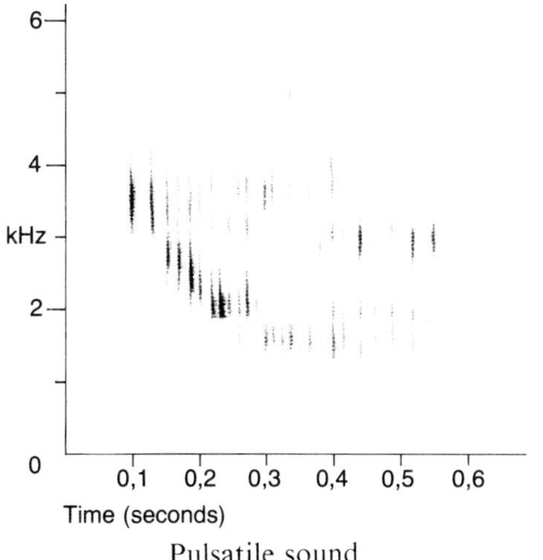

Pulsatile sound

Drawing a fingernail across the teeth of a comb produces a pulsatile noise depicted as a series of discrete marks. Compare these with the continuous blackening produced by the flute and horn in Example 1.

By listening to the record while examining the corresponding sonagrams, the reader will soon become proficient at 'reading' sound patterns, and will then be in a position to evaluate call differences directly from the sonagrams. It is extremely difficult to assess differences between calls on a purely aural basis, but when represented pictorially, the differences are at once evident.

Nomenclature

The present work is not a formal systematic treatment of the South African Amphibia. The nomenclature and systematic arrangement adopted by J. C. Poynton in *The Amphibia of Southern Africa: A Faunal Study* has been followed, and justification for the few deviations which were considered necessary is given in the text. Synonyms are provided only in cases where the nomenclature differs from that employed by Poynton. It was not considered necessary to duplicate the exhaustive treatment of synonyms contained in the above study.

In cases where a species comprises several described subspecies, these have not been treated separately, but rather as part of the total morphological variability of the species as a whole. The application of subspecific status is discussed in the first chapter. No attempt is made in the present work to validate all the described subspecies, but subspecific nomenclature is given in the text in order to stimulate further work in this direction. The morphological differences between presently recognized subspecies are tabled in the Appendix.

English common names have been included for each species. In all cases, a group name is applied to each genus, and this is qualified by a second descriptive name. Where possible, the latter name refers to a recognizable feature or habit of the species.

Many common names have been used for South African frogs, and all the published names known to the authors are listed in the text. New names have been coined only in those few instances where none existed previously, or where none of the earlier names were, in our opinion, appropriate. The most important sources of common names are *The Frogs of South Africa* by V. A. Wager, and *The Reptiles and Amphibians of Southern Africa* by W. Rose. Names have also been taken from the works of Broadley, Cochran, Hewitt, Pienaar, Poynton, Stewart, Channing and Van Dijk.

Vernacular names in other South African languages have been omitted, as it would have been impossible to have covered these comprehensively.

The Key

The descriptions of the species have been divided into sections based on generic groups. A key is provided to aid the reader, when identifying a frog, to establish the genus to which it belongs, and hence locate the section in which it is described. The key has been devised for use on living animals, and complete reliance has been placed on external characters. Positive identification is sometimes difficult on the basis of such features alone. The key is therefore not infallible, and identification should always be substantiated by reference to the illustrations and the listed diagnostic characters of the species concerned.

Maps

For each species, distribution maps have been provided in which shaded areas enclose all recorded localities in South Africa. Where the pattern appears to be discontinuous, and the intervening area has been poorly collected, arrows are used to indicate the probable over-all distribution.

SPECIES AND SUBSPECIES

THE SPECIES

In the majority of animals the sexes are separate, and male and female individuals must meet in order to reproduce. This encounter of the sexes is of fundamental importance, and without it sexuality could not effectively be involved in reproduction. The fact that different kinds of animals exist implies that, under natural conditions, sexually reproducing individuals mate 'each after their own kind'. The Latin word 'species' means literally 'a particular kind', and 'each after its own species' describes accurately the situation in animals, where mating almost always occurs between members of the same species.

Given that mating occurs between conspecific sexual partners, it follows that males and females of each species must be capable of meeting and recognizing one another. Numerous adaptations have evolved to ensure that this occurs on a regular and efficient basis. These varied adaptations consist essentially of signals and specially tuned responses between conspecific males and females. Paterson, who has contributed significantly in this field, has called these signal systems specific mate recognition systems (SMRS). Each sexually reproducing species is equipped with its own SMRS which is essential in organisms which reproduce in this fashion.

The action of the SMRS allows for a very precise choice of mating partners, and mistakes are rare under natural conditions. The system ensures that genes are exchanged only between members of the same species, and the species can therefore be thought of as comprising a 'gene pool'. The definition of species in terms of 'a closed gene pool' is widely accepted, but it is the SMRS which prescribes the limits of the gene pool by controlling the pattern of gene exchange between individuals. Paterson has therefore defined the species as *a group of organisms which share a common mate recognition system*.

This definition is an acceptable one in biological terms. It does not imply that species are inflexible units that do not change in the course of time. Furthermore, it does not define the species in terms of its possession of a particular set of observable characters. It therefore accommodates the fact that considerable phenotypic variation occurs in all species.

Fairly extensive morphological variation within a single species is a well-established fact. For example, humans vary considerably in many aspects of external appearance, yet there is no doubt that they all comprise one species. Conversely, there are valid biological species that are morphologically very similar and are difficult to distinguish by ordinary means. These are generally called *sibling species*. Because of their similarity to other related species, they are often discovered by accident, and only on close inspection do small differences in appearance then become evident. There is no reason to believe that species must be vastly different from one another in their appearance. The species concept defined above does not rely on particular distinctive phenotypic characters, and it succeeds in establishing the distinctness of sibling species. Furthermore, by using mate recognition signals to distinguish species, we are using the very same methods that the animals themselves are, and it is likely that reliable decisions will be made. Another important attribute of the SMRS is that it is stable, since any individual departing from the norm would not find a mate and would leave no progeny. The genes governing this 'radical departure' would therefore not be represented in future generations. Reproductive success would be limited to those individuals displaying the typical mate recognition system for the species concerned. Only those genes governing the normal mate recognition system would be represented in the offspring. In this way the mate recognition system is self-stabilizing and therefore subject to little variability within species.

The process of mate recognition is often very complex. Elaborate display and courtship patterns are common and involve visual recognition, and touch, sound and chemical attractants. In the great majority of species we know very little about inter-mate signalling, and in most cases investigation and characterization of the signals is difficult and may require sophisticated equipment and exhaustive observation. The mate recognition systems of frogs centre around acoustical signalling, and the sounds involved are loud, distinct and well within the range of human hearing. The most commonly heard sounds are the mating calls of the males which facilitate the meeting of the sexes. These important auditory cues are common night sounds which are regularly produced and easily analysed. In view of this, frogs are an excellent group in which to examine the real implications of the word *species*.

The Subspecies

The subspecies is a frequently used taxonomic category in frogs, and it is important to examine the implications of this taxonomic rank in the light of the species criteria outlined in the previous section.

Until fairly recently, species criteria had a purely morphological basis, as did subspecies criteria. Where the degree of morphological difference between two forms was extensive, they were considered distinct at the species level. Where only small morphological differences were evident, the forms were often considered to be only subspecifically distinct from one another. The employment of the subspecific category in this way is undesirable, because it assumes that species will differ extensively from one another in terms of their morphology. As discussed above, there is no reason why this should be the case.

Subspecific rank can be meaningfully applied where two populations of a species are geographically isolated from each other, and exhibit consistent differences. The isolates could differ in colour, pattern, behaviour or many other traits or combinations of them. The extent of the differences would depend on the nature of the environment and the length of the period of isolation. They would however, share a common mate recognition system. These subspecies are best regarded as *incipient species*. Depending on future events like climatic and topographical change or change in vegetation, any isolated population may equally develop into a new species, or be reabsorbed into a single homogeneous population if the geographical barriers break down.

In reality, few species appear to be physically divided into isolated populations which can be shown to be independent of one another. In addition, few populations appear to have known fixed limits. We therefore know very little about the extent of gene flow between adjacent populations and no purpose is served by the erection of subspecies under these circumstances.

Within the geographical range of a widespread species, characters may vary in a *clinal* fashion, i.e. in the form of a smooth character gradient from one end of the range to the other. This variation is due to the presence of environmental gradients. The recognition of subspecies at various points along the cline is impossible. In reality the concepts of clines and subspecies are separate issues, and they are best not confused.

Situations have been described where the character gradient, e.g., in colour, is not smooth from one end of the range to the other, but shows distinct steps. Each of these has then been treated as a separate subspecies. However, each 'subspecific step' may intergrade with the next to some extent, and the allotted subspecific rank then does nothing more than recognize a particular, and often rather hazily defined, portion of the total variation in the character concerned. If formal recognition was accorded to each portion of the variation in every character, a totally chaotic situation would result.

It is not being suggested that morphological variation within species is unimportant, or that it should be ignored. On the contrary, morphological variation is prevalent in most species, and the nature of this variation and its causes remain just as important in the absence of subspecific recognition — and perhaps biologically more intelligible.

The morphologically based subspecies has drawn attention to the variability within many taxa and there is a pressing need to re-examine a large proportion of our frog fauna using characters other than external morphology. This approach will undoubtedly reveal that some of the presently recognized subspecies represent nothing more than a loosely demarcated portion of the total specific variation, while in other cases, good species are probably veiled by the subspecific label.

FROG SOUNDS

Most species of frogs are capable of producing a variety of sounds which comprise what may be loosely termed a small 'vocabulary'. The different components do not constitute speech as we know it, and they should not be considered as comparable to words in human language. Nevertheless, the different categories of sounds do convey information and they are useful and important in the lives of these animals.

Sounds and Species

The most commonly heard vocabulary component is the mating call. The mating calls of all species examined to date differ significantly from each other. These calls are therefore species-specific and highly characteristic. The mate recognition system here has two essential parts which are closely connected:

1. The production of a unique species-specific signal by the male.
2. The approach of a conspecific female in response to the call, with the subsequent pairing of the sexes.

The importance of species-specific mate recognition systems has been discussed in the previous section, and the finding that calls differ extensively between species makes them highly reliable as characters upon which to base the diagnosis of species.

Sound Production

The production of sound is seldom a simple process, but in essence it consists of the following:

1. Inflating the lungs to a greater capacity than is the case during normal breathing.
2. A rapid shift of this air from the lungs to the buccal cavity, setting the vocal cords of the larynx vibrating.
3. The sound thus produced is usually intensified by resonance in a thin-walled extension of the buccal cavity — the vocal sac.
4. Most of the air in the vocal sac is then shunted back to the lungs and utilized repeatedly in the production of subsequent calls.

N.I. Passmore

N.I. Passmore

Transfer of air between lungs and vocal sacs

Several different vocal sac configurations are evident. A rigid categorization of these is inadvisable, since many intermediate conditions occur. However, three broad groups are recognizable on the basis of external form, and these are described below.

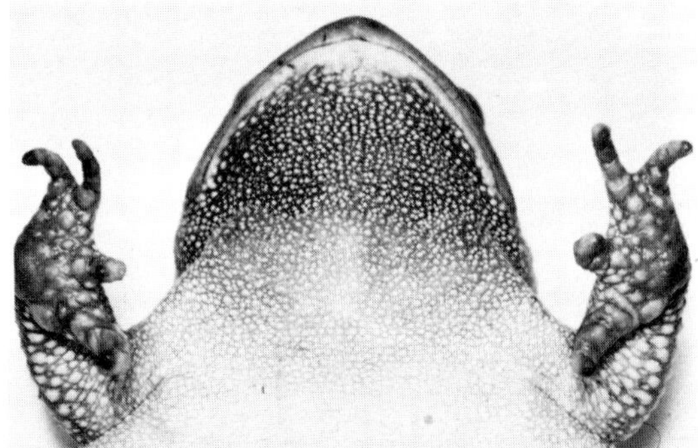

Median subgular sac

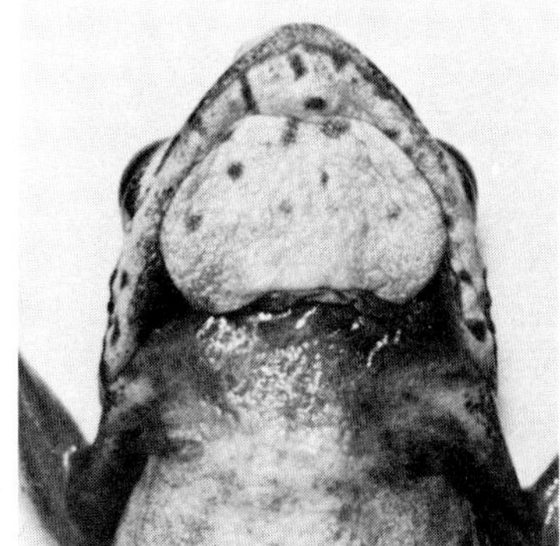

Median subgular sac with gular disc

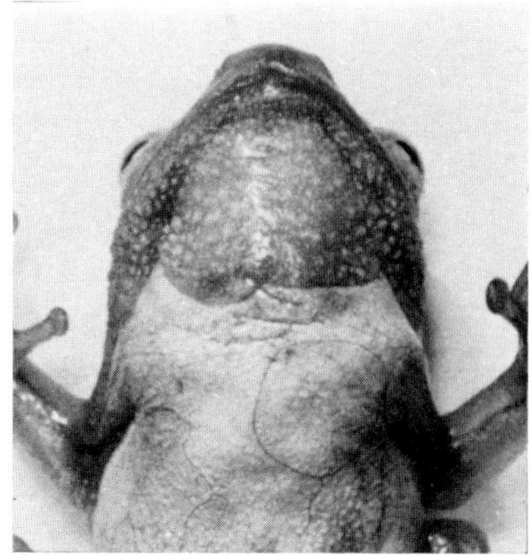

Paired subgular sac

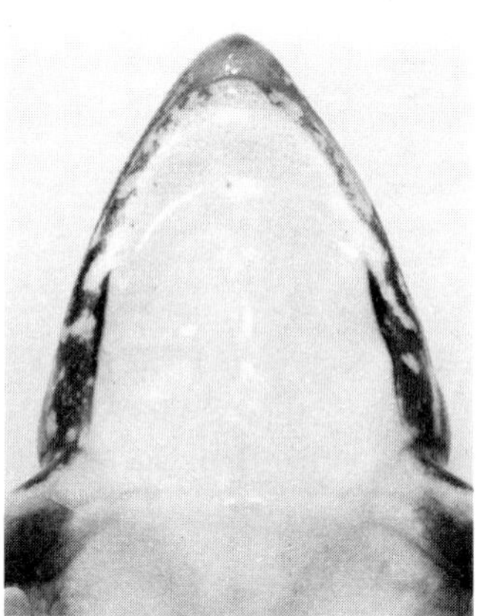

N.I. Passmore

Paired lateral sacs

The *median subgular sac* is single, and located beneath the throat. The majority of South African species possess this type of sac. The external covering ranges from unmodified gular skin to a thin membranous lining of muscle and skin. The *paired subgular sac* has two lobes separated by a median partition. In some cases the two lobes are distinct, but their separation is less clear in others, which appear to be intermediate between the single and paired condition. The *paired lateral sacs* are unmistakable. They are thin membranous structures which emerge from slits located on the side of the head, behind and below the angle of the jaws. Vocal sacs are absent in *Xenopus*, where the calls are produced under water.

A Classification of some Frog Calls

1. *The Mating Call*

Mating calls are produced only by adult males during the breeding season. Males aggregate at the breeding site and produce this call in concert with others, thereby forming a chorus. As mentioned previously, the principal role of the mating call is the attraction of conspecific females to the calling males, with the resultant pairing of the sexes. Other effects of this call include directing the movements of other males towards the breeding site and regulating their distribution relative to one another during calling.

Mating calls vary little within species, but both temperature and size of the caller do have some influence on call structure, and should therefore be considered when comparing calls of different species. In view of the importance of the mating call in the mate recognition system of frogs, only those species which differ adequately in call would be capable of co-existing sympatrically.

The intensity of the mating call varies from species to species, but it is usually clearly audible to the unaided ear, and in some species may reach levels capable of causing discomfort to nearby humans.

2. *The Male Release Call*

In the majority of species males clasp both females and other males indiscriminately and sex recognition occurs only after mounting has been accomplished. If the individual that is seized is a male, its protestations take the form of a writhing or struggling movement, accompanied by the emission of short sounds. These are different from the mating call, but are also species-specific and appear to evoke the release of the inadvertently clasped male. In contrast, if the seized individual is a sexually receptive female, no such protestations are evident and no sound is produced. Male release calls function essentially as *sex* recognition signals, the importance of which on dark nights is immediately evident. Male release calls can often be elicited by grasping a male with the thumb and forefinger in the region of the axilla.

3. *Female Release Call*

This vocabulary component has been reported in some species and has no doubt been overlooked in others. It is uttered by *sexually unreceptive* females in response to being clasped by a male.

4. *The Territorial Call*

Calls that function in the maintenance of spacing between calling individuals have been reported in a number of species. In some cases this function is served by the mating call, but in others special territorial calls are produced. Territorial calls are usually uttered only when adjacent calling males are closely located, and they result in the silence or retreat of one or both of the interacting individuals. These are relatively uncommon vocalizations in most species and are really only detectable with careful and extensive observation.

5. *The Distress Call*

This constitutes a further call type which has been reported in many genera. They are often given on being seized by a predator, and although experimental proof is lacking, it has been suggested that they may put other frogs in the vicinity on the alert.

The Co-existence of Frog Sounds

The aquatic habitats utilized by frogs for purposes of breeding are many and varied. Very often a number of different species utilize the same body of water concurrently and therefore share the total resources of the breeding locality in both time and space. Situations where only one species is breeding at a time are the exception rather than the rule, and in South Africa it is not uncommon to find ten or more species breeding synchronously.

Breeding occurs principally in shallow water. Calling animals are therefore often concealed by vegetation. Furthermore, calling is mostly a nocturnal activity and in these circumstances chance encounters of the sexes are virtually eliminated. There is almost complete reliance on the mating call to facilitate the meeting of the sexes.

Because the function of mating calls is to act as species-specific mate attractant signals, all sympatric species breeding synchronously have to signal their mates differently. This is achieved by utilizing calls which differ in terms of their physical structure, and by temporal separation of the calls or spatial separation of the callers.

Structural Differences in Mating Calls

1. *Frequency Separation*

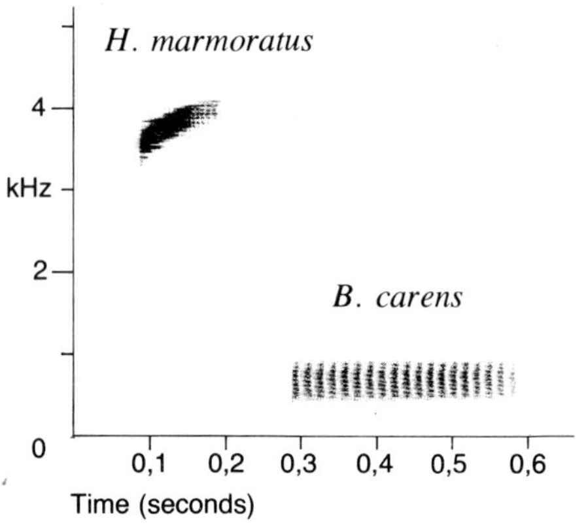

High- and low-pitched calls

The acoustical complexity in the environs of the breeding site is reduced because different species utilize different frequencies for the transmission of their calls. Some have high-pitched calls, e.g., *Hyperolius marmoratus*, and others lower pitched calls, e.g., *Bufo carens*. It has been shown in many species that the female's receptor (the ear) is preferentially receptive to the frequency range over which the conspecific male's call is transmitted.

This separation reduces acoustic 'jamming' which would result if many species were utilizing the same frequency band.

Differences in pitch are important, but there are limitations on the frequencies that can be effectively utilized in natural environments. For example, high frequencies attenuate more rapidly than do lower ones. The use of high frequencies for call transmission would therefore result in the loss, or at least substantial decrease, in the distance over which the call is effective. This is probably part of the reason why the principal frequencies employed by most frogs are below about 4-5 kHz.

2. *Call Pulse Rate*

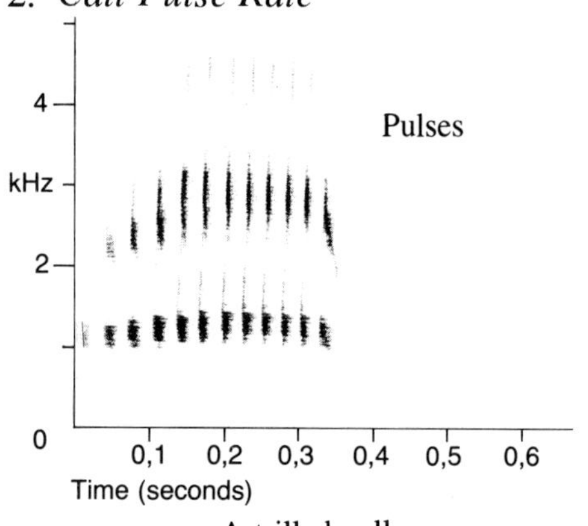

A trilled call

Most frog calls are trilled, i.e. they are divided up into successive bursts of sound, known as pulses, rather than being a continuum of sound. Where a number of species call together, calls could differ in the pattern of pulses. The most convenient measure here is the pulse rate, which is the number of pulses per unit time. Substantial differences usually exist between the pulse rates of different species, and at least in some species, females can distinguish conspecific males solely on the basis of this character.

In the great majority of grassland birds and frogs, the calls are trilled or pulsatile. It has been suggested that in savanna, selection favours information transfer in terms of temporal factors rather than in terms of signal frequency. The reasons for this are that high frequencies attenuate more rapidly and that sound frequencies are distorted by phenomena like air turbulence and temperature conditions. Frequency coding would, therefore, be less efficient.

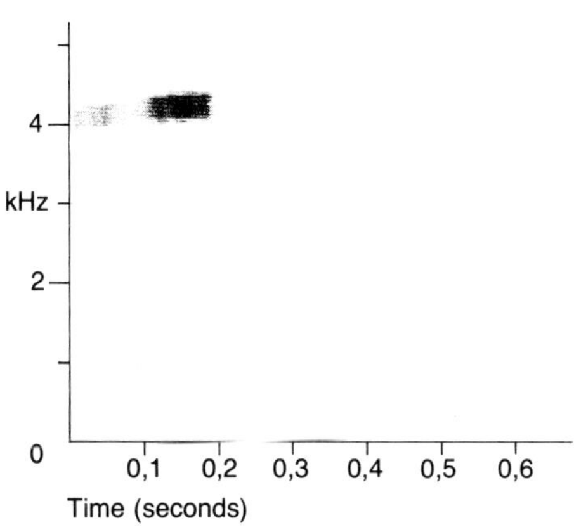

A pure tone-like forest call

In forest however, call reception may be more efficient for pure tone-like calls, against the background of wide band noise of rustling leaves. The forest atmosphere is relatively more stable with regard to temperature and air movements. This may permit the concentration of sound energy into a narrow band, which results in a pure tone-like call. This concentration of sound energy would result in a greater call volume and therefore more efficient long-distance communication.

3. *Call Duration*

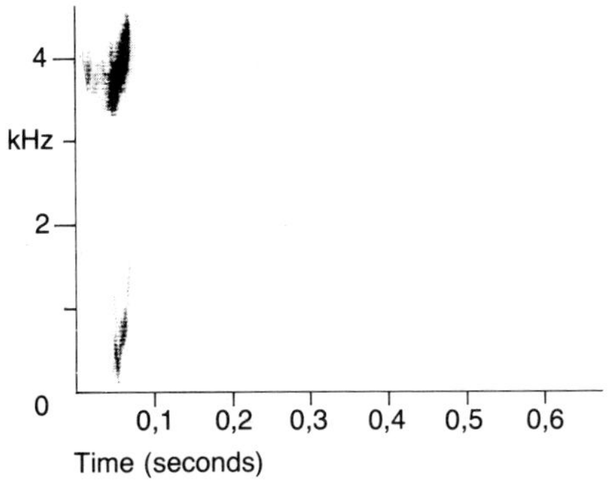

The short call of a *Rana*

Species differ considerably in the length of their calls. Some toads produce a single call that lasts a minute or more, while many other species have calls lasting less than 0,1 seconds.

Many of the South African species of *Rana*, where vocal sacs are inconspicuous, have extremely short calls. A concentration of the available sound energy into a call of short duration may compensate for the loss in amplitude associated with poorly developed vocal sacs.

4. *Frequency Modulation*

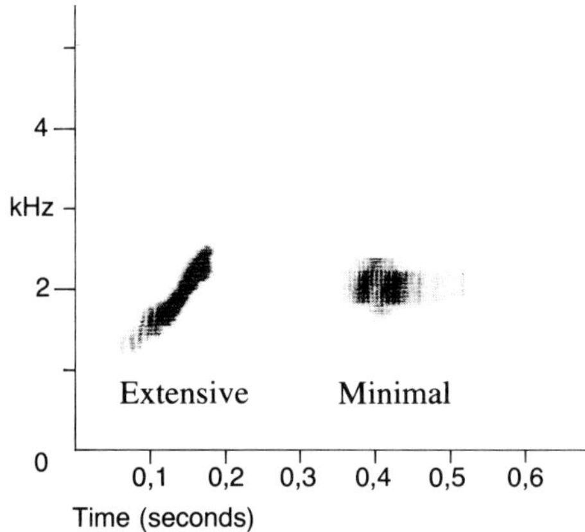

Calls differ both in the presence or absence, and in the extent, of frequency modulation. Some calls are markedly frequency modulated, while others show little or no frequency modulation. To the best of the authors' knowledge it is not known whether females can discriminate between species on the basis of this character or not. Nevertheless it remains a character which varies between species and warrants investigation.

Temporal and Spatial Separation

Where several species are calling together, the acoustical environment can become rather complex. The different unique signals can overlap each other in time, thus interfering with the effectiveness of the information transfer. In addition, the signals of those species with less intense vocal capabilities could feasibly be masked, or even obliterated, by the louder calls of other species. Acoustical complexity can be alleviated by *temporal* and *spatial separation* of the calls of the various individuals. There are several ways in which this can be achieved:

1. *Gross Separation of Times of Active Calling*

Where species diversity is high, there are often obvious differences in the periods during which the different species are most active.

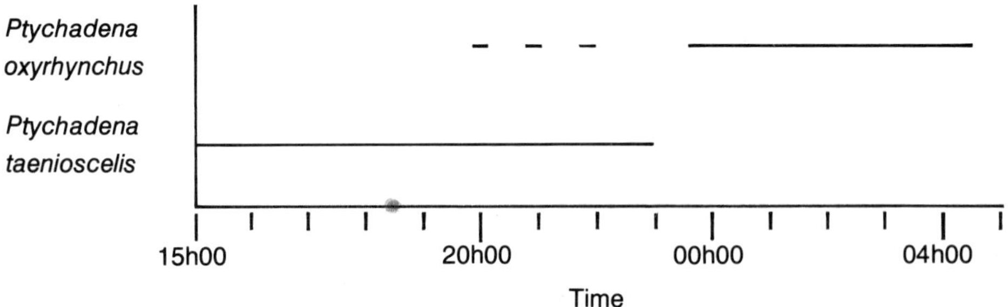

Periods of active calling in two species of *Ptychadena*

Different preferred calling times have the effect of simplifying the acoustics of the breeding site considerably and it appears to be a useful arrangement which one might expect to encounter frequently. However, many of the species observed by the authors do not appear to have markedly different preferred calling times. Although tendencies in this direction are sometimes noticeable, there is invariably considerable overlap in the calling times of different species. In general in South Africa, the majority of species reach peak calling levels before midnight.

2. *Antiphonal Calling between Conspecific Individuals*

Temporal factors appear to be equally important *within* species. Consider the following situation: Six conspecific males are located fairly close to one another, and are separated by 20-30 cm. If calls were uttered simultaneously by each of the six callers, then the resulting temporal overlap in the signals of each would greatly increase the conglomerate noise around an approaching female. Females appear to locate males simply by using their ears and 'homing in' on the caller. A situation where six calls are presented concurrently, and from different directions, will certainly make the task of finding a mate more difficult.

On the other hand, temporal separation of the calls of adjacent males in a sequential or antiphonal manner would provide a sonically polarized situation — one in which location of a calling male would seem to be considerably more simple and effective.

Many frogs call in an antiphonal manner and duets or even trios of calling males are commonplace, at least during portions of the chorus. A comparable arrangement has also been observed between different species. Two species calling concurrently often consistently partition the available time in such a way that the calls of one species regularly occur during the intervals between successive calls of the other.

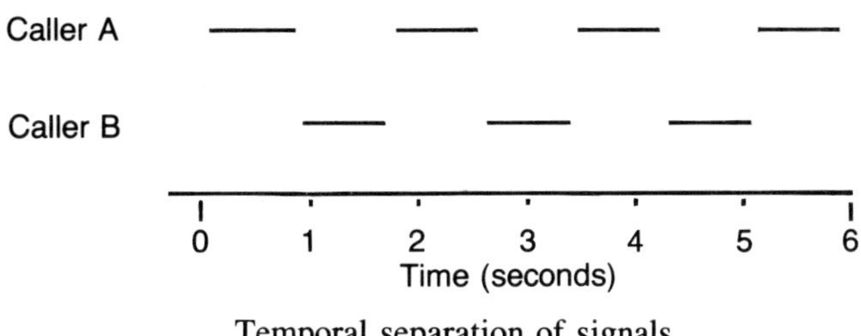

Temporal separation of signals

3. *Spatial Separation of Calling Males*

This is yet a third way of reducing gross acoustical complexity, and it can take a number of forms:

(a) The formation of aggregates. The distribution of calling males over the breeding site is seldom haphazard, and callers of particular species are often found grouped together in aggregates, despite the fact that the same 'calling niche' is available elsewhere. In such cases, the signals of the various species would emanate from different portions of the breeding site. This appears to be an approach towards gross polarization of breeding site acoustics.

(b) Calling site preferences. The location occupied by the calling male is highly variable between species, but usually fairly consistent within species. Tree Frogs call at various elevations above the ground, often from branches or leaves overhanging the water. A number of other species also have elevated call sites, but show distinct preferences for emergent sedges and reeds. The majority of South African species call from ground level, but here many different 'calling preferences' occur.

Many species call from the ground at the water's edge, but while some will habitually occupy exposed call sites in this region, others will seek more sheltered sites beneath overhanging vegetation or within grass tussocks.

Some species call while sitting in the water near the shore, or while clinging to emergent vegetation some distance from it. Calling while floating on the water is less common, but is the preferred position of some toads. Platannas vocalize under water and produce clearly audible sounds despite the absence of a vocal sac. Finally, subterranean calling is exhibited by some species and calls are produced from within their burrows.

In some closely related sympatric species, striking differences are evident in call site utilization. If the respective females show similar preferences with regard to the types of area they will enter when seeking a mate, then differences in calling position could be effective in facilitating conspecific matings. Although consistent call site preferences are not always present in closely related sympatric species, and this factor may not always play a primary role, it appears nevertheless to have some importance in this regard.

Another important consideration with regard to call sites is that the preferential occupation of particular sites amounts to further spatial separation of the different categories of callers, with the effect of increasing the gross polarization of the chorus. Calls of different species will emanate from different elevations, different portions of the shore depending on the vegetation, different regions of the water depending on its depth and the vegetation available for the bodily support of the caller.

In conclusion, although the way in which various concurrently produced signals can remain effective is not initially evident, this appears to be facilitated by a number of factors, the importance of which is not generally recognized. A large amount of useful work still remains to be done in this regard.

Examples of call sites

MATING

Much has been said in the previous sections about the attraction of the female to the male and the importance of vocalization in this process. The choice of a mate rests almost entirely with the female, and males simply call until a female arrives. In some species, the female is required to approach closely, or even touch the male, before clasping is attempted. In others however, the male literally pounces on the female as soon as she appears, or may even pursue her for some distance prior to pairing being accomplished.

Males of many species are largely indiscriminate with regard to what they will attempt to mate with. Some males may attempt to clasp any moving object in the vicinity which even remotely resembles a frog. The sentiments of herpetologist D. L. Jameson describe fairly accurately the apparent 'designs' of some male frogs: "If it is not small enough to eat nor large enough to eat you, and does not put up a squawk about it, mate with it."

This indiscriminate clasping behaviour seems to emphasize the importance of *inter-specific* territoriality at the breeding site. If males of two species are close to one another during calling, and a female is 'homing in' on one call type, she stands an equal chance of being clasped by the conspecific male or by the male of the other species. This is clearly an undesirable situation and one which would be alleviated to some extent by the methods of spatial separation of callers outlined in the previous pages.

The authors have found that the territorial calls of some sympatric species are similar and may therefore be more universally understood. The possibility exists that these calls may act to facilitate conspecific matings by influencing the distribution of calling males of different species relative to one another.

Amplexus is the clasping of the female by the male during mating. It differs from copulation in that fertilization is external and the male does not possess an intromittent organ serving to introduce the spermatozoa into the female reproductive ducts. Males are usually considerably smaller than the females and three types of amplexus occur.

1. *The Axillary Clasp*

Here the male straddles the female, clasping her with his forelimbs in the region of the axilla. Nuptial pads on the thumb or forearm of the male provide for an efficient 'grip' on the female until amplexus is terminated.

These are elevated roughened areas on the skin, which become enlarged during the breeding season. The relatively smaller size of the male and the axillary clasp allow for a close juxtaposition of the cloacae of the two sexes — an important feature because fertilization is external. Eggs and spermatozoa need to be deposited in close proximity to each other to ensure a high frequency of fertilization, since the effective life of spermatozoa in fresh water is short.

Forms displaying this type of clasp often initiate pairing whilst out of the water, and the male in this position does not appear to restrict the movements of the female, either in the initial approach to the water, or during the subsequent process of egg-laying. This is true even in the most agile of leapers.

2. *The Inguinal Clasp*

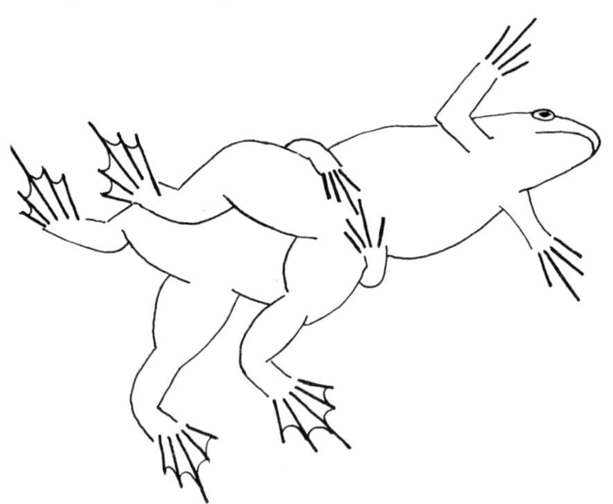

This occurs in the more primitive families, where the male clasps the female around the waist. Inguinal amplexus is typical of species that pair exclusively in the water, e.g., Platannas. In this type of amplexus, the cloacae of the male and female are not close together. Once the eggs are extruded, they pass posteriorly along the venter of the male and over his cloaca.

3. *Adhesion*

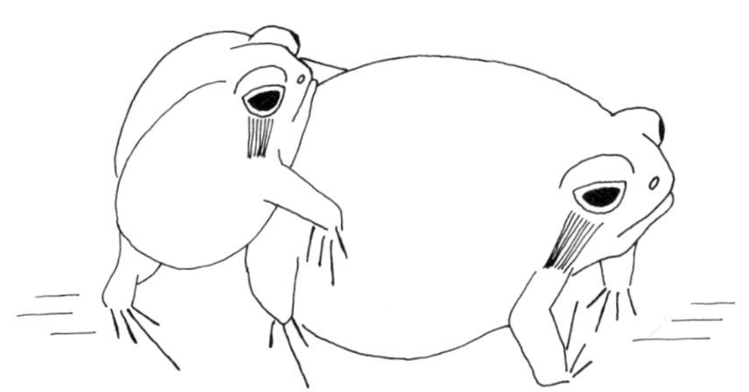

An unusual type of amplexus is exhibited by the Rain Frogs where the male becomes glued to the female for the duration of the process. This probably represents a modification of the axillary clasp associated with the stout body and short limbs of Rain Frogs.

There is considerable variability in the length of time the sexes remain in amplexus and there may be a delay between the initiation of clasping and the onset of egg-laying. In some species, the whole process of amplexus and egg-laying is completed in as little as 30 minutes, while in others it may last a few weeks. In the majority of forms, however, it is completed within several hours. The male generally remains silent during the process, and his main activity is usually a more or less continual 'pumping' or 'prodding' of the flanks of the female with his forelimbs.

At the moment of egg release, synchronized movements of both sexes occur. These appear to ensure the close proximity of eggs and spermatozoa. The movements vary from species to species, but where the clasp is axillary, the following general remarks apply.

1. Prior to the initiation of the egg-laying sequence, the female adopts a posture where the back is straightened or ventrally arched, and the two cloacae are more or less closely opposed.
2. This movement is accompanied by the ejection of eggs.
3. The ejaculation of seminal fluid by the male follows.

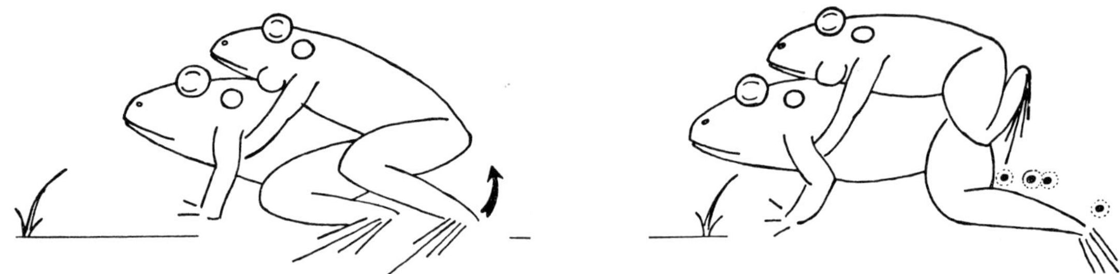

The egg-laying sequence

In many species, the male positions his feet over the juxtaposed cloacae at the moment of egg release. This allows for a funnelling of the seminal fluid over the freshly-extruded eggs. This egg-laying sequence is repeated, sometimes a large number of times, with each resulting in the deposition of a small batch of eggs. When oviposition has been completed, the female usually signals the dismissal of the male by a prolonged arching of the back or by a tonic stretching of her body, whereupon the male releases his grasp and the pair separates.

Where the inguinal clasp is employed, the cloacae of the two sexes are not close together at the time of egg release. The following procedure has been observed in Platannas. After emerging from the cloaca of the female, the eggs pass posteriorly along a shallow groove on the ventral surface of the male and pass his cloaca. Ejaculation by the male is presumably stimulated by this movement.

SPAWN

EGGS

Frog eggs are usually small and spherical, averaging 1-2 mm in diameter and they contain food reserves in the form of yolk. This provides for the nourishment of the embryo until the stage when the young organism is capable of abstracting its own food material from the environment.

Where the eggs are laid in water, the upper or animal hemisphere is fairly densely pigmented and may range in colour from shades of grey through brown to black. In contrast, the lower or vegetal hemisphere is far less densely pigmented and is usually yellow to grey-yellow in colour. The two areas shade into each other in the equatorial region of the egg. This phenomenon of *countershading* is consistently exhibited by open water breeders and does not appear to be an accidental occurrence. Consider that a predator looking into the water from above will see a darkly pigmented animal hemisphere against the predominantly dark background of the pond bottom. Equally, an aquatic predator, viewing the egg from beneath, will see the light coloured vegetal hemisphere against the bright background of the sky. This pattern of egg coloration would afford considerable protection to the egg by camouflaging it. This strategy is by no means peculiar to frog eggs; a host of other aquatic animals exhibit the same pattern of coloration, both in their larval and adult stages.

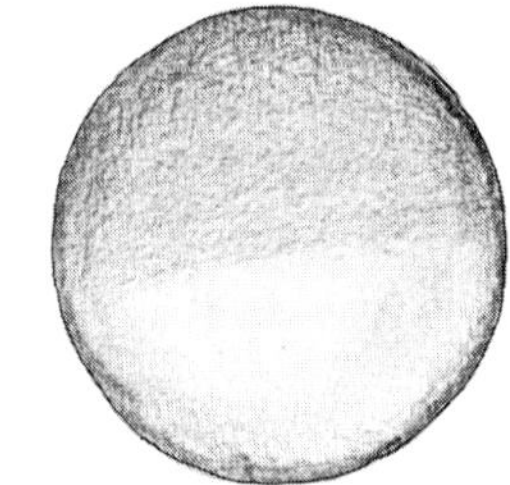

Countershaded egg

Egg pigment may also function in preventing excessive ultraviolet irradiation of the eggs, when these are exposed to strong sunlight in open water.

Where eggs are laid in burrows or nests on land, the advantages of pigmentation no longer apply, and the eggs are usually uniformly pale. In such cases, where an active foraging larval stage is absent, the eggs are very large and house large quantities of yolk.

EGG JELLY

As the egg passes down the oviducts of the female, prior to its expulsion to the exterior, a jelly-like oviducal secretion is deposited around it. This egg jelly is initially flaccid and translucent, but may thicken, enlarge and become less clear as development proceeds. The jelly may surround each egg individually, producing a translucent capsule with the egg at the centre, or the jelly envelopes of successive eggs may coalesce to form either egg cakes, clusters or strings.

Egg cake of Kloof Frog

Strings of toad eggs

Many advantages of the jelly covering are apparent. It is often sticky when the eggs are laid. This allows them to attach or be attached to objects in the water, thereby preventing translocation by water currents, or perhaps settling into anoxic areas less suitable for development. The adhesiveness also provides for some measure of concealment, by allowing adherent particles of detritus to break up the outline of the egg, thereby rendering it less visible to predators. The jelly is also shock-absorbent and prevents damage to the embryo by mechanical shock.

In a few species the egg jelly has some more bizarre uses. In Leaf-folding Frogs the eggs are laid on leaves, which are folded over and glued together by the jelly, thereby enclosing the brood in a leaf chamber. In Foam Nest Frogs, the oviducal secretion is beaten up into a stiff foam, producing a dehydration resistant nest in which the eggs develop out of water.

N. I. Passmore

Nest of Leaf-folding Frog

Foam Nest

In some of the terrestrial breeders, the egg capsules are very large. These, together with supernumerary 'egg-less' capsules, function to restrict dehydration in the burrows where they are laid.

Subterranean egg nest (Rain Frog)

In some species the jelly contains an antibiotic factor which acts to reduce bacterial growth. It may also offer physical protection from small predators, e.g., leeches.

Oviposition Sites

Eggs and the positions in which they are laid are subject to almost endless variation and provide a fascinating field of study. Attempts have been made to categorize modes of reproduction in frogs, and although boundaries between different proposed categories are sometimes rather indistinct, the categories make considerations of fecundity and ovum size more meaningful.

1. *Aquatic Development*

This includes the following:

(a) Species which deposit their eggs in open water and do not construct nests (e.g., Toads and the majority of South African species).

(b) Species constructing nests of some sort in the water, e.g., Leaf-folding Frogs.

(c) Species constructing nests on land or in trees overhanging the water, from which tadpoles hatch and migrate to the water, e.g., Foam Nest Frogs.

(d) Species where eggs are carried by a parent before advanced tadpoles are released into the water (no South African examples).

2. *Terrestrial Development*

(a) Species which construct nests in moss, under logs, etc., or in burrows. No aquatic larval stage. Parental care often evident, e.g., Rain Frogs.

(b) Eggs carried by parent, as in *(d)* above, but no free larval stage and the young emerge as froglets (no South African examples).

Numbers of Eggs

The number of eggs produced varies considerably with both mode of reproduction and the size of the female. Understandably, within species, larger females will produce more eggs than smaller females. Another general relationship is that larger species produce more eggs than do smaller ones, provided that comparison is limited here to species displaying the same mode of reproduction, i.e. both laying their eggs in open water, or both in nests beneath the surface. In species displaying terrestrial development, as outlined above, fecundity is greatly reduced and only a small number of eggs are produced. Some Rain Frogs lay 25-50 eggs, roughly 5 mm in diameter. This decrease in egg number is offset by parental care and the fact that the young are removed from aquatic predation. In contrast, many of the species showing aquatic development in open water produce many thousands of small eggs. The Guttural Toad for example, lays about 20 000, the great majority of which perish long before development is completed.

DEVELOPMENT AND TADPOLES

Embryonic Development

Adult amphibians are multicellular and the first and most obvious requirement is the transformation of the fertilized egg, which is a single cell, into a multicellular structure. This is accomplished by rapid successive mitotic division of the zygote — a process known as *cleavage*. It is an easy and thoroughly fascinating exercise to observe this process, with the aid of a hand lens, in freshly collected eggs.

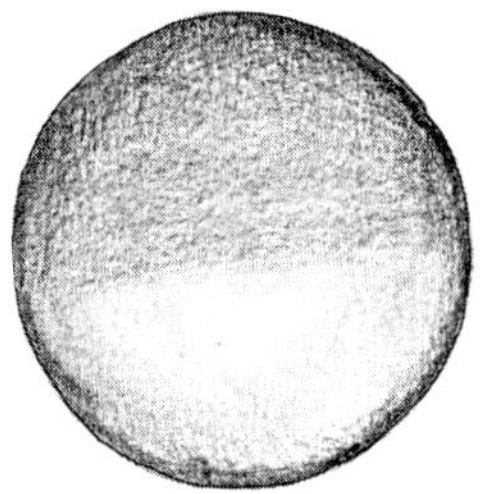
Egg

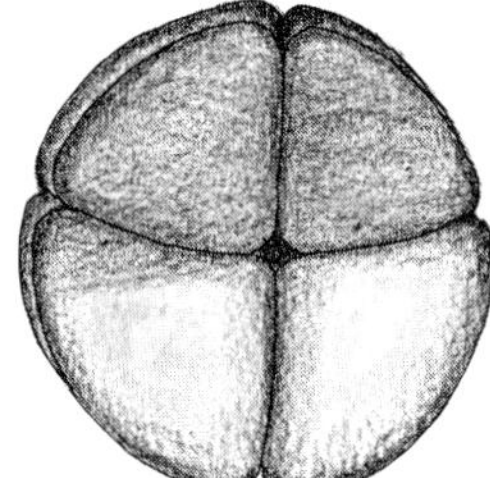
8 cell stage

Later cleavage

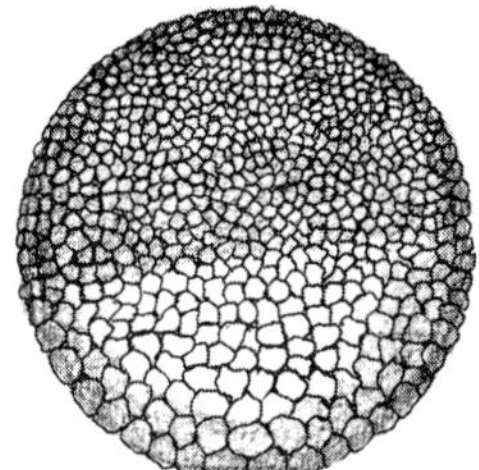
Multicellular embryo

Following the achievement of multicellularity, the embryo undergoes the process of *gastrulation*, after which it possesses the three body layers characteristic of most animals. Next, the rudiments of organs are laid down during the process of *organogenisis*.

Fine hair-like cilia develop on the surface of the body and these enable the embryo to rotate within the capsule, and they may assist in its respiration. However, the gills soon develop and assume the latter function.

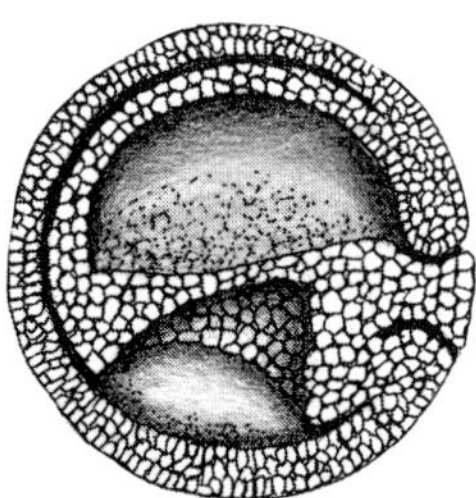
Gastrula
3 body layers present

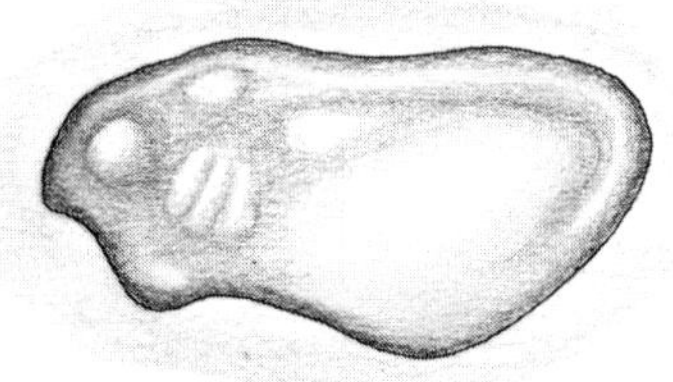
Early larva
organ rudiments present

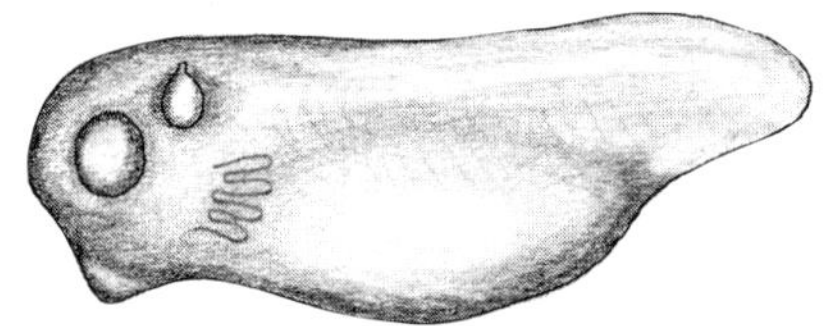
Early larva
tail developing, gills present

In time, the process of *hatching* takes place and the embryo escapes from the membranes and jelly which previously surrounded it. Hatching is accomplished by various combinations of enzymatic action, wriggling with the aid of newly-formed muscles, and ciliary action. A fully functional adhesive organ is present in most embryos by this stage, enabling attachment to objects in the water and thereby reducing the effects of water currents. Following hatching, the young animal is usually referred to as a *tadpole* or *larva*.

Tadpole Types — An Ecological Distinction

There are a number of different categories of tadpoles which occupy different broad aquatic niches:

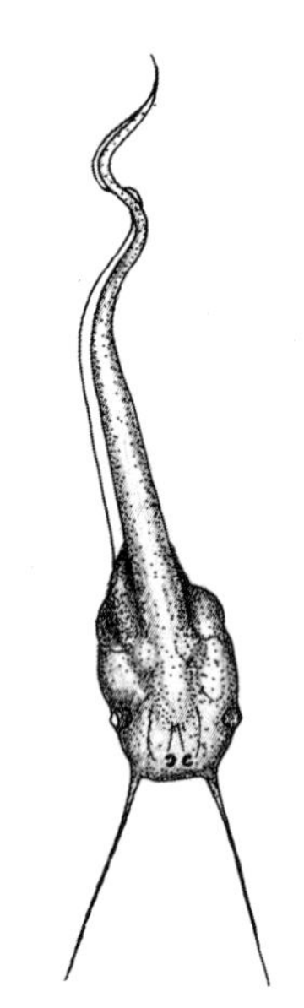

1. *The Nektonic Tadpole*

This tadpole type is an open-water dweller in lentic environments and remains continually suspended in the water by means of the active swimming movements of the enlarged tail. There is a tendency towards body transparency. They are plankton feeders and often assume characteristic orientations in the water.

2. *The Benthonic Tadpole*

These are bottom dwelling tadpoles with ventral mouths. They feed on algal crusts, leaves, detritus and periphyton. It is the common and 'typical' tadpole type of many species, and occurs mainly in the shallower regions of standing water. In some species (non-South African) these tadpoles are modified into active predacious carnivores by the development of large beaks and teeth.

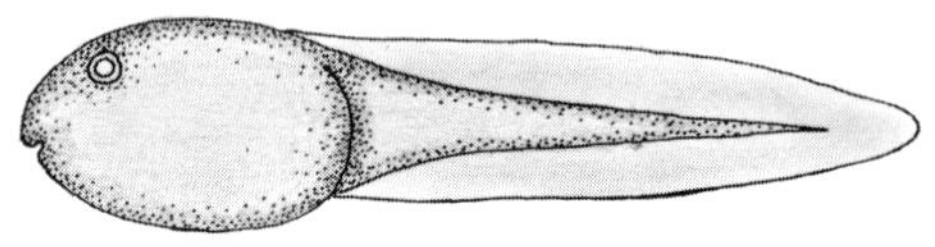

3. *Stream Dwelling and Torrent Tadpoles*

These are dorsoventrally flattened with ventral sucker-like mouths. This tadpole type is adapted for living in rapidly flowing water. The body is powerful, and the sucker acts as a holdfast, allowing the animal to attach to submerged objects and avoid being washed downstream.

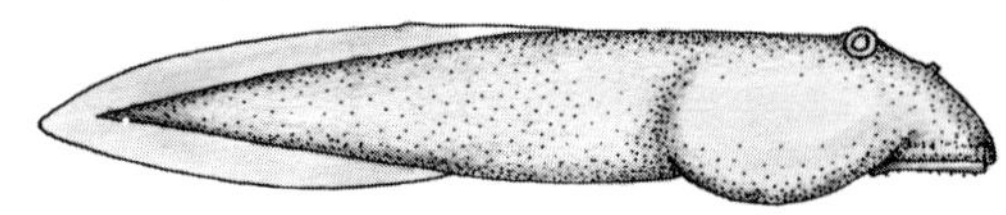

4. *Terrestrial Nest Tadpole*

These larvae complete their development in subterranean nests. They emerge as metamorphosed froglets, without having undergone an aquatic tadpole stage. They do not feed in the nest, and the mouth parts are consequently reduced. The tail is elongated and the fins are poorly developed.

Tadpoles in these different broad niches exploit the aquatic habitat in a variety of ways, and therefore utilize largely different portions of the available resources. This results in far less interspecific competition. Competition is further reduced by differences in breeding periods of the adults and the preferential exploitation of different microhabitats within the broad niches themselves. A recent study by Heyer has led to the conclusion that competition among tadpoles does not occur to any marked extent in nature.

It is therefore not surprising that tadpoles differ, not only in gross external appearance and proportions of body parts, but also in the structure of the feeding apparatus. Tadpole mouths reflect both the broad niches outlined above, and in many cases differences in microhabitat preferences as well. Mouth structure is therefore often a good systematic character and it is extremely useful in tadpole identification. More detailed treatments of tadpoles are given in the works of Van Dijk and Wager.

The Length of the Larval Life

The larval period varies considerably between species. In arid areas where water bodies persist for short periods of time, the larval life is often correspondingly short and may be completed within 3 weeks. In the majority of species the tadpole life lasts for 4-12 weeks, but it may be very much longer amongst species which breed in permanent waters. *Rana angolensis*, for example, commonly has a larval period of 9 months, but this may be extended to 2 or more years. Both low temperature and scarcity of food retard growth and extend the length of time spent as a larva.

Metamorphosis

At the end of the larval life, the tadpole metamorphoses into a small frog. The process involves a number of gross changes, which occur in a relatively short period of time, at this late developmental stage. Together these processes constitute a drastic change in form, resulting from both regressive and constructive processes.

The regressive changes involve the loss of organs that are functional in the larva but redundant in the adult. Such organs include: gills, tail, fin folds, horny structures of the larval mouth and others.

Many of the constructive processes are initiated during the larval period prior to the onset of metamorphosis, e.g., limbs and lung development, but at metamorphosis these organs develop at an accelerated rate and become functional. Other organs which make their appearance at this time are the tympanum, eyelids, tongue and a cornified skin. These are all fairly obvious morphological changes, but it is important to realize that the process involves profound physiological modifications as well. There is, for example, a change from ammonia excretion to urea excretion, and a change from a basically herbivorous to a carnivorous diet. Different species vary in the size attained by the tadpole prior to the onset of metamorphosis. In some groups, such as the toads, the tadpole does not reach very large proportions compared to the size of the adult, and since the size of the newly metamorphosed froglet is dependent on tadpole size, the resulting froglets are very small. In other species, particularly those with extended larval lives, the tadpole often grows to enormous proportions, and the froglets are not very much smaller than the adults.

The metamorphic process is hormonally mediated. The hormones of the thyroid and pituitary gland control this complex and highly co-ordinated process. The speed of the changes is important, since while they are occurring the individual is vulnerable and ill-adapted to both life in water and on land. While the alimentary tract, for example, is being 'refitted' all feeding may be halted for periods of days. While the tail is being resorbed, the young froglet often flounders about and may easily be taken by a predator.

Metamorphosis and emergence from the water are sometimes synchronized within populations, resulting in an *en masse* exodus of many individuals. It has been suggested that this may allow a few to escape under the cover of those captured by predators.

COLOUR

Frogs are very colourful animals, but the physical basis and functions of coloration are seldom appreciated.

The Physical Basis

The colours of many animals, including frogs, are due to the presence of pigment cells or chromatophores in the skin. There are three different types of chromatophores. Two of these contain pigments of various types associated with sub-cellular organelles. The last contains minute reflecting platelets which, by the reflection and diffraction of light, are responsible for so-called 'structural colours'. The colour of a particular skin area will depend on the distribution of pigment associations and reflecting structures within it.

Colour Change

Most species are able to effect considerable changes in skin colour over short periods of time. Colour change occurs as a result of changes in the distribution of the pigment containing organelles within the chromatophores, and the effect of such changes on the chromatophores which reflect light. When the pigment is dispersed throughout the cell, the skin colour will be dark. When the pigment is condensed within the cells into small compact masses, the skin colour is light. It is not known how the changes in pigment dispersal *occur* in frog skin chromatophores, but these changes are *caused* by hormones produced by the animal. Colour change may occur in response to many stimuli, e.g., changes in light intensity, temperature or background colour. In addition, colour may be associated with the emotional state of the individual.

The Functions of Colour

1. *The Protective Function*

Cryptic coloration

The advantages of concealment resulting from body colour are obvious, and concealment is important both when the frog is acting as a predator and when it is itself potential prey for other predators. Concealment involves blending with the physical environment, and this can be achieved by matching skin colour with that of the background where this is fairly uniform, or by matching colour patterns with environmental patterns. Examples of the former case, the matching of tones, are: the dorsal coloration of Platannas matching the muddy pond bottom, and the uniform green skin colour matching the background of green vegetation.

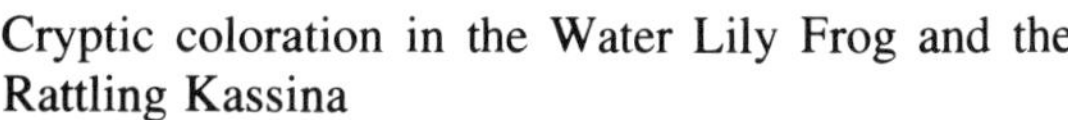

Cryptic coloration in the Water Lily Frog and the Rattling Kassina

Concealment due to the matching of patterns is often very striking in frogs. In grassland, by the very nature of the vegetation, patterns of light and shadow will be elongated, and many grassland species have longitudinally arranged light and dark stripes. In more thickly vegetated areas, the patterns of light and shadow will tend to be more 'blotchy', and many species in such areas display similar colour patterns.

Limbs which display transverse banding and an absence of longitudinal stripes are common in frogs. One may wonder why the limbs do not display the same pattern as the rest of the body. When the limbs are folded however, the position and orientation of the bands is such that they coincide with each other to form stripes.

Transverse banding on the limb of the Berg Stream Frog; eye stripe in the Plain Stream Frog

All the colour patterns mentioned above tend to break up, or disrupt, the outline of the animal, making it more difficult to see. Many species have a dark line passing through the eye. This is common in vertebrates and it serves to reduce the conspicuousness of the eye.

Most frogs have a light-coloured ventral surface and a darker dorsal surface. This phenomenon of countershading has been dealt with under eggs on page 17.

Flash colours

Flash colours in the Arum Lily Frog

Colours may also be concealing in other ways. The so-called 'flash colours' are bright patches of colour, that are concealed when the animal is resting, but are vividly displayed when it moves. The function of flash colours has been explained in the following way: when a predator disturbs a resting frog, the bright flash colours are revealed as the frog attempts to escape. The predator sees the flash colour, and continues to look for it, but the frog is again at rest with the flash colour concealed, and is again camouflaged by its cryptic pattern.

Aposematic coloration

Aposematic coloration in the Banded Rubber Frog

Animals that are toxic to others if eaten, venomous or unpalatable often display bright warning colours that make them conspicuous in natural environments. The colours usually employed for this function are black, white, red and yellow, and their use amounts to advertisement of the undesirable properties of the bearer. Predators learn to recognize these colours, and avoid repeatedly taking the distasteful prey.

An extension of the function of warning colours is seen in mimicry. If palatable species resemble noxious ones, they will presumably enjoy the same protective effect of the aposematic coloration.

2. *The Sex Recognition Function*

In many animals the males and females are strikingly different in their coloration and these differences allow for recognition of the sexes. Obviously colour and visually mediated sex recognition are more important where breeding takes place during the day than they would be where it occurs at night. In the majority of frogs the only obvious colour difference between the sexes is the darker colour of the throat in males. But since breeding is invariably nocturnal, it is questionable whether the colour of the throat and vocal sac are important.

3. *The Thermoregulatory Function*

A dark-coloured frog will, when exposed to the sun, absorb more heat than a light-coloured one. In addition, where its temperature is higher than that of the surroundings, a dark frog will lose heat more rapidly than a light one. Thus, if colour change is possible, a frog can exert some control over the amount of heat absorbed during the day and the amount of heat lost at night. Many species of Reed Frogs often assume a light coloration when exposed to the sun, and become considerably darker when in the shade.

Colour change in the Arum Lily Frog

4. *The Radiation Protection Function*

Coloration may also act to prevent damage to tissues by certain wavelengths of radiant energy. Dark pigmentation in the skin and the peritoneum are both important in avoiding excessive irradiation of the tissues.

Colour Pattern Polymorphism

Polymorphism is widespread amongst animals and many South African frogs are polymorphic in dorsal colour pattern, i.e. several different colour patterns occur, and persist, within populations. Polymorphism in colour is very conspicuous in some genera and as much as a half of the local frog species are probably polymorphic to some extent. In *Hyperolius*, where dorsal pattern has been used as a major systematic character, a large number of subspecies have been erected, many of them probably artificially. Colour can be a reliable systematic character, but the extent of intraspecific variation must be known and considered.

The Puddle Frog is a good example of a species which is polymorphic for colour pattern (see page 166). Within populations of this species, some individuals have a uniform mottled brown dorsum, while in others there is a coloured vertebral stripe or band. A vertebral stripe or band is a disruptive pattern (see page 26).

In grassland the striped pattern would be cryptic amongst the elongated shapes and shadows of the grasses. On the other hand, the uniform pattern provides very effective camouflage against a substrate of bare mud. Stewart reports that in arid areas in Malawi, where vegetation is less abundant, the frequency of striped patterns is lower than it is in more grassy regions. In areas where grasses prevail for the greater part of the year, higher frequencies of striped morphs were encountered.

In grassland habitats there is often considerable seasonal variation in the state of the vegetation. During the dry season, when there is little grass, the uniform morphs are concealed from predators, and the green striped individuals are perhaps more conspicuous. Conversely, when green grass is abundant during the wet season, the striped morphs would probably be subject to less predation than the uniform ones. Morphs with green stripes would presumably enjoy the greatest protection at this time of the year.

Many bird and snake predators have acute vision, and some have been shown to employ a learned *search image* in seeking their prey, i.e. they search for, and are more efficient in finding, prey morphs that they have already caught. The search image of such predators would be for the commonest morph present at the time. This familiar form would be preferentially preyed upon, and the other morphs would remain unrecognized and escape predation. In this way only a portion would be removed by any particular predator at any time. If the previously common morph becomes less abundant as a result of the predation, the predator could develop a new search image for another morph, or seasonal vegetational changes could make another morph more conspicuous. This would then be preferentially preyed upon and the original morph could recover numerically.

TEMPERATURE, WATER AND THE SKIN

Desiccation is one of the major environmental stresses facing all terrestrial organisms. Air is a dehydrating environment and continued existence requires regular replenishment of lost moisture. On the other hand, fresh water organisms face a different problem — one of flooding of the body, due to the continual influx of water by the process of osmosis. Both of these factors are very relevant in the life of frogs. Aquatic types (e.g., Platannas) must cope with continual hydration, while the more exclusively terrestrial forms (e.g., Sand Frogs) face severe desiccation problems. The many species which spend part of their time in water and the remainder on land must cope with both extremes of the water problem.

The skin is the major organ involved in both the gain and loss of water. Its structure offers little or no restriction to the passage of water in and out of the animal. Whilst on land, water loss from the skin surface is continual, irrespective of local humidity conditions. In water, the kidneys function to expel excess fluid from the body. Given that some frogs function effectively in arid areas, it is tempting to suggest that their skins are less permeable to water than those of more aquatic frogs. This does not however appear to be the case, and many studies have reported an equal skin permeability in frogs from a variety of habitats. Species from more terrestrial habitats are, however, capable of tolerating a *greater total water loss* than other species. In certain terrestrial forms the bladder acts as a water reservoir. So although frogs from wet and dry areas lose water at basically comparable rates, those from dry regions *tolerate* water loss better than others do.

Clearly, the rate of water loss will vary in different habitats, e.g., it will be low in burrows and high in exposed sites on reeds. It will also be far greater during the day than at night. The behaviour of many species is often correlated with evaporative conditions in the environment.

Body temperature is important in frogs and all other animals because the chemical processes of living systems are temperature dependent. Body temperature in this group is affected by a complex of factors, most of which fall beyond the scope of this work. A few of the important considerations are, however, mentioned.

Frogs are ectothermic vertebrates, i.e. they depend on environmental heat sources rather than metabolic heat sources to maintain their body temperature. Temperature control is behaviourally regulated. In general, most frogs will seek to avoid exposure to high temperatures by creeping away in the ground or by moving to water or shade. By confining their activity to the hours of darkness, the problem of exposure to high daytime temperatures is further alleviated. These are some of the many ways in which body temperature can be *behaviourally* regulated.

Heat is gained from the environment by basking and conduction and lost principally by the evaporation of water from the surface of the skin. Basking in open sunlight is common, but due to the high rate of water loss under such conditions it is usually only indulged in when there is ready access to water. Many species can tolerate a wide range of environmental temperatures, provided that they are not in water stress.

The amphibian skin, like that of other vertebrates, consists of an outer layer, the epidermis, and an inner dermal layer. The epidermis itself consists of several cellular layers, the outermost of which is known as the stratum corneum. Being the outer layer of the skin, and that which is in contact with the environment, the stratum corneum serves a protective function. It is a layer of dead, cornified cells which is periodically shed during the process of moulting, and is replaced by the new stratum corneum which develops beneath it.

Frogs moult at regular intervals throughout the year. The frequency of moulting varies, but it usually occurs every four to eleven days. Some species actively remove the old stratum corneum, and frequently adopt a characteristic 'hunched up' posture while doing so. Movements of both the fore and the hind limbs assist in pulling off the old stratum corneum in many species, and it may come off either in large sheets or in smaller pieces. The moult is frequently eaten immediately, and ingestion may assist in its removal. In some species, however, no effort is made to remove the moult, and it appears to fragment and float free in these circumstances.

FEEDING

Structures Associated with Feeding

Frog mouths are generally large, with a substantial gape. In all but the exclusively aquatic forms, the tongue is well developed. It is usually attached anteriorly to the floor of the mouth, with its free end pointing towards the pharynx. The tongue is principally an organ involved in the ingestion of food, and in most species it can be rapidly flipped out of the mouth in picking up food items.

Glands in the mouth produce sticky secretions which cover the tongue. These, together with partial entanglement in the long tongue, facilitate the transfer of food items to the mouth.

Teeth are generally small and degenerate, and are completely absent in some genera. In most forms they are present in the upper jaw only. Frogs do not masticate their food but swallow it whole, and the teeth function mainly to restrain the struggling prey prior to swallowing. In the Bullfrog, a pair of large projections on the lower jaw serve a similar function (see page 115) but these are not true teeth.

Food

Adult frogs are carnivores and usually feed only on live moving prey. They are largely insectivorous and many studies have shown that they are unselective feeders, taking whatever prey happens to be available. This is reflected in that, when stomach contents are examined, the proportions of different types of food articles often resemble their relative proportions in the habitat of the species concerned. From this observation one may conclude that the different species may compete with one another for the same food. But this is probably not really the case.

There are a number of factors which could act to reduce the extent of interspecific competition for food.

1. *Size*

Large frogs have large mouths, and a large gape facilitates the ingestion of large prey items. Small species would be confined to relatively smaller prey. The largest South African frog, the Bullfrog, includes such things as mice, lizards and even other large frogs in its diet. Clearly the Bullfrog has no competitors amongst other frogs for prey of this type. This is obviously an extreme example, but differences in adult size will limit competition for particular size classes of food.

2. *Foraging Area*

Species often feed in areas which are quite different in respect to the composition of the insect fauna. A number of species forage actively in the grassland some distance from the water. Other species spend the daylight hours at the water's edge and do not move much, if at all, from this position during the process of feeding. Although these species may occur sympatrically, they effectively utilize different portions of the insect fauna. In those species foraging in the savanna, Orthoptera would constitute the greater portion of the diet, and aquatic or aquatic associated insects would be unimportant. The reverse would be the case where foraging occurred at the water's edge. In a similar way arboreal species would utilize an essentially different portion of the insect fauna to that used by burrowing forms.

Substantial differences may therefore be present in the feeding behaviour of sympatric species, and these are important when attempting to assess the extent of interspecific competition for food.

FIELD KEY TO THE GENERA

The key consists of a series of numbered couplets of alternative statements. To identify the group or genus to which a specimen belongs, the reader should start at couplet 1 and select the statement applicable to the specimen. This will either indicate the genus, or it will direct the reader to the number of the next couplet to be considered. In the former case, a page reference for the genus is given and the species can then be identified by comparing the descriptions and photographs of the members of the genus. If the statement leads to another couplet the process should be repeated until the genus of the animal has been established.

NOTE: This key is not infallible. Conclusions drawn from it should always be confirmed by comparison with other evidence in the text.

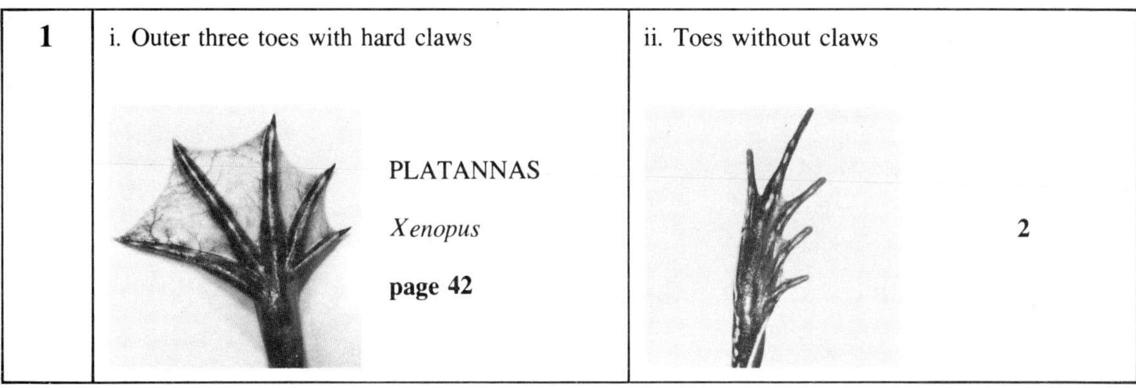

1	i. Outer three toes with hard claws PLATANNAS *Xenopus* **page 42**	ii. Toes without claws **2**

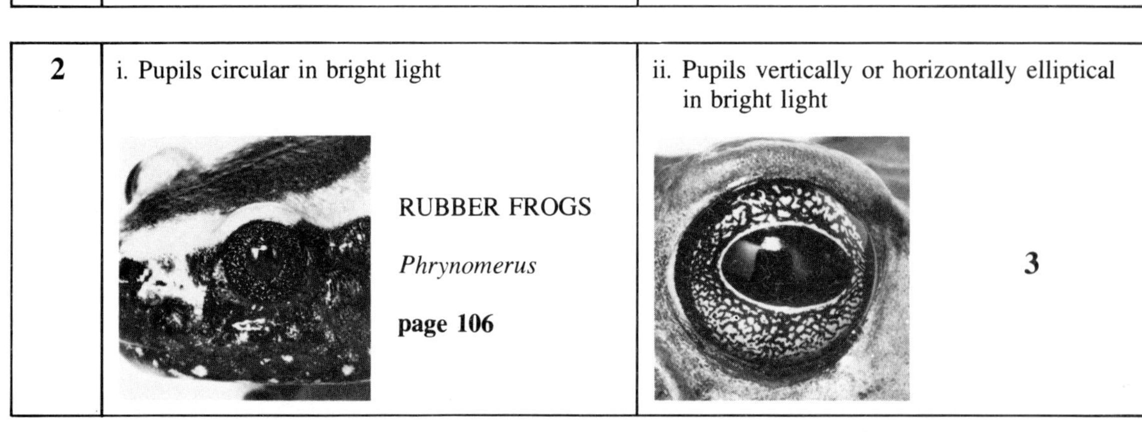

2	i. Pupils circular in bright light RUBBER FROGS *Phrynomerus* **page 106**	ii. Pupils vertically or horizontally elliptical in bright light **3**

3	i. Pupils vertical in bright light **4**	ii. Pupils horizontal in bright light **9**

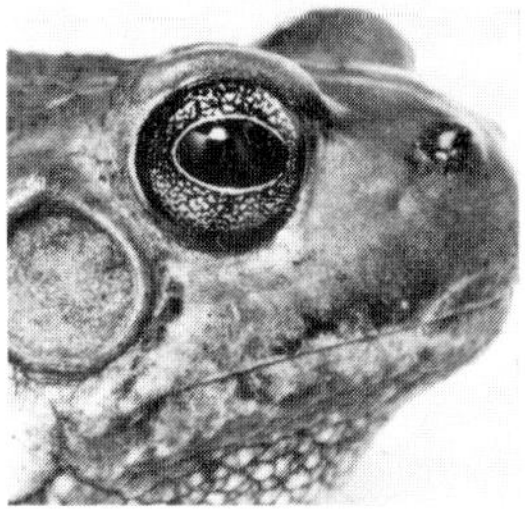

4	i. Shank longer than half the body length (a > ½b in figure) GHOST FROGS *Heleophryne* **page 50**	ii. Shank shorter than or just equal to half body length (a < ½b in figure) **5**

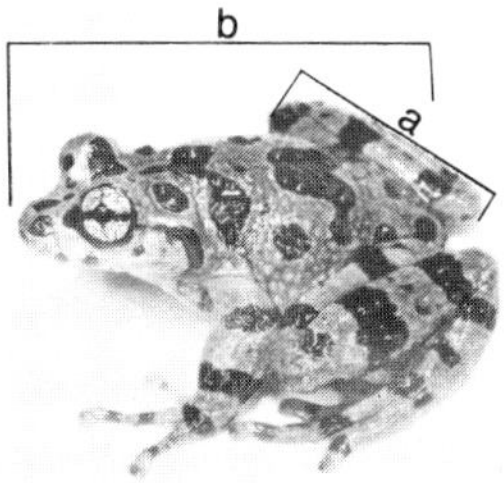

5	i. Snout acutely pointed and flattened; eyes small and barely elevated above forehead SHOVEL-NOSED FROGS *Hemisus* **page 210**	ii. Snout normal; eyes large and bulging **6**

6	i. Toes terminate in discs **7**	ii. Toes not terminating in discs KASSINAS (part) *Kassina senegalensis* *Kassina wealii* **pages 228, 230**

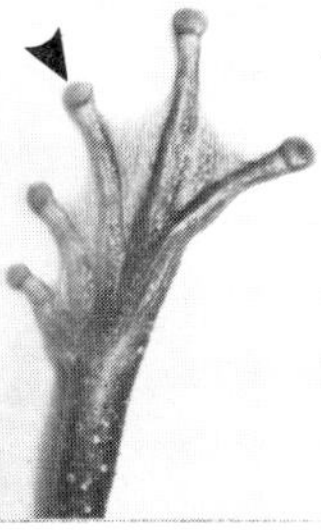

	i.	ii.
7	i. Scarlet colouring on groin and axilla  KASSINAS (part) *Kassina maculata* **page 226**	ii. No scarlet colouring on groin or axilla  **8**
8	i. Tympanum easily discernible  TREE FROGS *Leptopelis* **page 216**	ii. Tympanum not visible  LEAF-FOLDING FROGS *Afrixalus* **page 232**
9	i. Toe tips expanded into discs or bulbs 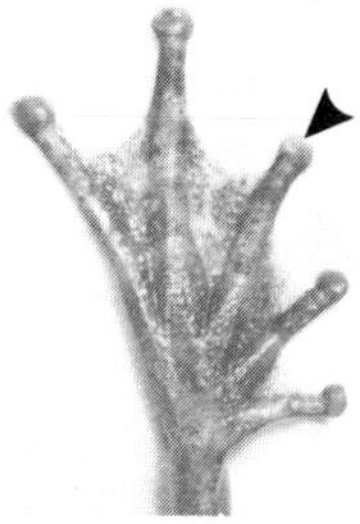 **10**	ii. Toes not terminally expanded  **13**
10	i. A tubercle present well up on the tarsus; terminal expansion of toes small and bulbous  PUDDLE FROGS (part) *Phrynobatrachus acridoides* **page 168**	ii. No tubercle on upper tarsus; terminal discs conspicuous  **11**

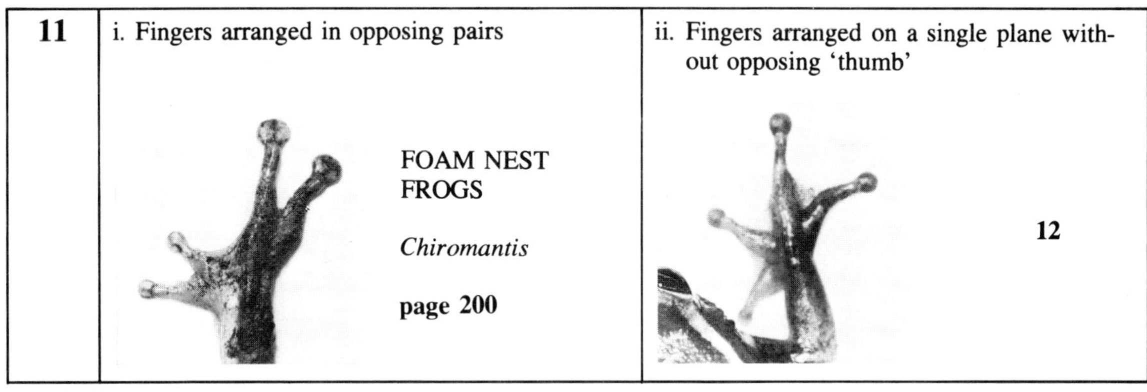

11	i. Fingers arranged in opposing pairs	ii. Fingers arranged on a single plane without opposing 'thumb'
	FOAM NEST FROGS *Chiromantis* **page 200**	**12**

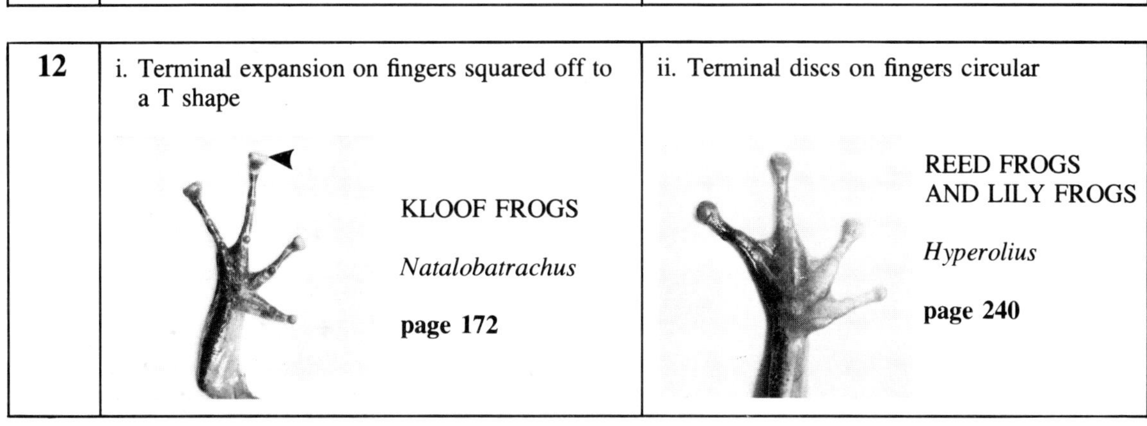

12	i. Terminal expansion on fingers squared off to a T shape	ii. Terminal discs on fingers circular
	KLOOF FROGS *Natalobatrachus* **page 172**	REED FROGS AND LILY FROGS *Hyperolius* **page 240**

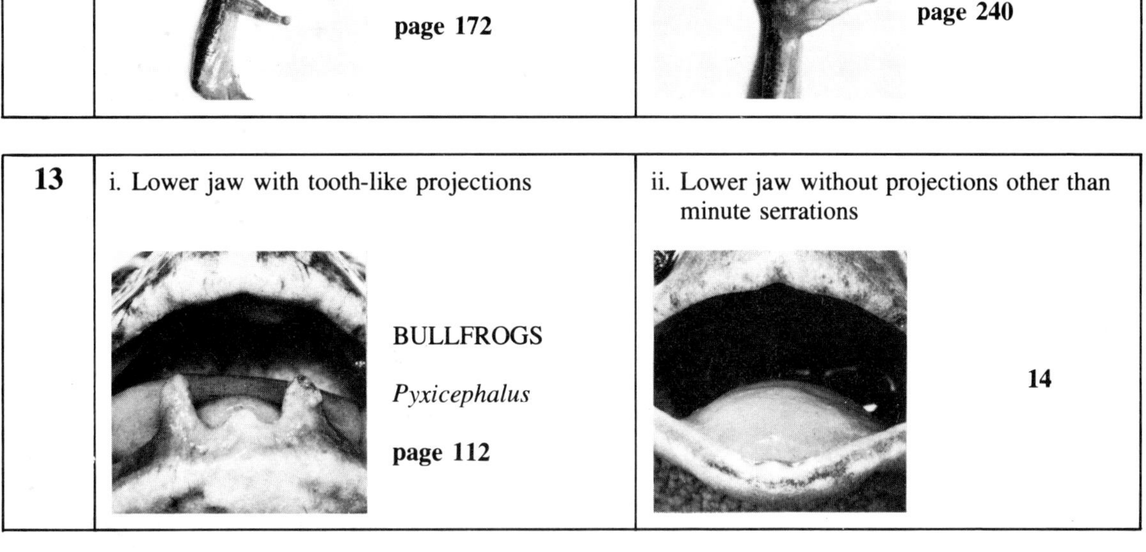

13	i. Lower jaw with tooth-like projections	ii. Lower jaw without projections other than minute serrations
	BULLFROGS *Pyxicephalus* **page 112**	**14**

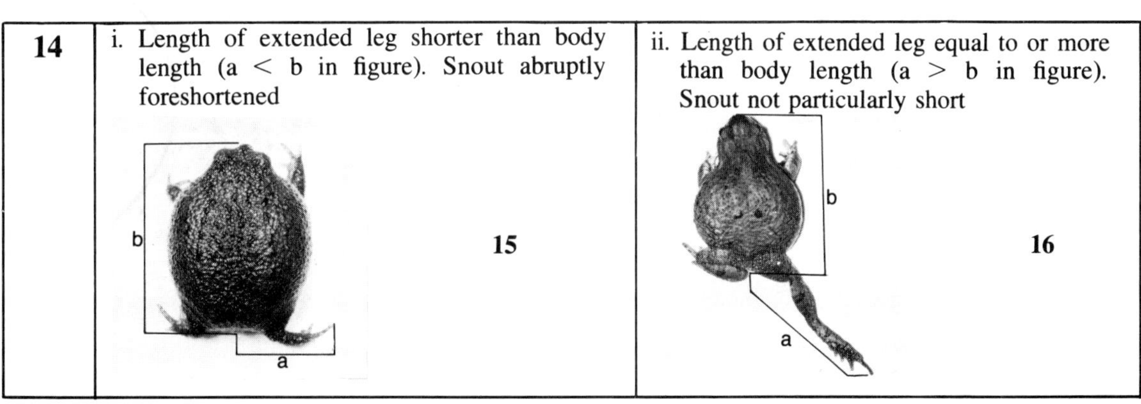

14	i. Length of extended leg shorter than body length ($a < b$ in figure). Snout abruptly foreshortened	ii. Length of extended leg equal to or more than body length ($a > b$ in figure). Snout not particularly short
	15	**16**

	i	ii
15	i. Parotid glands present TOADS (part) *Bufo angusticeps* and occasionally individuals of other species **pages 60, 58**	ii. Parotid glands absent RAIN FROGS *Breviceps* **page 82**

	i	ii
16	i. Toes webbed at the base (at least to the extent illustrated) **17**	ii. Toes without webbing **23**

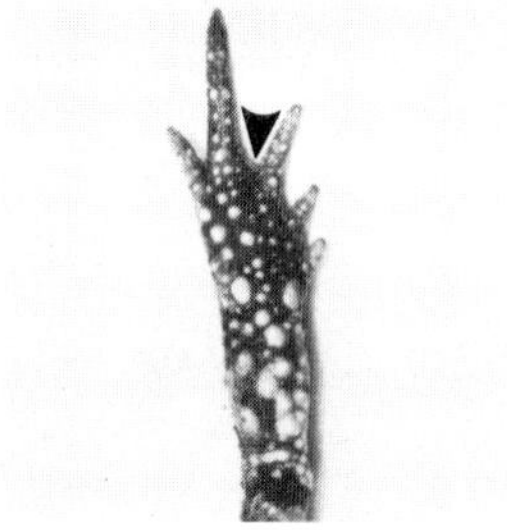

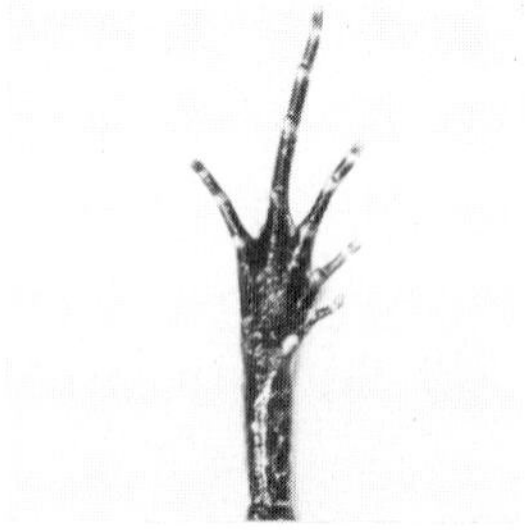

	i	ii
17	i. Skin granular on belly TOADS (part) *Bufo* **page 58**	ii. Skin smooth on belly **18**

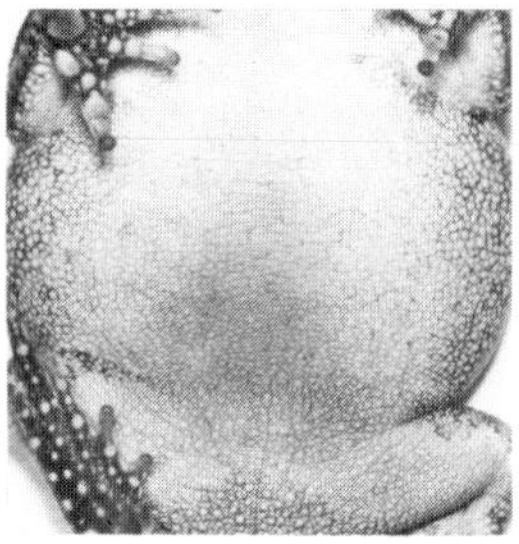

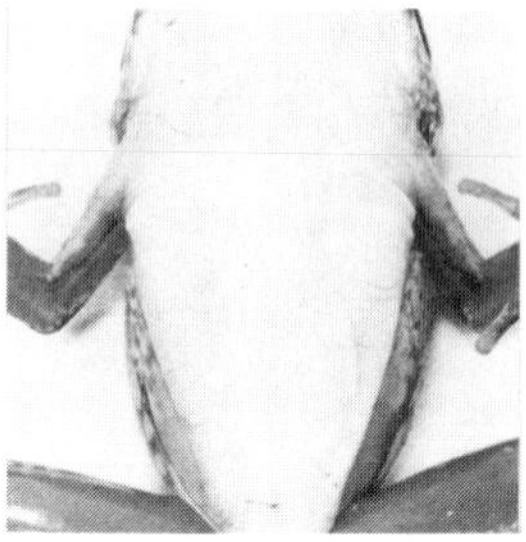

	i	ii
18	i. A distinctive pair of white Y-shaped marks on a black throat 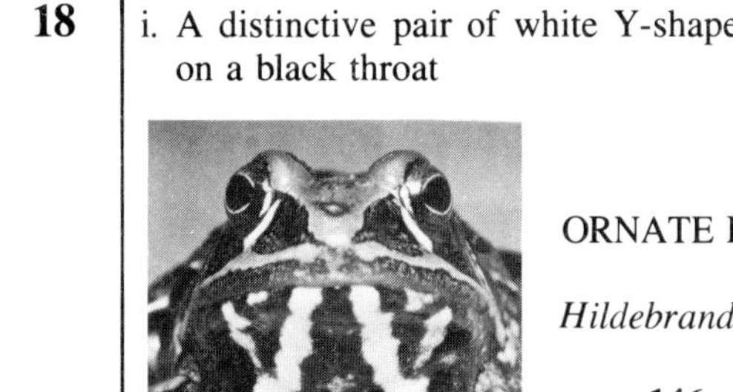 ORNATE FROGS *Hildebrandtia* **page 146**	ii. Throat plain or with any pattern other than 18 i 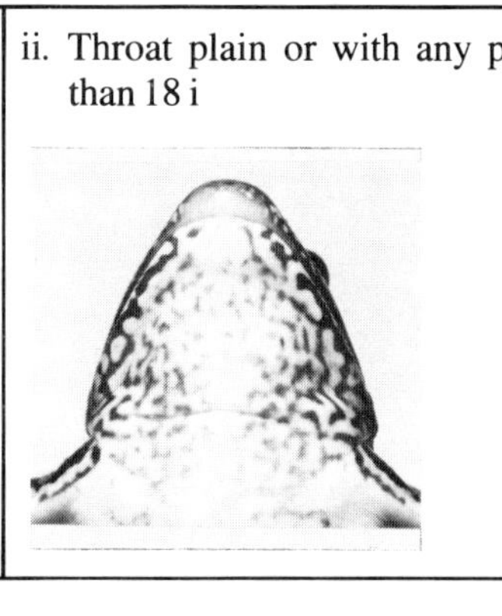 **19**

	i.	ii.
19	i. Inner metatarsal tubercle large and flanged SAND FROGS *Tomopterna* **page 116**	ii. Inner metatarsal tubercle not flanged; usually small **20**

	i.	ii.
20	i. A tubercle present well up on the tarsus as well as inner and outer metatarsal tubercles PUDDLE FROGS *Phrynobatrachus* **page 164**	ii. No tubercle on upper tarsus and only one metatarsal tubercle (either inner or outer) **21**

	i.	ii.
21	i. Shank less than half body length (a < ½b in figure) MICRO FROGS *Microbatrachella* **page 176**	ii. Shank more than half body length (a > ½b in figure) **22**

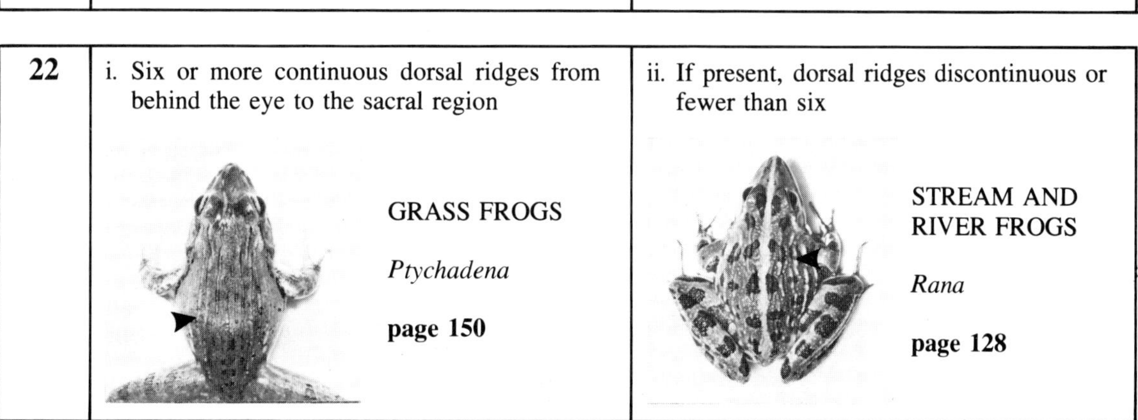

	i.	ii.
22	i. Six or more continuous dorsal ridges from behind the eye to the sacral region GRASS FROGS *Ptychadena* **page 150**	ii. If present, dorsal ridges discontinuous or fewer than six STREAM AND RIVER FROGS *Rana* **page 128**

23	i. Skin on ventral surface granular	ii. Skin on ventral surface smooth
	SQUEAKERS *Arthroleptis* **page 204**	**24**

24	i. Ventral pattern consisting of dark spots, sometimes elongated, on a white background	ii. Ventral pattern in any variation except distinct spots
	CACOS *Cacosternum* **page 180**	**25**

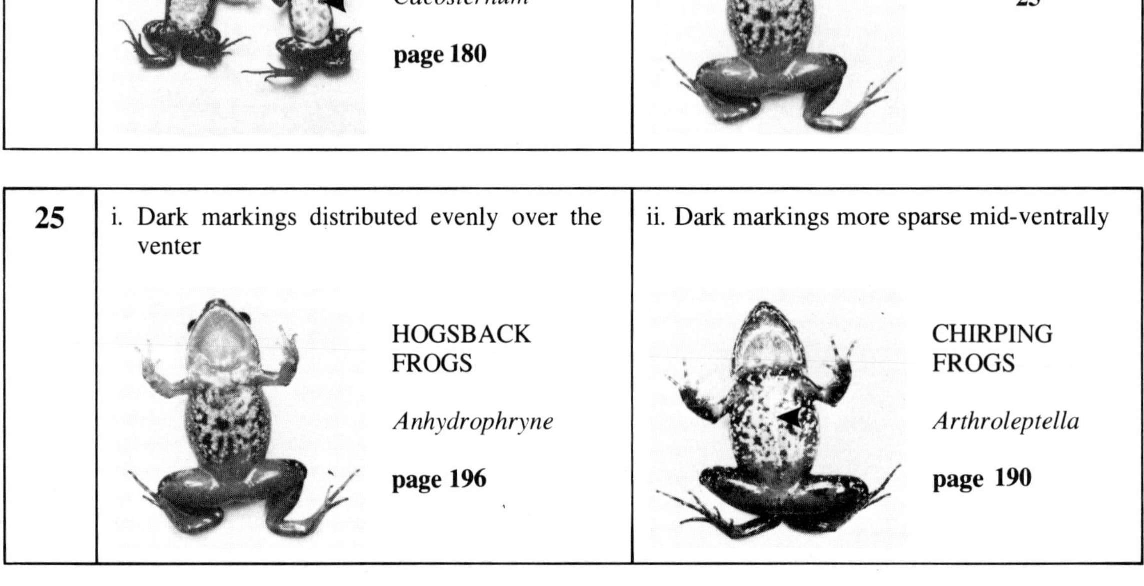

25	i. Dark markings distributed evenly over the venter	ii. Dark markings more sparse mid-ventrally
	HOGSBACK FROGS *Anhydrophryne* **page 196**	CHIRPING FROGS *Arthroleptella* **page 190**

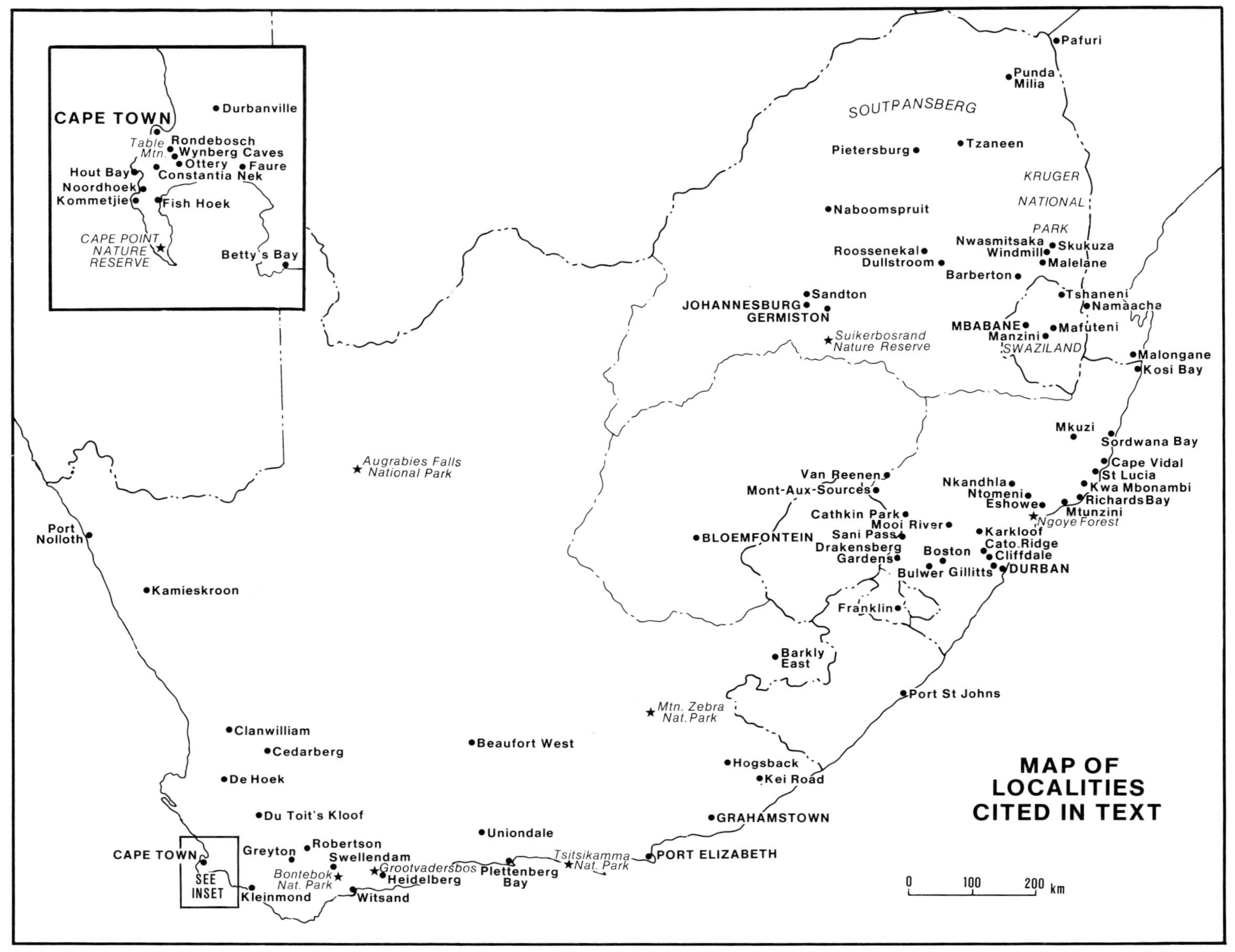

CAPE TOWN
Durbanville
Table Mtn.
Rondebosch
Wynberg Caves
Ottery
Faure
Constantia Nek
Hout Bay
Noordhoek
Kommetjie
Fish Hoek
CAPE POINT NATURE RESERVE
Betty's Bay
Pafuri
Punda Milia
SOUTPANSBERG
Pietersburg
Tzaneen
KRUGER NATIONAL PARK
Naboomspruit
Roossenekal
Dullstroom
Nwasmitsaka
Windmill
Skukuza
Malelane
Barberton
Sandton
JOHANNESBURG
GERMISTON
Tshaneni
Namaacha
MBABANE
Manzini
Mafuteni
SWAZILAND
Suikerbosrand Nature Reserve
Malongane
Kosi Bay
Mkuzi
Sordwana Bay
Cape Vidal
St Lucia
Kwa Mbonambi
RichardsBay
Mtunzini
Ngoye Forest
Augrabies Falls National Park
Van Reenen
Mont-Aux-Sources
Nkandhla
Ntomeni
Eshowe
Cathkin Park
Mooi River
Karkloof
Cato Ridge
Cliffdale
BLOEMFONTEIN
Sani Pass
Drakensberg Gardens
Boston
Bulwer
Gillitts
DURBAN
Port Nolloth
Kamieskroon
Franklin
Barkly East
Port St Johns
Mtn. Zebra Nat. Park
Clanwilliam
Cedarberg
Beaufort West
Hogsback
Kei Road
De Hoek
MAP OF LOCALITIES CITED IN TEXT
Du Toit's Kloof
GRAHAMSTOWN
Uniondale
CAPE TOWN
Greyton
Robertson
Swellendam
Tsitsikamma Nat. Park
PORT ELIZABETH
SEE INSET
Bontebok Nat. Park
Grootvadersbos
Heidelberg
Plettenberg Bay
Kleinmond
Witsand
0
100
200 km

PLATANNAS

Xenopus Wagler

- ★ Conspicuous lateral line sense organs are present ▲.
- ★ The pupil is circular.
- ★ Tympanum is absent.
- ★ Fingers lack webbing.
- ★ Three of the toes are clawed.
- ★ Toes are fully webbed.

Three species occur in South Africa. All species are totally aquatic and emergence onto land is restricted to occasional migrations to adjacent bodies of water. The genus occurs at both high and low altitudes in many different types of water bodies.

External features are remarkably consistent within the genus and represent specializations associated with the aquatic environment. Tympanum, tongue and movable eyelids are lacking, being of reduced importance in water. In contrast, lateral line sense organs are well developed as they are in other aquatic vertebrates. The body is streamlined and slippery and this, together with the powerful hindlimbs with fully webbed toes, provides for efficient progression through the water. Three of the toes of the foot terminate in conspicuous black claws. The adults are both predators and scavengers, and in the absence of a tongue, the forelimbs are employed in the ingestion of food. No vocal sac is visible during calling. Amplexus is inguinal and, like calling, occurs below the surface.

Sexual Dimorphism

Skin folds around the vent are smaller in males than females.

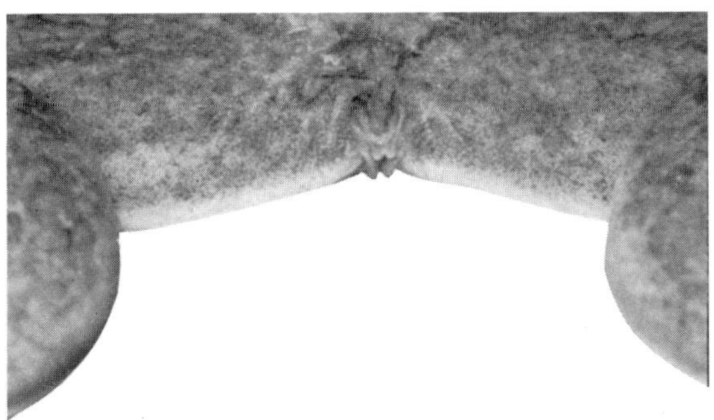

Male vent

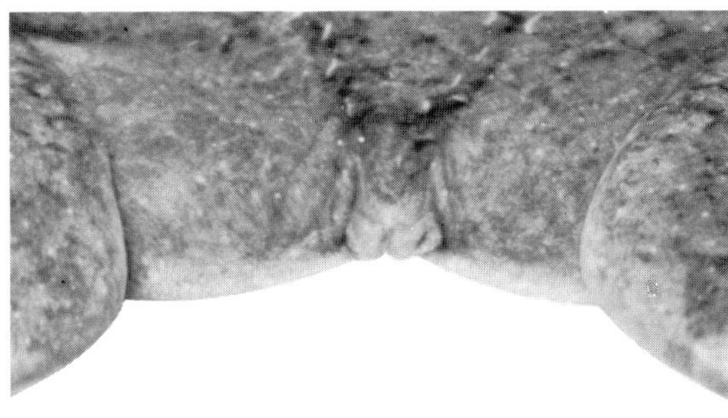

Female vent

Eggs

Eggs are small, heavily pigmented and enclosed in individual jelly capsules. They are attached to submerged objects at oviposition.

Tadpoles

All species have characteristic nektonic tadpoles which lack horny mouthparts and feed on plankton in the water. The body is largely transparent, with a well developed highly motile tail. A pair of filamentous tentacles is present in the mouth region. They are often gregarious and adopt a characteristic 'head down' attitude in the water.

Distribution

The genus comprises fifteen species and subspecies. Living forms are restricted to sub-Saharan Africa and a fossil form has recently been discovered in South America.

COMMON PLATANNA *Xenopus laevis* (Daudin) 1802

Clawed Toad
Clawed Frog
Upland Clawed Frog

Subspecies
The form in South Africa is *Xenopus laevis laevis* (Daudin). Other subspecies are recognized elsewhere in Africa.

COMMON PLATANNA *Xenopus l. laevis* Sandton, Transvaal

BREEDING HABITAT

Any more or less permanent bodies of water.

VOICE

Soft, undulating buzzes emitted under water. About one per second.

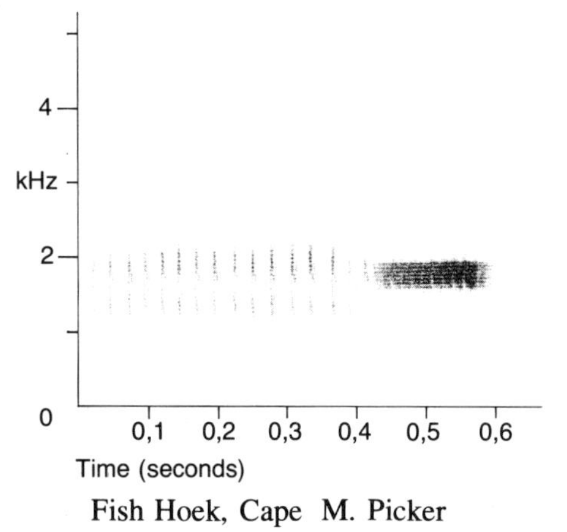

Fish Hoek, Cape M. Picker

- ★ Dark dorsal patches are variable in size and shape but never include an elongated pair between the eyes and over the shoulder as in *X. gilli*.
- ★ A sub-ocular tentacle ▲ is present but inconspicuous — cf. *X. muelleri*.

LIFE SIZE Sandton, Transvaal

- ★ The venter is greyish white, sometimes tinged with yellow posteriorly. Grey spots are sometimes evident, particularly in younger specimens.

Sandton, Transvaal

- ★ Webbing is grey and occasionally yellow tinged but not conspicuously orange-yellow as in *X. muelleri*.
- ★ The claws are noticeably smaller than those of *X. muelleri*.
- ★ The inner metatarsal tubercle ▲ is an elevated ridge.

Sandton, Transvaal

TROPICAL PLATANNA *Xenopus muelleri* (Peters) 1844

Northern Platanna
Mueller's Clawed Frog

TROPICAL PLATANNA *Xenopus muelleri* Skukuza, Kruger National Park

BREEDING HABITAT

A wide variety of permanent bodies of water.

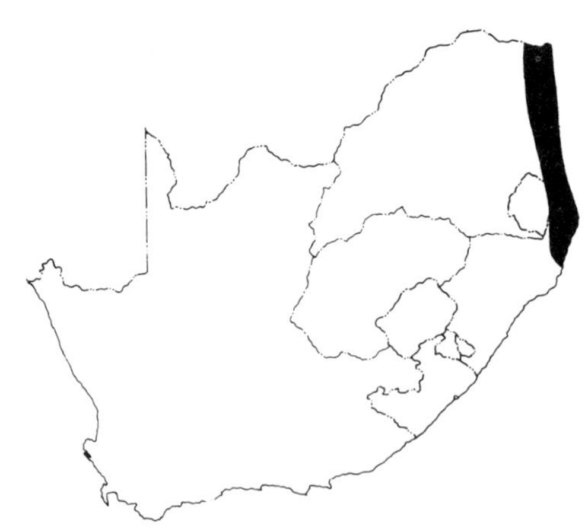

VOICE

A series of tapping sounds emitted under water. About two calls per second.

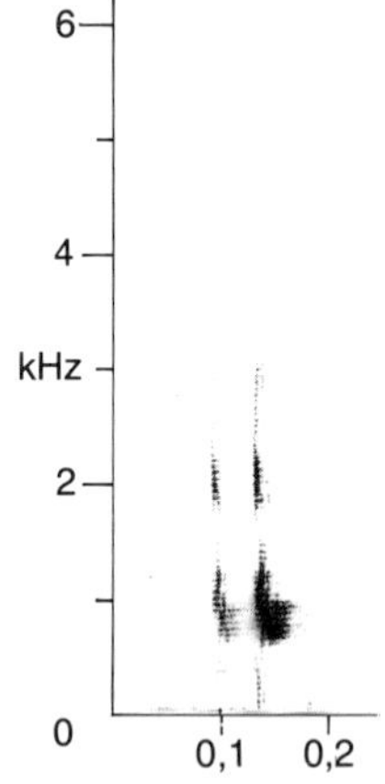

Kruger National Park, Transvaal M. Picker

★ Dark dorsal patches are variable in size and shape but never include a conspicuous elongated pair between the eyes and over the shoulder as in *X. gilli.*

★ The sub-ocular tentacle ▲ is long and conspicuous — cf. *X. laevis.*

LIFE SIZE Skukuza, Kruger National Park

Tshaneni, Swaziland

★ The venter is light grey on the pectoral region, blending to deep orange-yellow on the belly and legs. Grey spots are often evident.

★ Webbing is orange-yellow.

★ The claws are longer and more pointed than those of *X. laevis.*

★ The inner metatarsal tubercle ▲ is a small finger-like projection.

Tshaneni, Swaziland

CAPE PLATANNA *Xenopus gilli* Rose and Hewitt 1927

CAPE PLATANNA *Xenopus gilli* Betty's Bay, Cape

BREEDING HABITAT

Pans in the south-western Cape.

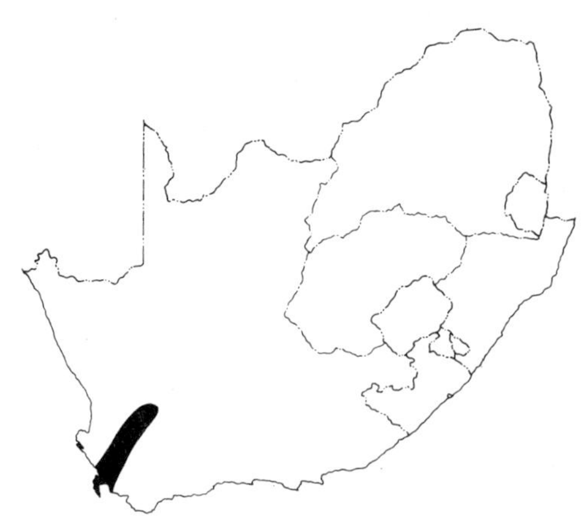

VOICE

Metallic buzzes emitted under water. About two per second.

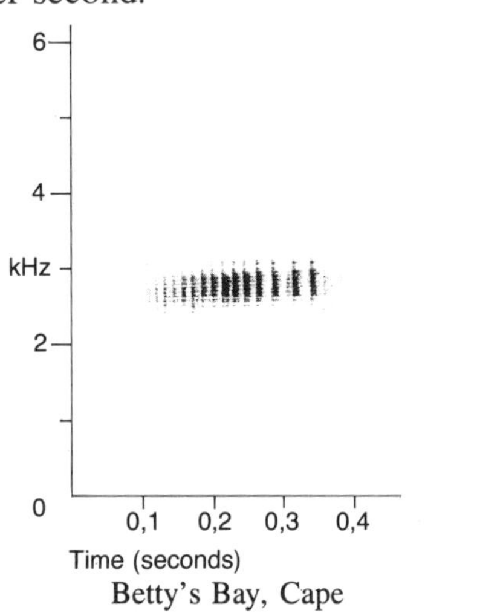

Betty's Bay, Cape

- ★ A pair of elongated dorsal patches extends from between the eyes over and beyond the scapular region.
- ★ There is no sub-ocular tentacle as in other species.
- ★ The lateral line sense organs are less conspicuous than those of other species.

LIFE SIZE Betty's Bay, Cape

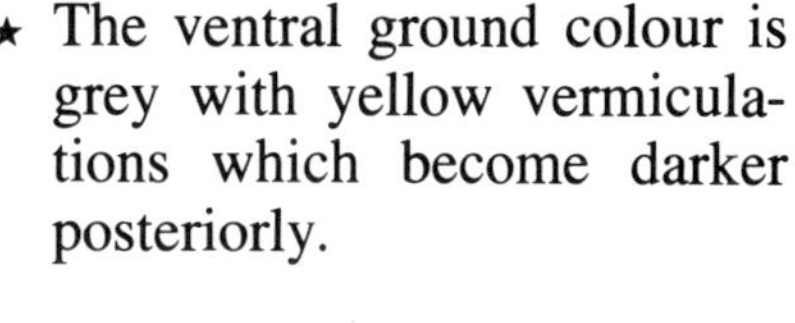

- ★ The ventral ground colour is grey with yellow vermiculations which become darker posteriorly.

Betty's Bay, Cape

- ★ The webbing is grey.
- ★ The inner metatarsal tubercle ▲ is barely discernible.

Betty's Bay, Cape

GHOST FROGS

Heleophryne Sclater

- ★ A glandular fold ▲ is present behind the eye.
- ★ The pupil is vertical.
- ★ The tips of the fingers and toes are expanded and spatulate.
- ★ Fingers lack webbing.
- ★ Toes are extensively webbed.

There are three species of *Heleophryne*. The genus is confined to swiftly flowing permanent streams.

The head and body are depressed, facilitating concealment in narrow rock crevices. The limbs are long and the digits are terminally expanded and spatulate, thereby providing purchase on slippery surfaces. The tips of the fingers are somewhat wider than those of the toes. The toes are extensively webbed and the frogs are efficient swimmers. Well developed tubercles are present on both hands and feet. Dorsal coloration is cryptic and variable.

Sexual Dimorphism

Males in breeding condition bear elongated nuptial pads along the length of the forearm. In *H. purcelli* spines are present along the margin of the lower jaw in males and in *H. natalensis* similar spines are present on the fingers and in the axilla.

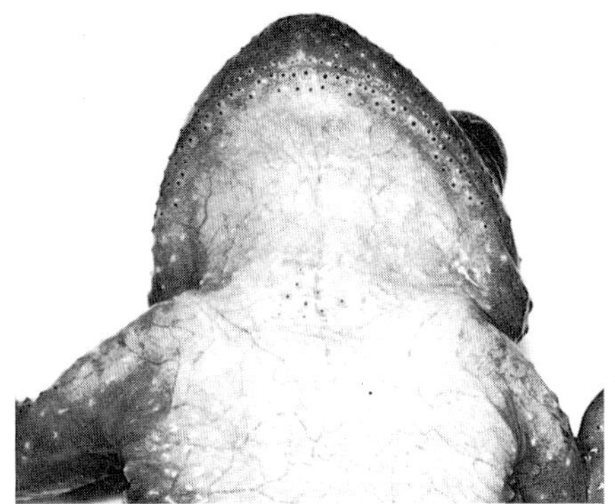

Spines on jaw of male *H. purcelli*

Spines on fingers and axilla of male *H. natalensis*

Eggs

Eggs have been observed only in the case of one species, *H. purcelli*. They are large and yolky and are laid either in shallow pools or out of the water on wet gravel beneath stones (Visser, 1971).

Tadpoles

All species have characteristic torrent adapted tadpoles with large sucker-like mouths which afford purchase on the substrate. They feed by grazing over algae covered rocks. The body is depressed and capable of strong swimming movements. The larval life is reported to be comparatively long (Wager, 1965).

Distribution

The genus occurs only in the mountainous regions of the Cape and along the eastern escarpment. It is not found outside South Africa.

THUMBED GHOST FROG *Heleophryne rosei* Hewitt 1925

THUMBED GHOST FROG *Heleophryne rosei* Wynberg Caves, Cape

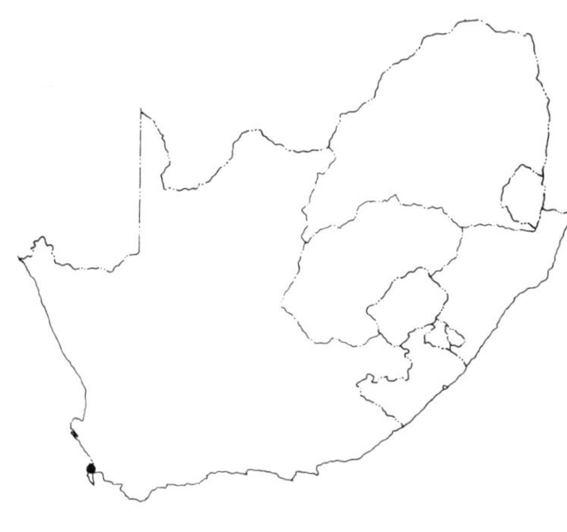

BREEDING HABITAT

"Known from forested gorges with perennial streams on the eastern slopes of Table Mountain. Several adults have been found at different times of the year in caves on top of the mountain" (C. Gow, personal communication).

★ The dorsum is marked with reddish-brown reticulations on a green ground colour.

LIFE SIZE Wynberg Caves, Cape

★ The ventral surface is granular except on the throat. The belly is whitish and the underside of the limbs, pink.

Wynberg Caves, Cape

★ A vestigial 'thumb' ▲ is present on the hand — cf. other members of the genus.

Wynberg Caves, Cape

★ The last phalanx of the 5th toe is free of webbing ▲.

Wynberg Caves, Cape

CAPE GHOST FROG

Heleophryne purcelli Sclater 1899

Subspecies
Heleophryne purcelli purcelli Sclater
Heleophryne purcelli depressa FitzSimons
Heleophryne purcelli orientalis FitzSimons
Heleophryne purcelli regis Hewitt
See page 257

H.p. purcelli Du Toit's Kloof, Cape

H.p. orientalis Swellendam, Cape

CAPE GHOST FROGS *Heleophryne purcelli*

BREEDING HABITAT

Streams in the forested, boulder-strewn gorges in the mountains of the southern and western Cape. Calling males remain concealed in rock crevices.

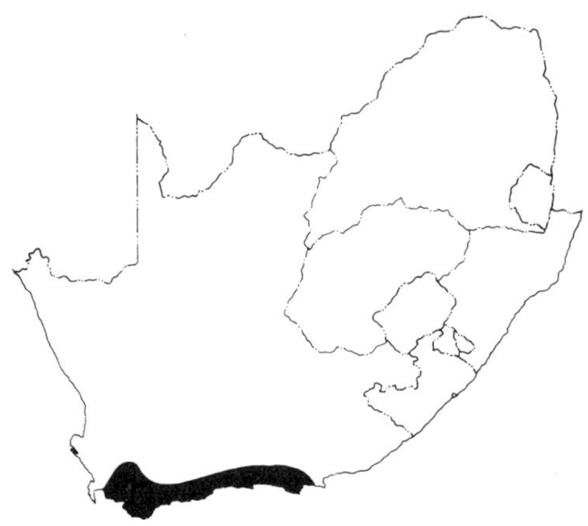

VOICE

A clear high-pitched ringing note, produced at regular intervals of one per second.

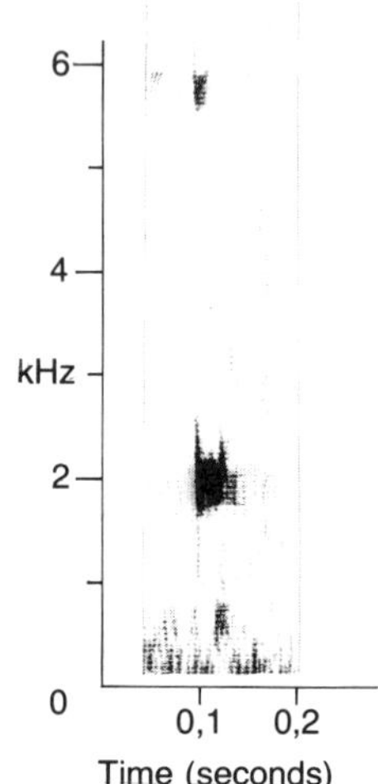

Du Toit's Kloof, Cape

★ The dorsum is conspicuously marked with dark spots and patches of variable size on a greenish ground colour.

LIFE SIZE Swellendam, Cape

★ The ventral surface is densely granular except on the throat. The belly is whitish in colour and the underside of the limbs is fleshy-orange.

Swellendam, Cape

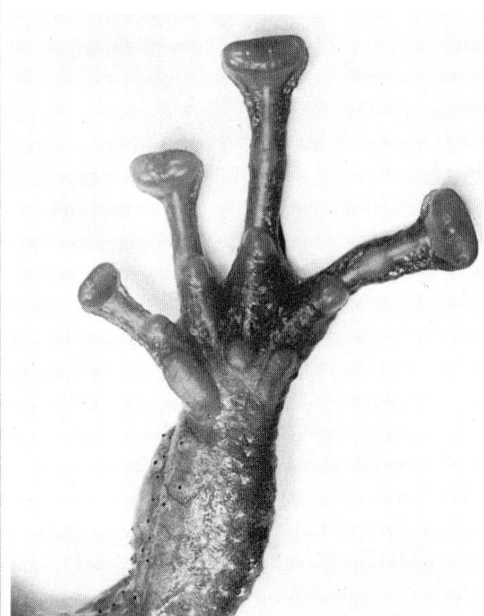

★ No vestigial 'thumb' can be distinguished — cf. *H. rosei.*

Du Toit's Kloof, Cape

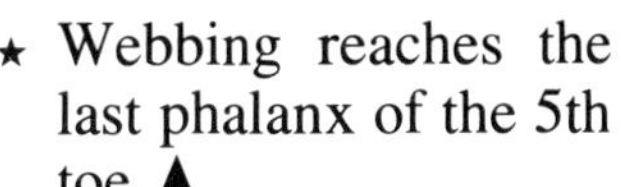

★ Webbing reaches the last phalanx of the 5th toe ▲.

Du Toit's Kloof, Cape

NATAL GHOST FROG *Heleophryne natalensis* Hewitt 1913

Heleo Frog

NATAL GHOST FROG *Heleophryne natalensis* Karkloof, Natal

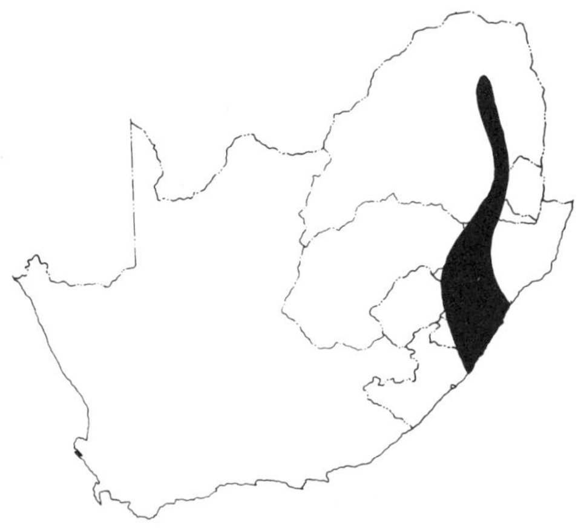

VOICE

A gentle clear note. About two per second.

BREEDING HABITAT

Forested streams in Natal and on the eastern Transvaal escarpment.

★ The dorsum is purplish-brown, usually with green or yellow speckles which are very variable in size and colour intensity.

LIFE SIZE Boston, Natal

★ The ventral surface is less granular than in the other species. The belly is whitish, and the undersides of the limbs are dark chocolate.

Karkloof, Natal

★ No vestigial 'thumb' can be distinguished — cf. *H. rosei*.

★ Fingers are less abruptly squared-off than in the other species.

Karkloof, Natal

★ The last phalanx of the 5th toe may or may not be webbed.

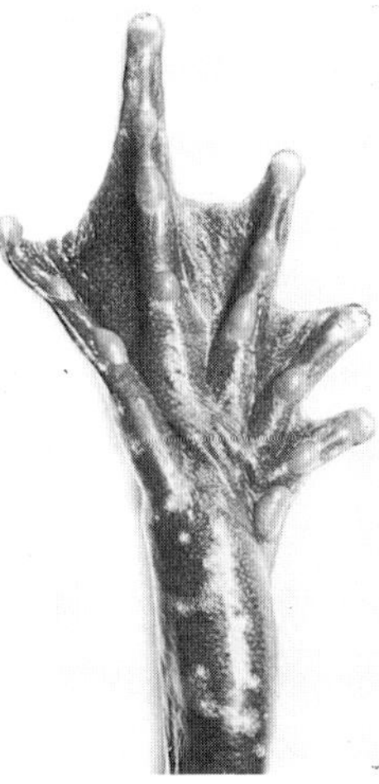

Karkloof, Natal

TOADS

*Bufo** Laurenti

- ★ The skin is rough and dry in appearance with numerous elevations on the dorsum.
- ★ Parotid glands ▲ are present, except in *B. carens.*
- ★ The pupil is horizontal.
- ★ The ventral skin is granular.
- ★ Fingers lack webbing.
- ★ Fleshy webbing is present between the toes, although it is rudimentary in some species.

Eleven species occur in South Africa. With few exceptions, toads inhabit open country, where they are usually abundant and successful. They are often found in dry situations some distance from water.

In over-all appearance, toads are stout of habit with short slender limbs and the basic body form varies little within the genus. The skin is rough and dry with numerous protuberances on the dorsum. Parotid glands are characteristically present behind the eyes of most species, and the parotid secretion is irritant, toxic and defensive in function. They usually hop or run, and are incapable of the long leaps exhibited by many other genera.

*Some workers place *B. carens* in a separate genus *Schismaderma*.

Dorsal coloration is cryptic, and follows a similar pattern in many of the species. Although the ability to change colour is not as well developed as in other genera, colours do become extremely dark prior to sloughing and the pattern may become obscured. Teeth are lacking and prey is ingested with the aid of a long tongue. A variety of aquatic habitats are utilized for breeding.

Sexual Dimorphism

Breeding males can be distinguished by the presence of nuptial pads on the thumbs. In *B. gutturalis*, *B. rangeri*, *B. garmani*, *B. pardalis* and *B. maculatus,* the gular region of the male is darker than the rest of the venter. In *B. vertebralis* it is yellow. In the males of other species the folds of the deflated vocal sac are usually evident.

Eggs

Toad eggs are distinctive in that they are united into strings by copious amounts of jelly-like oviducal secretion. These are commonly entangled around aquatic plants during the oviposition process. As many as 20 000 eggs may be deposited by a single female.

Tadpoles

Standard benthonic tadpoles characterize most species. They are usually small and dark coloured. Those of *B. carens* differ in possessing a flange of skin around the crown of the head, and they congregate in tight, free-swimming clusters in open water.

Distribution

This is a very large genus endemic to Africa, Asia, Europe and North and South America.

SAND TOAD *Bufo angusticeps* Smith 1848

Common Cape Toad

SAND TOAD *Bufo angusticeps* Rondebosch, Cape

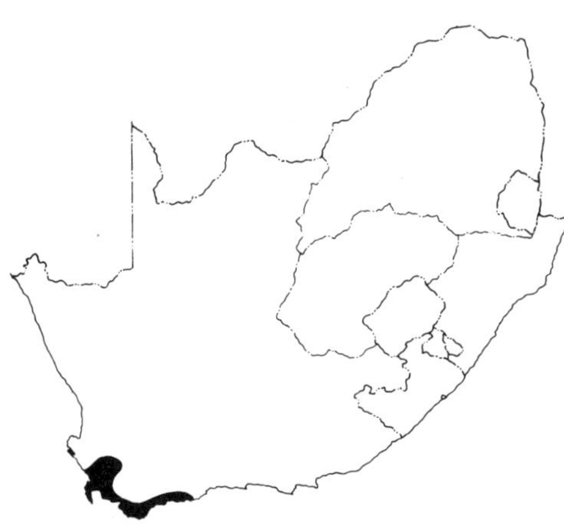

VOICE

"Muted mewing of sea-gulls" (C. Gow, personal communication).
"'Gaa, gaa, gaa' slowly with no appreciable dilation of the throat" (Rose, 1962).

BREEDING HABITAT

Temporary depressions in sandy areas along the southern Cape coast.

- ⋆ The dorsal coloration is variable, but includes more or less symmetrical pairs of dark paravertebral patches, and usually a thin vertebral line.
- ⋆ One of the pairs of patches appears on the snout — cf. *B. rangeri.*
- ⋆ Parotid glands ▲ are conspicuous.

LIFE SIZE Rondebosch, Cape

Rondebosch, Cape

- ⋆ The venter is white and granular except for the throat where the skin is much smoother.

- ⋆ The edges of the toes are fringed with webbing — cf. *B. amatolica.* Only 2 phalanges of the 3rd toe are free of the inter-digital webbing ▲ — cf. *B. gariepensis.*
- ⋆ The dorsal surfaces of the feet are usually yellow.

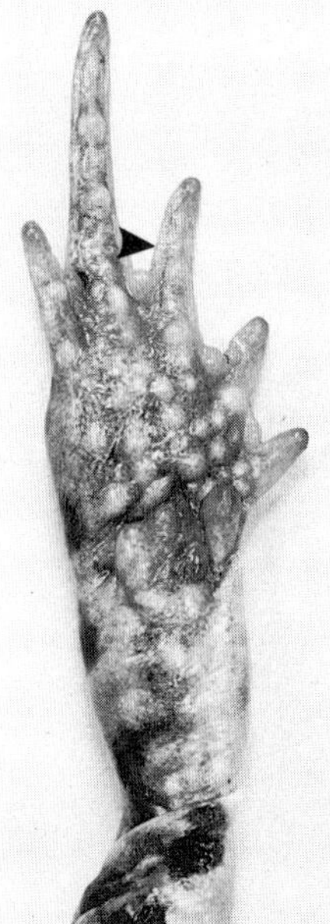

Rondebosch, Cape

AMATOLA TOAD *Bufo amatolica* Hewitt 1925

AMATOLA TOAD *Bufo amatolica* Hogsback, Cape

BREEDING HABITAT

Temporary rain pools and seepage in the Amatola Mountains.

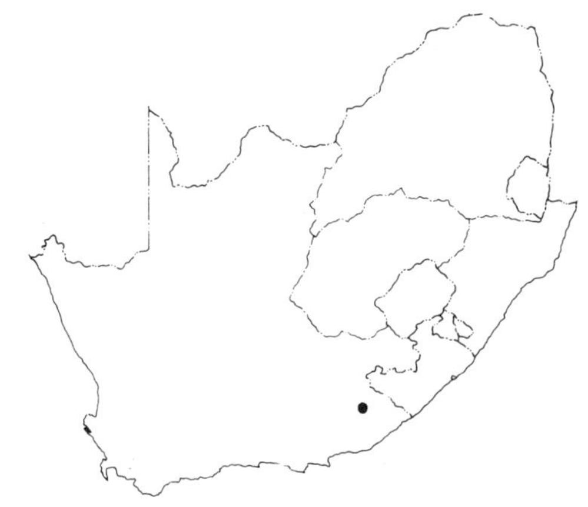

VOICE

A brief nasal squawk, uttered singly at long intervals.

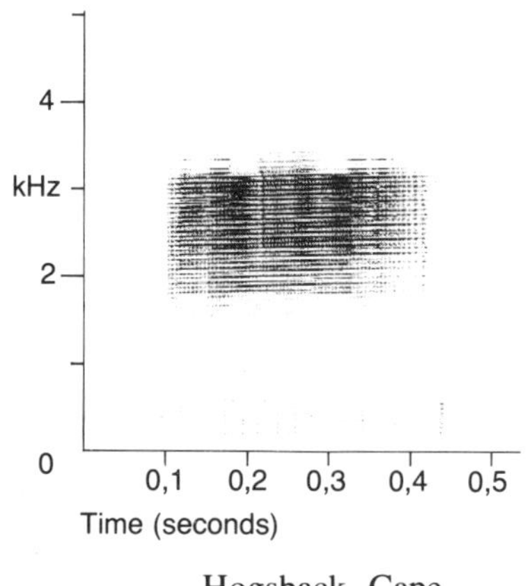

Hogsback, Cape

- ★ The dorsum is usually an over-all dark grey with or without a thin vertebral line. When a pattern is discernible it involves more or less symmetrical dark patches as in *B. angusticeps*.
- ★ The parotid glands ▲ are conspicuous.

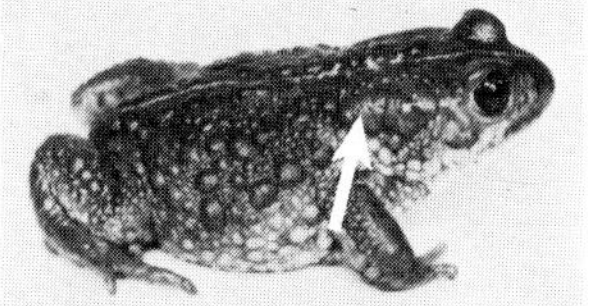

LIFE SIZE Hogsback, Cape

Hogsback, Cape

- ★ The venter is granular and white, occasionally with black spots. On the throat the skin is much smoother.

- ★ The toes are not fringed with webbing, or, if so, very poorly — cf. *B. angusticeps*.
- ★ The tarsal fold ▲ is flattened or slightly ridged — cf. *B. gariepensis*.

Hogsback, Cape

KAROO TOAD *Bufo gariepensis* Smith 1848

Gariep Toad

Subspecies
Bufo gariepensis gariepensis Smith
Bufo gariepensis nubicolus Hewitt
See page 257, 258.

B. g. gariepensis Beaufort West, Cape

Mountain Zebra National Park, Cape

B. g. nubicolus Mont aux Sources, Natal

B. g. gariepensis Mbabane, Swaziland

KAROO TOADS *Bufo gariepensis*

BREEDING HABITAT

Streams, waterholes or rain pools in Karoo scrub or grassland.

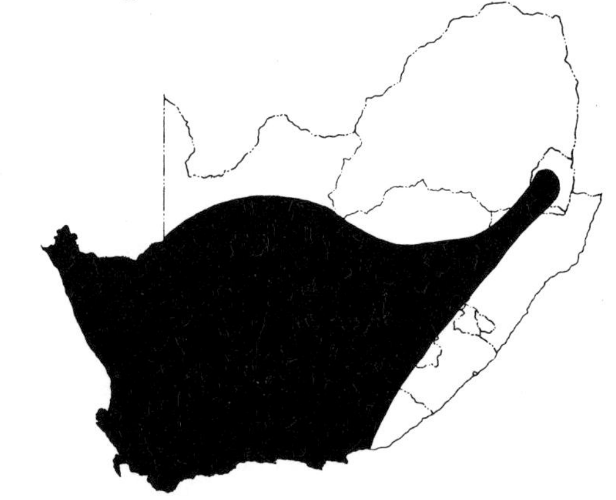

VOICE

A series of rasping squawks. One per second.

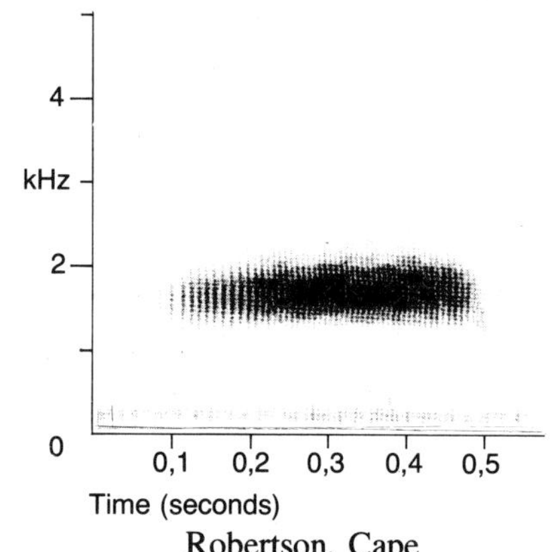

Robertson, Cape

- ★ There is considerable variation in dorsal pattern. In the central part of the range the dorsum usually displays asymmetrical dark patches on a tan ground colour. In the south-west a uniformly khaki coloration becomes common. In the north-east the dark areas merge and cover the entire dorsum leaving only small patches of light ground colour. In the latter part of the range this pattern is found on specimens at both moderate altitudes (*B. g. gariepensis*) and high altitudes (*B. g. nubicolus*).
- ★ The parotid glands ▲ are massive on specimens from the central and southern parts of the range, but become flattened in north-eastern material (both subspecies).

LIFE SIZE Uniondale, Cape

- ★ The venter is off-white and frequently covered with small indefinitely outlined spots particularly in young specimens. A blueish grey or green colour is sometimes evident in north-eastern specimens.

Beaufort West, Cape

JUVENILE Mountain Zebra National Park, Cape

- ★ The edges of the toes are not fringed with webbing, or, if so, very poorly.
- ★ The tarsal fold ▲ is massive, except in north-eastern specimens — cf. *B. amatolica*.

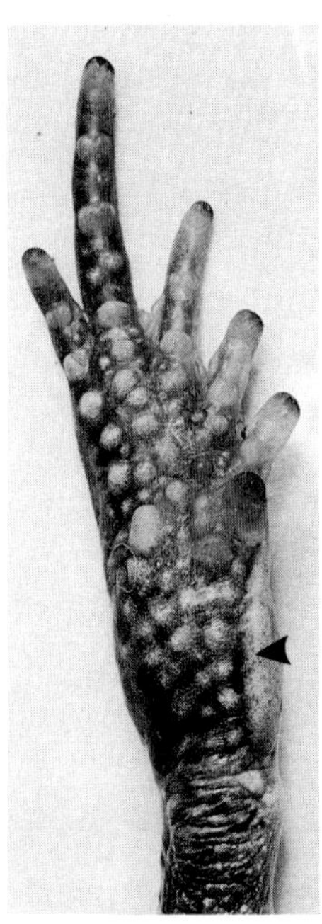

Mountain Zebra National Park, Cape

CAPE MOUNTAIN TOAD *Bufo rosei* Hewitt 1926

Striped Mountain Toad, Rose's Toad

CAPE MOUNTAIN TOADS *Bufo rosei* Cedarberg, Cape

BREEDING HABITAT

Moist depressions, vleis and springs on the grassland slopes and plateaux of the Cape mountains.

VOICE

A creaking squawk, often terminating in a sharp cheep. About one in three seconds.

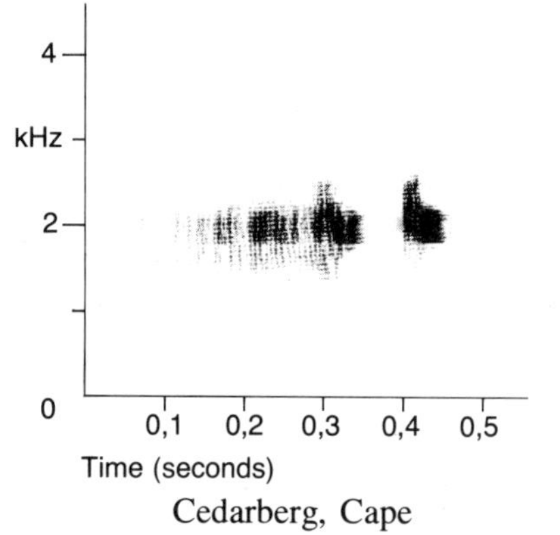

Cedarberg, Cape

- ★ The dorsal pattern is variable but usually includes a light vertebral line and a pair of irregular light longitudinal bands.
- ★ The snout is dark and a pale inter-orbital bar is present. This is intersected by the vertebral line.
- ★ The parotid glands ▲ are conspicuous and usually light orange coloured.
- ★ A glandular lump ▲ on the shank is distinctive.

LIFE SIZE
Cedarberg, Cape

- ★ The ventral pattern is variable from white with grey specks, to distinctly marbled. The skin texture is granular but less so on the throat.

Cedarberg, Cape

- ★ The toes lack webbing.

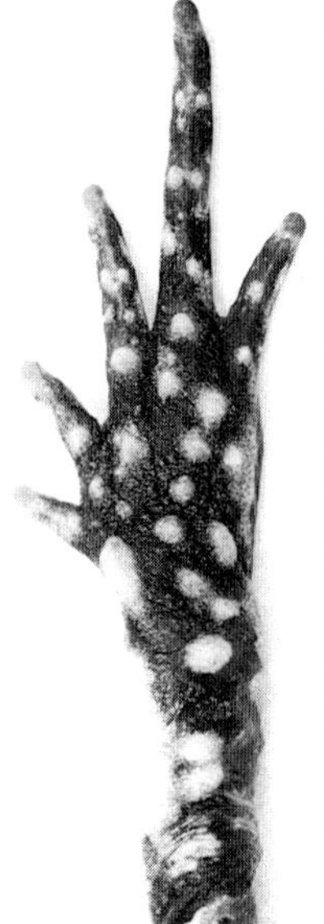

Cedarberg, Cape

GUTTURAL TOAD *Bufo gutturalis** Power 1927

Common Toad, Square-marked Toad Syn: *Bufo regularis* Poynton (non Reuss)
Leopard Toad

GUTTURAL TOAD *Bufo gutturalis* Sandton, Transvaal

BREEDING HABITAT

Open pools, dams, streams or other more or less permanent water. Males call from partly concealed positions around the perimeter of the breeding site.

VOICE

A vibrant snore of about one second is repeated constantly. About one in three seconds.

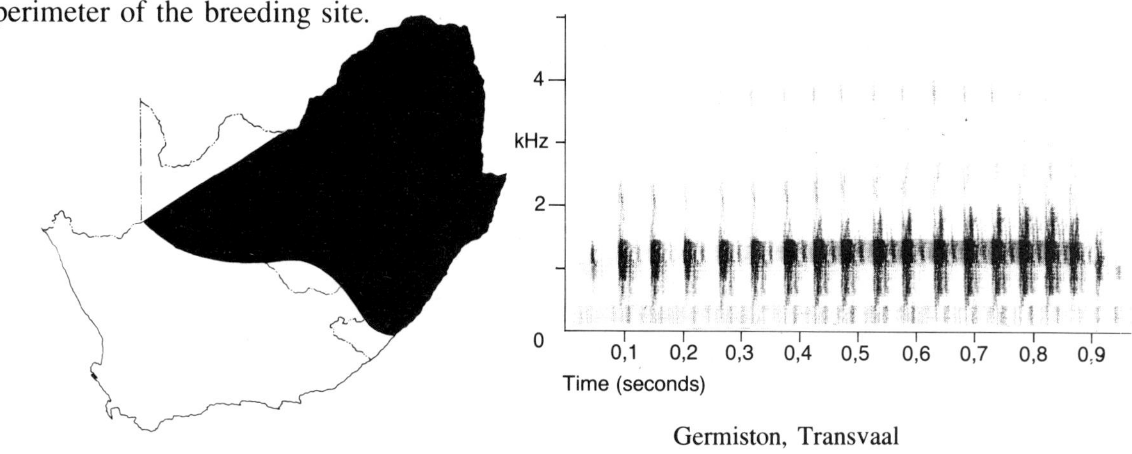

Germiston, Transvaal

*The use of *gutturalis* for material previously referred to *regularis* by Poynton (1964) and most other workers, follows Tandy and Keith (1972) and Blair (1972). On the basis of hybridization and call studies the southern African form has been separated from the northern *Bufo regularis*.

- ★ Pairs of symmetrical paravertebral patches are generally visible on the dorsum but may be poorly defined in some specimens. A thin vertebral line is common, particularly in small animals.
- ★ The top of the snout is characteristically marked with a pair of dark patches. These combine with another pair located posteriorly between the eyes to leave a cross shape of pale ground colour ▲ running from eye to eye and from nostril to occiput. The pair of inter-ocular patches are never fused as in *B. rangeri.*
- ★ Parotid glands ▲ are conspicuous and are distinct from the rest of the dorsum — cf. *B. maculatus.*
- ★ Irregular red infusions mingle with the ground colour on the back of the thighs — cf. other species except *B. garmani.*

LIFE SIZE Suikerbosrand Nature Reserve, Transvaal

Suikerbosrand Nature Reserve, Transvaal

- ★ The venter is granular and whitish. The throat is darkly pigmented in males.

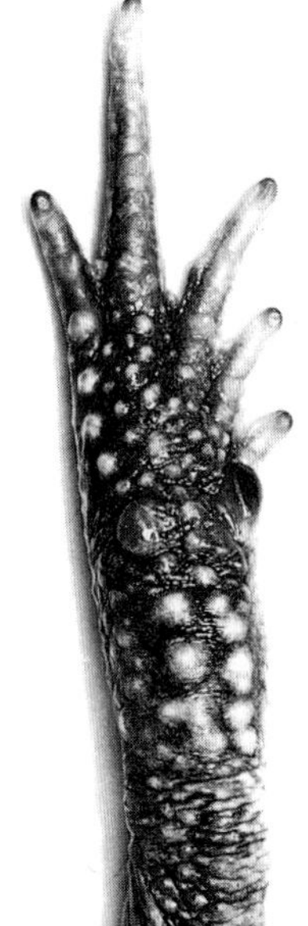

Sandton, Transvaal

- ★ The inter-digital webbing is scanty — cf. *B. rangeri.*

FLAT-BACKED TOAD — *Bufo maculatus** Hallowell 1854

Striped Toad
Lesser Square-marked Toad

Syn: *Bufo pusillus* Mertens

FLAT-BACKED TOAD *Bufo maculatus* — Malelane, Kruger National Park

BREEDING HABITAT

Rivers and streams in savanna. Males call from partly exposed positions on the banks.

VOICE

A raucous and rapidly trilled bray. About one per second.

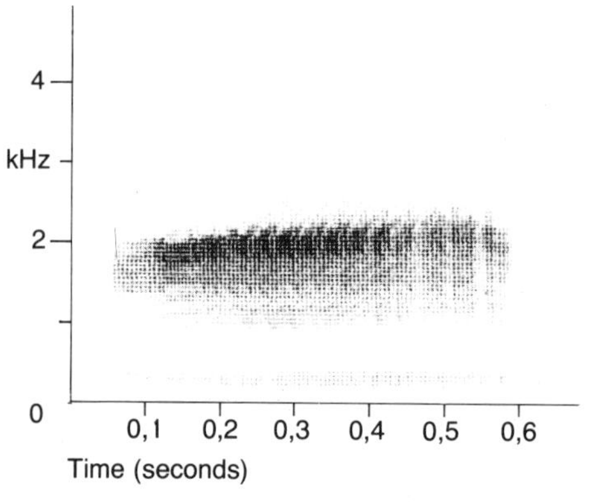

Kruger National Park, H. H. Braack

*The use of *maculatus* for material previously referred to *pusillus* by Poynton (1964) and other southern African workers follows Tandy (1972) and Tandy and Keith (1972). These authors found no significant differences between the mating calls of these two forms.

- ★ Pairs of symmetrical paravertebral dark patches are generally visible on the dorsum and a distinct vertebral line is present.
- ★ The top of the snout is marked with a pair of dark patches and there is another pair located between the eyes. A characteristic cross shape of pale ground colour ▲ is thus formed as in *B. gutturalis*.
- ★ The parotid glands ▲ are not elevated above the dorsum — cf. other species.
- ★ The back of the thighs have no red markings as in *B. gutturalis* and *B. garmani*.

LIFE SIZE Malelane Kruger National Park

Tshaneni, Swaziland

- ★ The venter is granular and whitish, often with flecks of dark grey. The throat in males is dark.

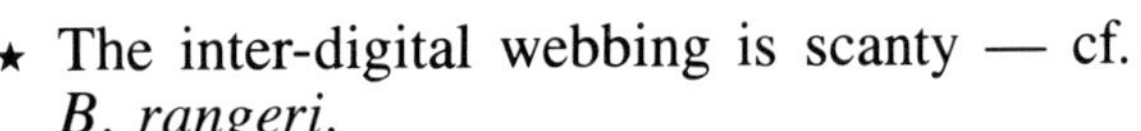

- ★ The inter-digital webbing is scanty — cf. *B. rangeri*.

Tshaneni, Swaziland

OLIVE TOAD *Bufo garmani* Meek 1897

Northern Mottled Toad
Light-nosed Toad
Garman's Square-marked Toad

OLIVE TOAD *Bufo garmani* Tshaneni, Swaziland

BREEDING HABITAT

Vleis, pans or dams in open or wooded savanna. Groups of males call from exposed positions at the water's edge.

VOICE

A loud bray, of about half a second, uttered repeatedly. About one per second.

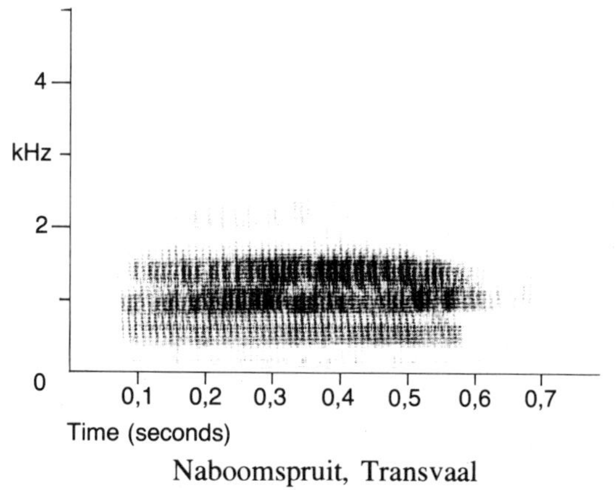

Naboomspruit, Transvaal

- ★ Dark dorsal markings may take the form of symmetrical paravertebral pairs or they may be broken up into an irregular pattern.
- ★ The top of the snout is characteristically free of dark markings except for an occasional asymmetrical dot — cf. *B. gutturalis*. The dark inter-orbital patches ▲ converge posteriorly, but do not actually fuse — cf. *B. rangeri.*
- ★ Parotid glands ▲ are conspicuous.
- ★ Irregular red infusions mingle with the ground colour on the back of the thighs as in *B. gutturalis* — cf. other species.

LIFE SIZE Tshaneni, Swaziland

Tshaneni, Swaziland

- ★ The venter is granular and whitish. The throat in males is darkly pigmented.

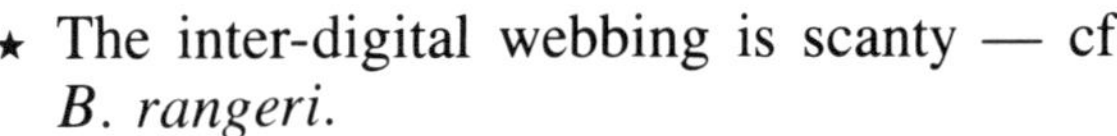

- ★ The inter-digital webbing is scanty — cf. *B. rangeri.*

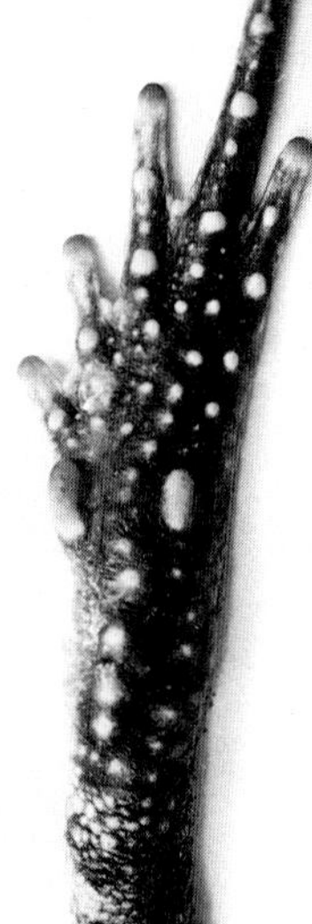

Tshaneni, Swaziland

RAUCOUS TOAD *Bufo rangeri* Hewitt 1935

RAUCOUS TOAD *Bufo rangeri* Sandton, Transvaal

BREEDING HABITAT

Breeding takes place in rivers and streams in grass or woodland. Groups of males call from exposed positions at the water's edge, or a few metres from it.

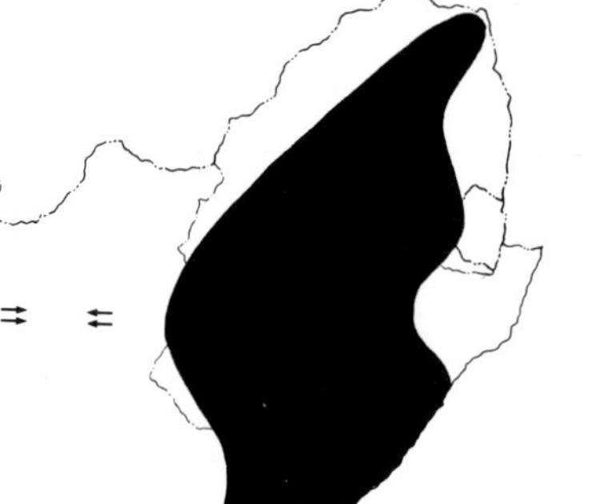

VOICE

Rasping quacks repeated constantly. About two per second.

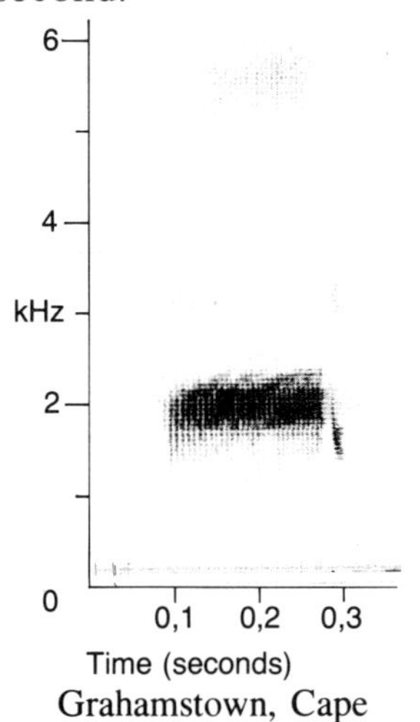

Grahamstown, Cape

- The pairs of dark symmetrical patches on the dorsum sometimes fuse together across the midline.
- The top of the snout is characteristically free of dark markings except for an occasional small asymmetrical dot. The inter-orbital patches ▲ are usually fused, forming a continuous bar — cf. *B. gutturalis*.
- Parotid glands ▲ are conspicuous.
- The backs of the thighs have no red infusions as in *B. gutturalis* and *B. garmani*.

LIFE SIZE Sandton, Transvaal

Suikerbosrand Nature Reserve, Transvaal

- The venter is granular and whitish. The throat in males is darkly pigmented.

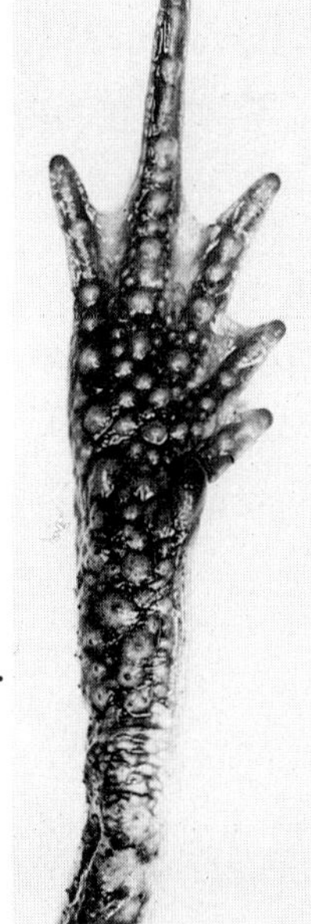

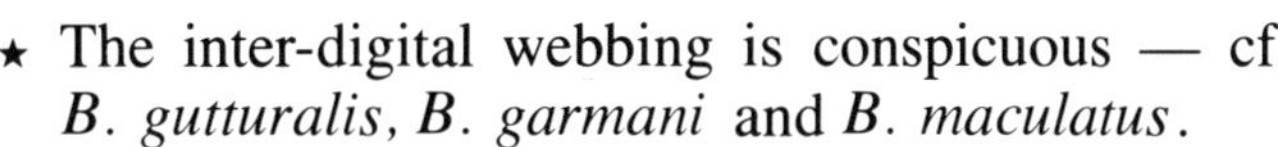

- The inter-digital webbing is conspicuous — cf. *B. gutturalis*, *B. garmani* and *B. maculatus*.

Suikerbosrand Nature Reserve, Transvaal

LEOPARD TOAD *Bufo pardalis* Hewitt 1935

Snoring Toad
August Toad

LEOPARD TOAD *Bufo pardalis* Noordhoek, Cape

BREEDING HABITAT

Permanent, usually deep waterholes and dams. The call is generally uttered from a floating position away from the bank.

VOICE

A deep, slowly pulsatile snore of about one second in duration. One call every three or four seconds.

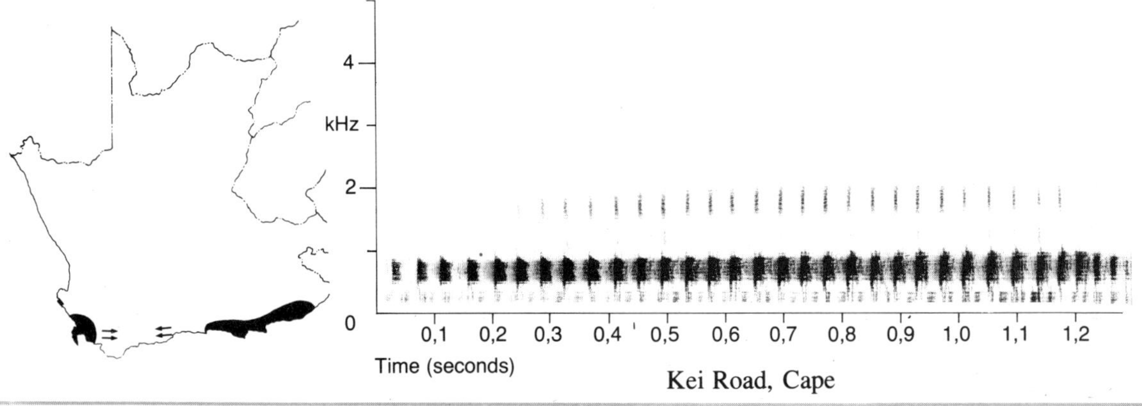

Kei Road, Cape

- The symmetrically paired paravertebral patches are distinct and a pale, often yellow, vertebral line is common.
- The top of the snout is characteristically free of dark markings except for an occasional asymmetrical dot — cf. *B. gutturalis*. The dark inter-orbital patches do not fuse, as in *B. rangeri*.
- Parotid glands ▲ are conspicuous.
- The backs of the thighs have no red infusions as in *B. gutturalis* and *B. garmani*.

LIFE SIZE — Noordhoek, Cape

- The venter is granular and whitish. The throat in males is darkly pigmented.

Noordhoek, Cape

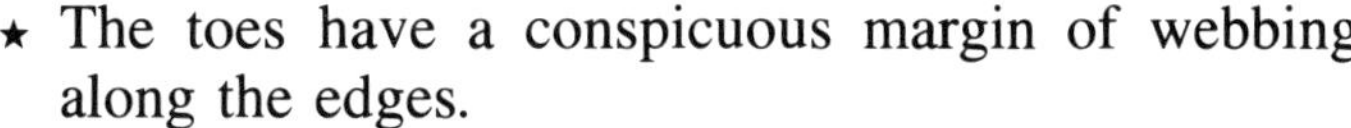

- The toes have a conspicuous margin of webbing along the edges.

Noordhoek, Cape

RED TOAD *Bufo carens* Smith 1848

RED TOAD *Bufo carens* Tshaneni, Swaziland

BREEDING HABITAT

Permanent, fairly deep waterholes in open or wooded savanna. Calling is done from a floating position usually with one hand or foot 'moored' to a reed.

VOICE

Very deep, muffled booming sounds of about one second in duration, uttered continuously. One call in about four seconds.

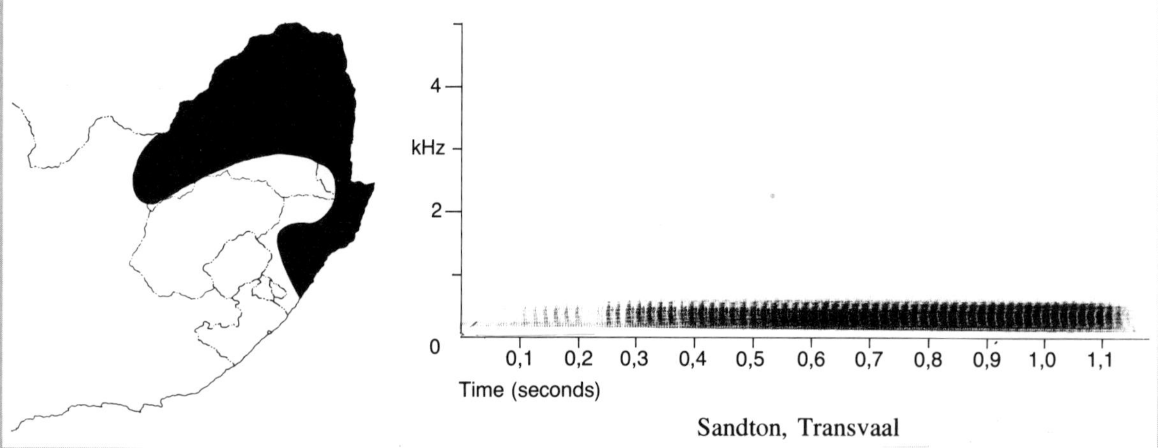

Sandton, Transvaal

- ★ The dorsum bears two characteristic dark spots in the sacral region ▲. If present, other dorsal markings are generally much less distinct.
- ★ A conspicuous glandular line ▲ runs dorso-laterally, and parotid glands are not visible as distinct structures.

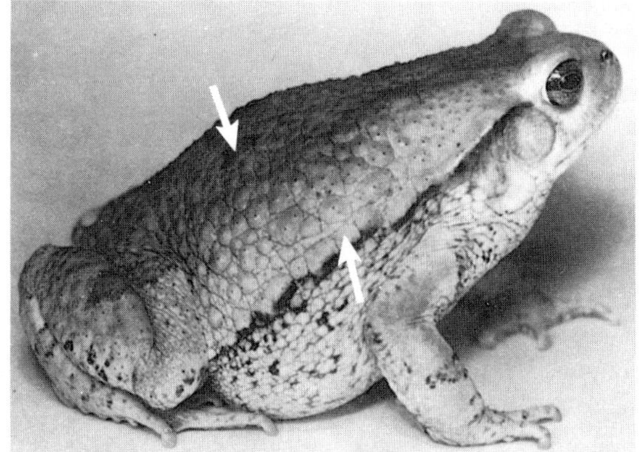

LIFE SIZE Sandton, Transvaal

Sandton, Transvaal

- ★ The venter is granular and white with grey flecks. The throat in males appears wrinkled and is sometimes pigmented.

- ★ The toes have a noticeable margin of webbing along their edges.

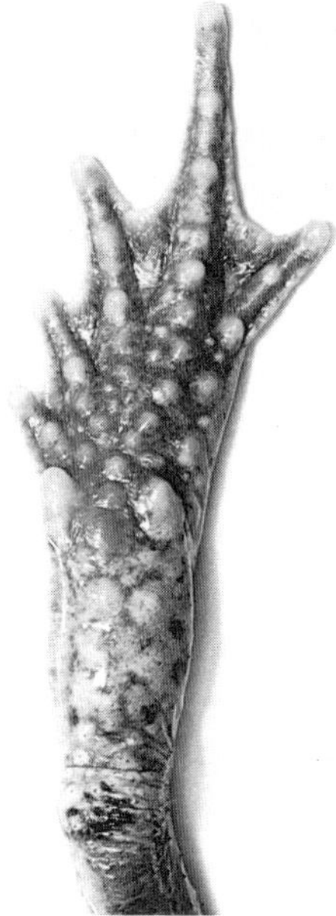

Sandton, Transvaal

PIGMY TOAD

Bufo vertebralis Smith 1848

Subspecies
Bufo vertebralis vertebralis Smith
Bufo vertebralis fenoulheti Hewitt and Methuen
See page 258

B.v. fenoulheti Eastern Swaziland

Pafuri, Kruger National Park

B.v. vertebralis
Mountain Zebra National Park

PIGMY TOADS *Bufo vertebralis*

BREEDING HABITAT

Temporary pools in stony, sometimes barren regions. Calling males can be found in very exposed sites at the edges of rain pools.

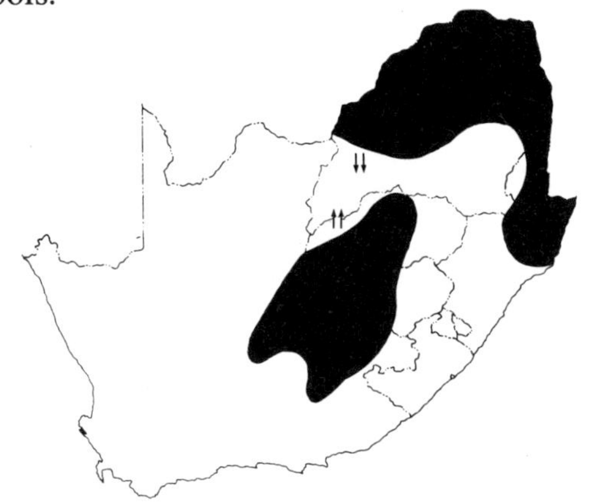

VOICE

A short, coarse, nasal rasping. About two calls per second.

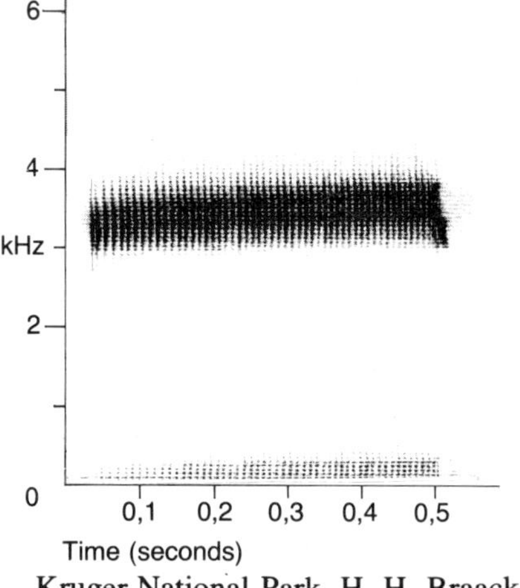

Kruger National Park, H. H. Braack

★ The dorsal colours and patterns are variable but markings are usually symmetrical about the midline. A light scapular patch ▲ is common but may be absent from specimens from the southern part of the range (*B.v. vertebralis*).

★ Parotid glands are inconspicuous. The skin on the dorsum is granular and lacks the large elevations found in most other species.

LIFE SIZE
Mountain Zebra National Park, Cape

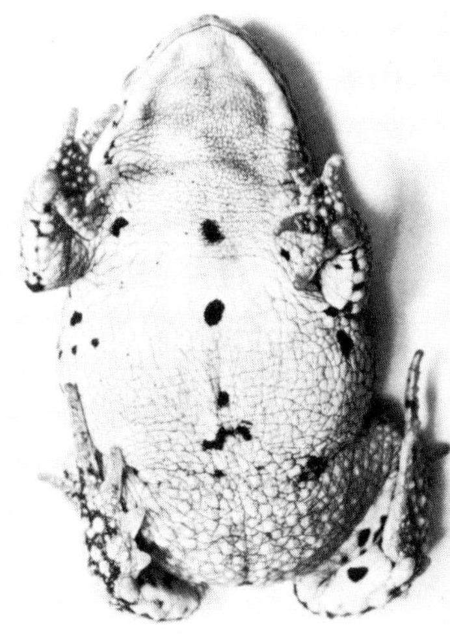

★ The venter is white and granular but less so on the throat which is bright yellow in males. In southern specimens (*B.v. vertebralis*) there are several clear black spots on the belly.

B.v. vertebralis
Mountain Zebra National Park

B.v. fenoulheti Tshaneni, Swaziland

★ The absence of a tarsal fold distinguishes this species from the other local forms.

★ The toes are scantily webbed and their edges are not fringed with webbing.

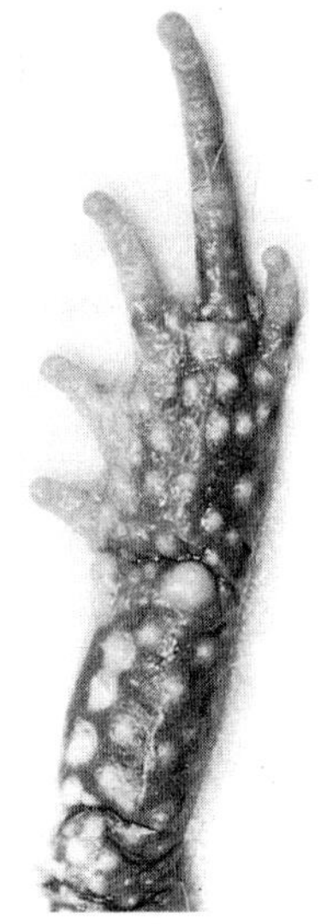

B.v. vertebralis
Preserved specimen
Transvaal Museum

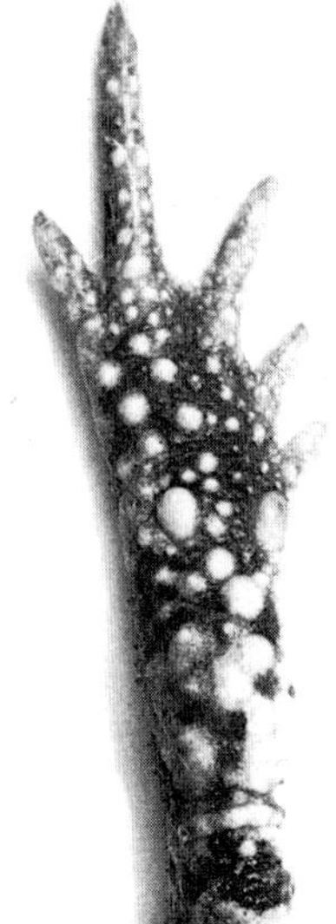

B.v. fenoulheti
Tshaneni, Swaziland

RAIN FROGS

Breviceps Merrem

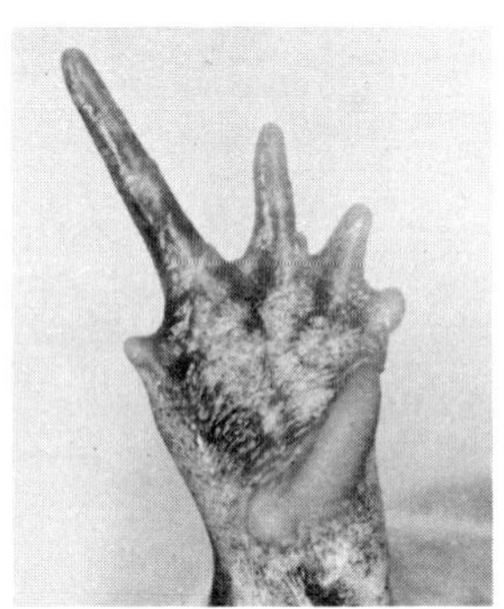

- ★ The pupil is horizontal.
- ★ The snout is short.
- ★ The limbs are shorter than the body width.
- ★ The fingers and toes lack webbing, except in *B. macrops*.

Eleven species occur in South Africa. Several of these are sylvicolous, living under the moist conditions of the forest floor, but most live in more open situations, and several species are successful in arid regions of the country.

The body is stout and almost globose, a feature which is accentuated by the ability to inflate the body with air when molested. The snout is short, and the eyes tend to be located anteriorly or antero-laterally. The mouth is narrow and terminal. The limbs are short and stout, and the inner and outer metatarsal tubercles are strongly developed in accordance with the burrowing habit. Burrowing is accomplished by a 'shuffling' movement of the hindlimbs, during which soil is displaced by the tubercles and feet. The dark coloration and patterning on the dorsum are cryptic. Amplexus is unusual in that, where it has been observed, the male becomes 'glued' to the posterior regions of the female. Their common name is derived from the fact that they seldom emerge from underground except during rainy periods.

Sexual Dimorphism

The throat in males is often darkly pigmented, and in some species deeply wrinkled.

Eggs

Eggs are very large and unpigmented, with thick and viscous jelly capsules. They are laid in subterranean nests or burrows in damp situations. The eggs, and a number of eggless capsules which frequently accompany them, adhere to one another forming a compact ball. The clutch comprises a comparatively small number of eggs.

Tadpoles

The larval stage is suppressed. It is passed within the egg jelly, and there is no foraging larva. Newly metamorphosed froglets emerge from the egg capsule, and the genus is therefore terrestrial throughout the life cycle.

Distribution

The genus is well represented in southern Africa, and a few species extend north into East Africa.

PLAINTIVE RAIN FROG

*Breviceps verrucosus** Rapp 1842

Syn: *B. maculatus* FitzSimons
Subspecies
Breviceps verrucosus verrucosus Rapp
Breviceps verrucosus tympanifer Hewitt
See page 258, 259

B. v. verrucosus Bulwer, Natal

B. v. tympanifer Hogsback, Cape

Drakensberg Gardens, Natal (previously *B. maculatus*)

PLAINTIVE RAIN FROGS *Breviceps verrucosus*

BREEDING HABITAT

Short, horizontal burrows (5-10 cm in Durban) just below the ground in and adjacent to natural riverine forests. Males call both from within burrows and in the open, sometimes clambering up onto stones or tussocks to call (Poynton and Pritchard, 1976).

VOICE

A thin, shrill, protracted whistle repeated slowly and usually alternating with other callers. About one call every three seconds.

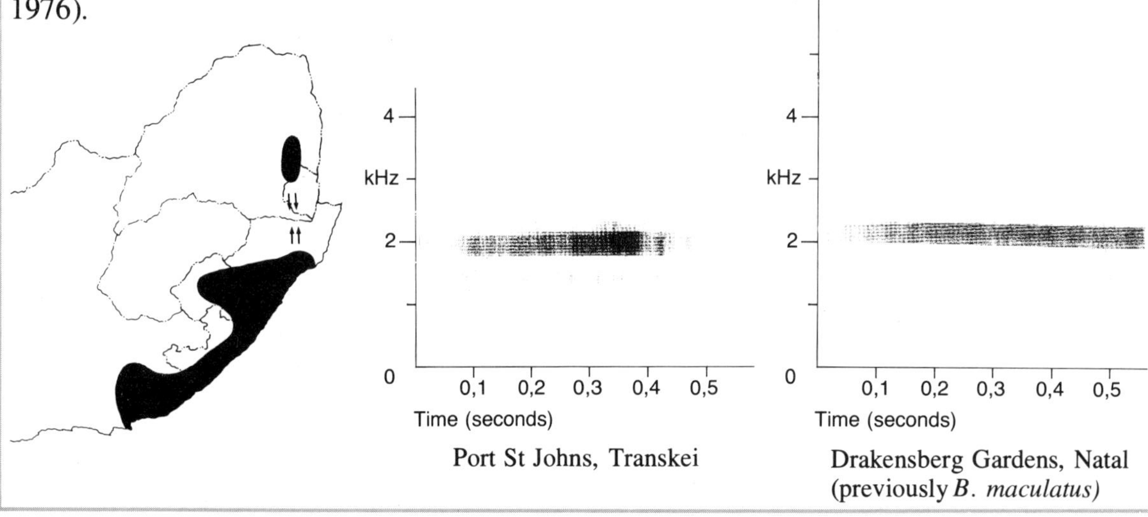

Port St Johns, Transkei

Drakensberg Gardens, Natal (previously *B. maculatus*)

*The close morphological similarity between *B. maculatus* and *B. verrucosus* is reinforced by the fact that they possess almost identical mating calls. On the basis of the limited amount of material that we have examined, we consider these forms to be conspecific.

★ Dorsal granules are large and pitted. The colour is usually uniform, but mottling on the flanks and an indistinct dorsal band or patches may be visible. A light line is present on the back of the legs in some southern specimens *(B. v. tympanifer)*.
★ The eye is comparatively small.
★ The tympanum ▲ is generally visible — cf. other species.

LIFE SIZE

Hogsback, Cape

Hogsback, Cape

★ The venter is densely granular, off-white and often mottled or speckled.

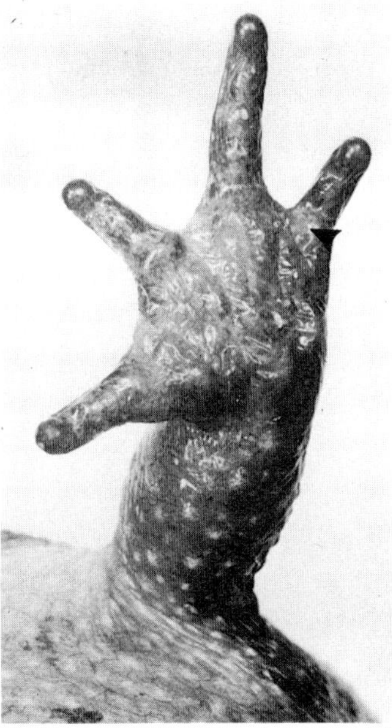

★ The palmar tubercles are moderately developed, and the basal subarticular tubercles ▲ are single.

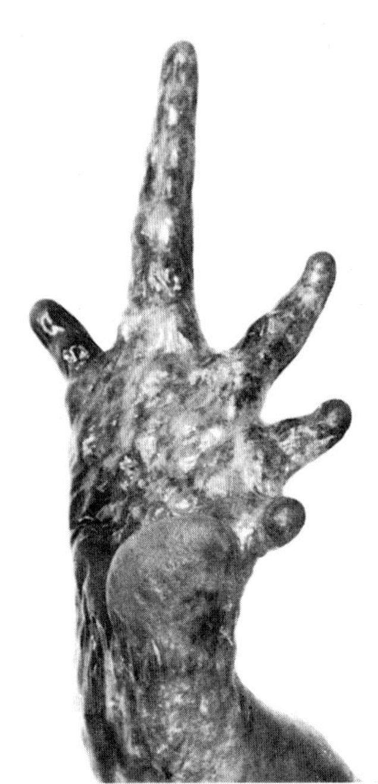

Hogsback, Cape

★ The inner and outer toes are noticeably longer than they are wide — cf. species other than *B. acutirostris*, *B. fuscus* and *B. sylvestris* which are either dorsally or ventrally distinctive.

STRAWBERRY RAIN FROG *Breviceps acutirostris* Poynton 1963

STRAWBERRY RAIN FROGS *Breviceps acutirostris* Heidelberg, Cape

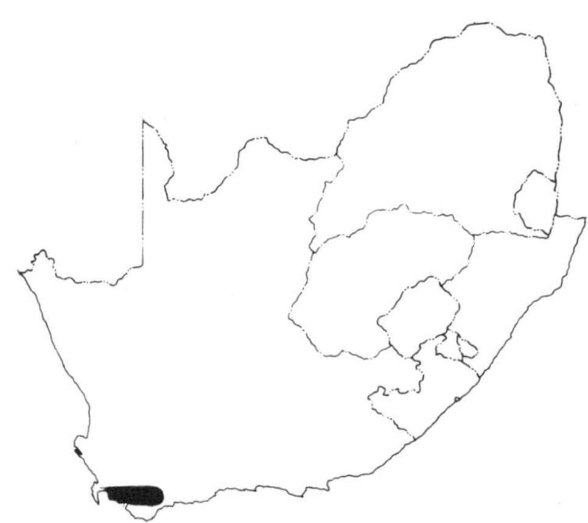

BREEDING HABITAT

Thick leaf beds on the floor of indigenous southern Cape forests where there is overhead canopy and undergrowth (H. Braack, personal communication).

- ★ The dorsum is brown or reddish and covered with black granules which become fused and dense in the vertebral region — cf. all the other species.
- ★ The eye is small and dark.
- ★ The tympanum is hidden.

LIFE SIZE
Heidelberg, Cape

Heidelberg, Cape

- ★ The venter is finely granular and plum coloured with white spots — cf. all other species. Granules are heavier on the throat in males.

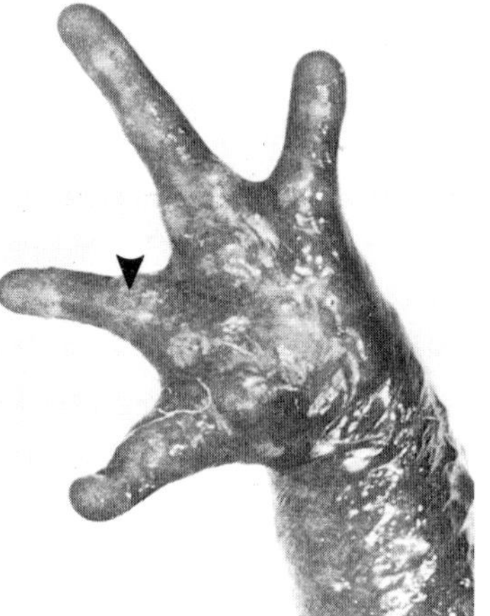

Heidelberg, Cape

- ★ The palmar tubercles are poorly developed, and the basal subarticular tubercles ▲ are single.

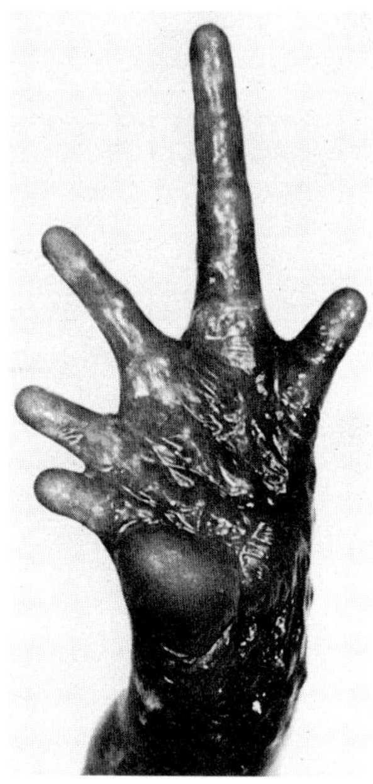

Heidelberg, Cape

- ★ The inner and the outer toes are noticeably longer than they are wide — cf. species other than *B. verrucosus*, *B. fuscus* and *B. sylvestris* which are dorsally and ventrally distinctive.

CAPE RAIN FROG

Breviceps gibbosus (Linnaeus) 1758

Blaasop
Jan Blom
Cape Short-head

CAPE RAIN FROG *Breviceps gibbosus* Rondebosch, Cape

BREEDING HABITAT

Burrows in sandy regions of the Cape Flats and Peninsula usually close to bushes, logs or rocks.

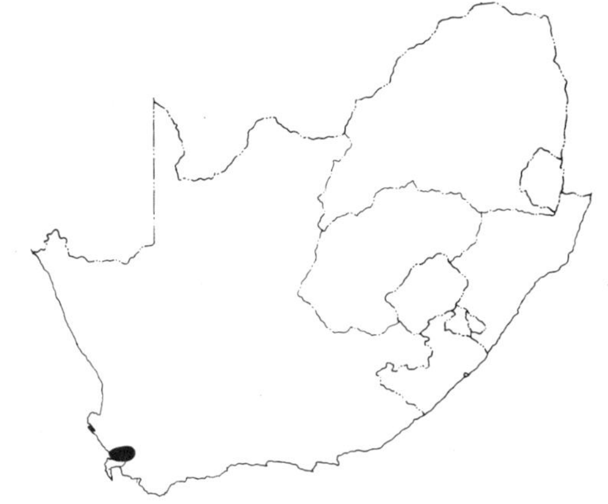

VOICE

A burred, alto squawk less than half a second in duration and repeated at short intervals. About one call per second.

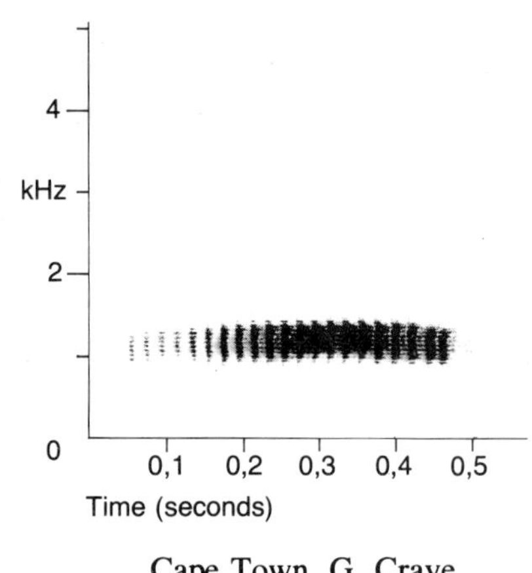

Cape Town, G. Craye

★ The dorsum is very granular particularly on the head. A cream band or series of cream patches is usually evident in the paravertebral region.
★ The eye is comparatively small.
★ The tympanum is hidden.

LIFE SIZE Rondebosch, Cape

Rondebosch, Cape

★ The venter is granular and mottled brown on cream. Granulation is heavier on the throat in males.

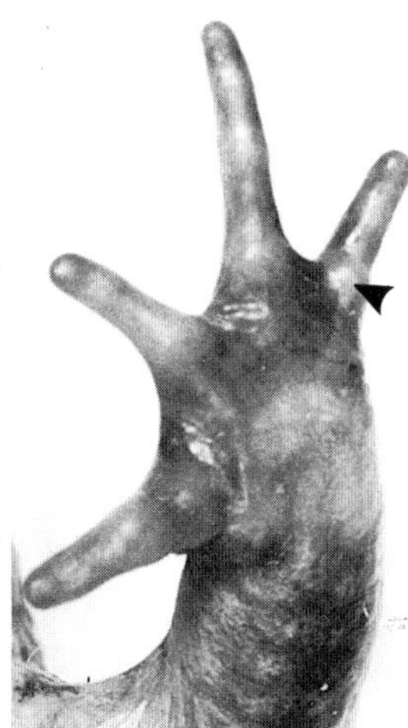

Rondebosch, Cape

★ Palmar tubercles are poorly developed, and the basal subarticular tubercles ▲ are single.

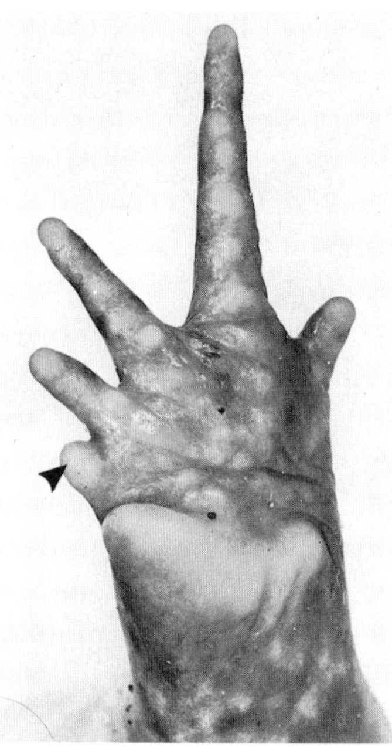

Rondebosch, Cape

★ The length of the inner toe ▲ is approximately equal to its width. The length of the outer toe is greater than its width — cf. all other species except *B.sylvestris* and *B.namaquensis.*

PLAIN RAIN FROG *Breviceps fuscus* Hewitt 1925

Jan Blom

PLAIN RAIN FROG *Breviceps fuscus* Plettenberg Bay, Cape

BREEDING HABITAT

Shallow tunnels (±15 cm) in the forest floor and in adjacent clearings in the southern Cape. Males call from the mouths of burrows which are generally located at the bases of trees (J. Clarke, personal communication).

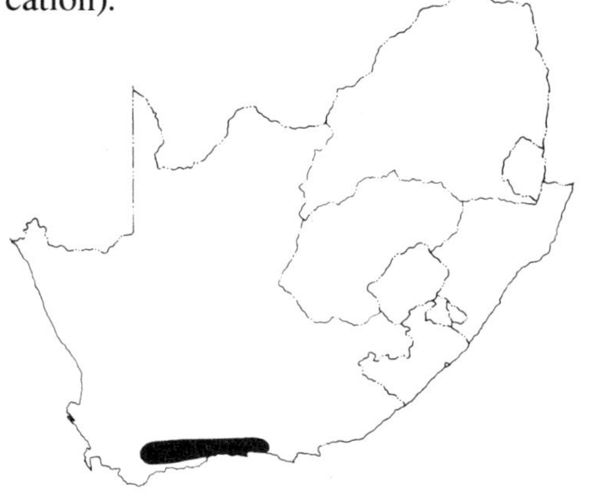

VOICE

A quick chirrup repeated at short intervals. About two calls every three seconds.

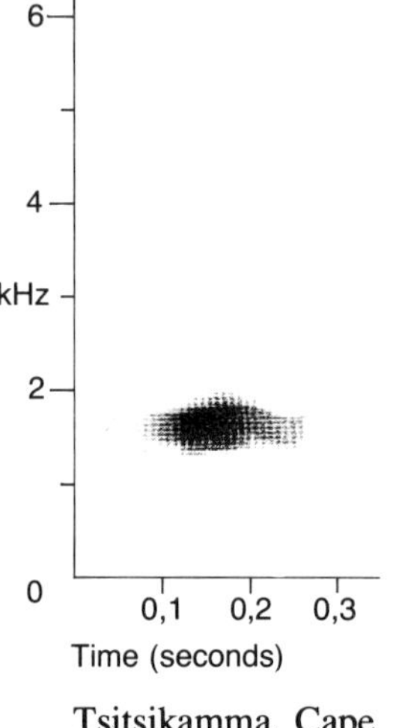

Tsitsikamma, Cape

★ The dorsum is covered in small pointed granules. The colour is uniform and varies from brown to charcoal.
★ The eye is small and dark.
★ The tympanum is hidden.

LIFE SIZE
Tsitsikamma National Park, Cape

★ The venter is purplish-brown and sparsely granular except on the throat — cf. all other species. The throat is very dark in males.

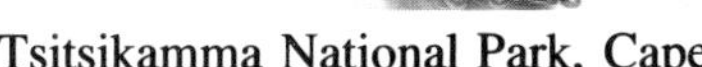

Tsitsikamma National Park, Cape

★ Palmar tubercles are moderately developed, and the basal subarticular tubercles ▲ are usually single.

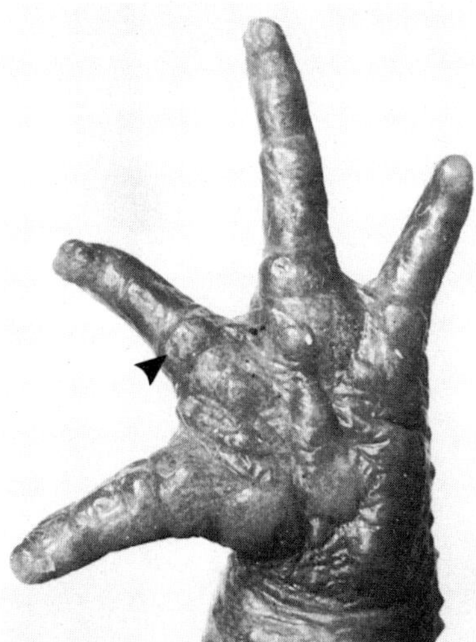

Tsitsikamma National Park, Cape

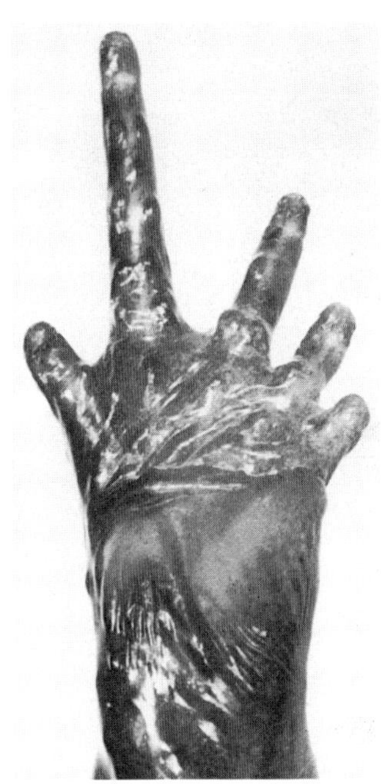

Plettenberg Bay, Cape

★ The inner and outer toes are noticeably longer than they are wide — cf. species other than *B. verrucosus*, *B. acutirostris* and *B. sylvestris* which are each ventrally distinctive.

TRANSVAAL FOREST RAIN FROG

Breviceps sylvestris FitzSimons 1930

Subspecies
Breviceps sylvestris sylvestris FitzSimons
Breviceps sylvestris taeniatus Poynton
See page 259

TRANSVAAL FOREST RAIN FROG *Breviceps sylvestris* Tzaneen, Transvaal

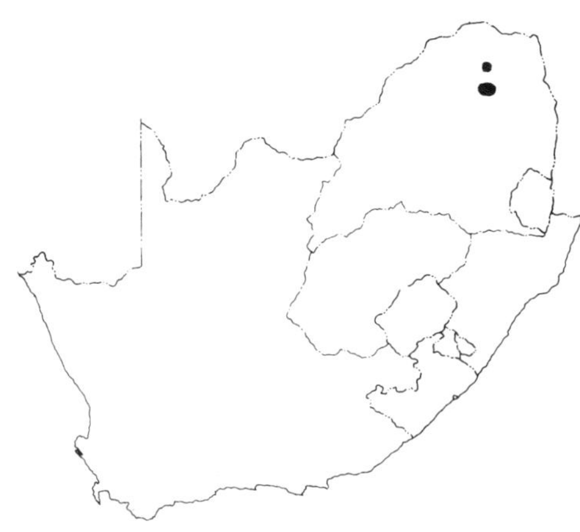

BREEDING HABITAT

Forest floor in the Tzaneen and Louis Trichardt districts.

- The dorsal granules are small and conical and paravertebral skin ridges ▲ are evident. Irregular light patches usually occur between the ridges and on the flanks.
- The eye is moderately sized.
- The tympanum is hidden within a conspicuous dark streak running from eye to armpit.

LIFE SIZE
Tzaneen, Transvaal

Tzaneen, Transvaal

- The venter is sparsely granular and mottled brown on white. Granulation is heavier on the throat.

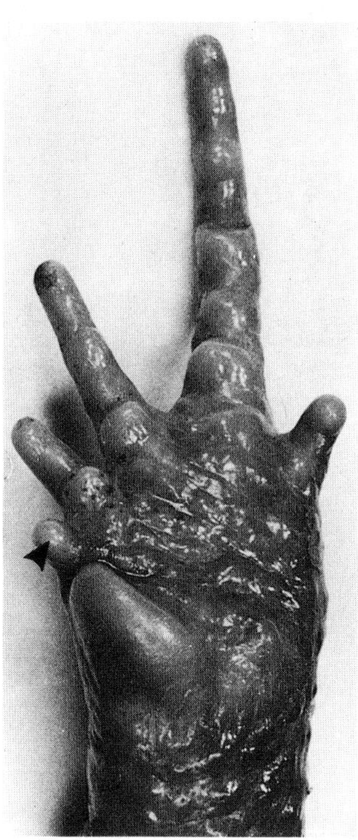

Soutpansberg, Transvaal
Preserved specimen
Transvaal Museum

- Palmar subarticular tubercles are well developed and the basal subarticular tubercle is single.

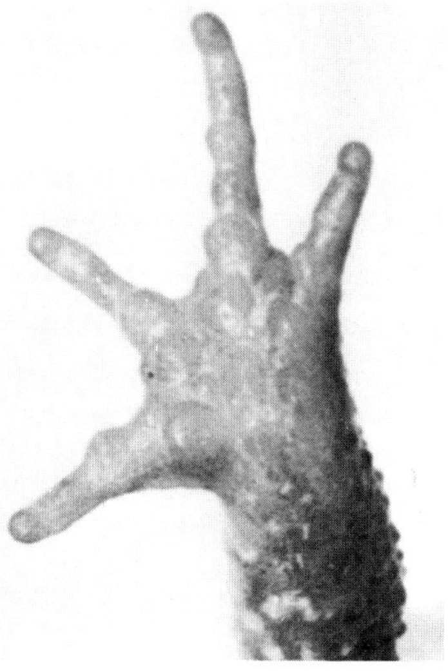

Tzaneen, Transvaal

- The length of the inner toe ▲ is approximately equal to its width. The length of the outer toe is greater than its width — cf. all other species except *B. gibbosus* and *B. namaquensis*.

CAPE MOUNTAIN RAIN FROG *Breviceps montanus* Power 1926

Mountain Blaasop

CAPE MOUNTAIN RAIN FROG *Breviceps montanus* Greyton, Cape

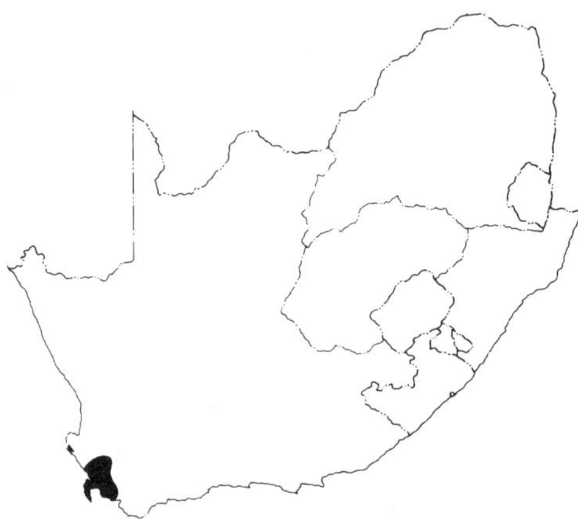

VOICE

A brief whistle. About one call per second.

BREEDING HABITAT

Stony, scrub-covered hillsides in the southern Cape. Males call from amongst outcrops of stones (H. Braack, personal communication).

- ★ The dorsum is finely granular. Light paravertebral patches fuse into a scalloped band with dark ridged edges — cf. *B. adspersus* and *B. mossambicus*. The dark streak from eye to armpit is distinct.
- ★ The eye is moderately sized.
- ★ The tympanum is hidden with a conspicuous dark streak running from eye to armpit.

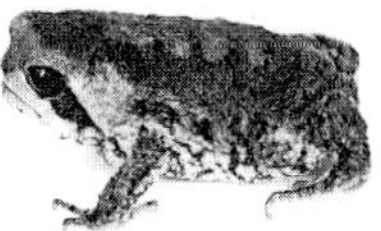

LIFE SIZE
Greyton, Cape

★ The venter is slightly granular and light beige coloured with dark flecks which are concentrated on the throat. Granulation is heavier on the throat and on both fore and hind limbs — cf. *B. rosei*.

Greyton, Cape

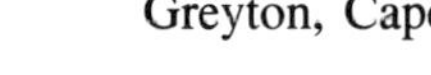

★ The palmar tubercles are well developed, and the basal subarticular tubercles ▲ are single.

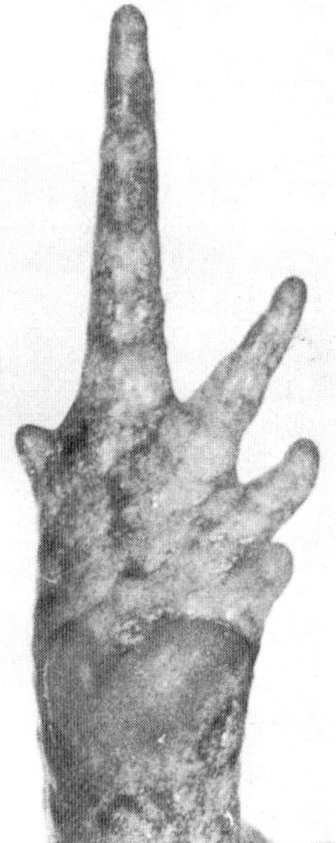

Greyton, Cape

★ The inner and the outer toes are not noticeably longer than they are wide — cf. species other than *B. rosei*, *B. adspersus* and *B. mossambicus* which are either dorsally or ventrally distinctive.

Greyton, Cape

SAND RAIN FROG

Breviceps rosei Power 1926

Subspecies
Breviceps rosei rosei Power
Breviceps rosei vansoni FitzSimons
See page 259

SAND RAIN FROGS *Breviceps rosei*

Witsand, Cape

BREEDING HABITAT

Sand dunes and fynbos in the Western Cape and sometimes on sandy slopes of the mountains. Males call from partly concealed positions amongst bush, sometimes clambering onto the low vegetation.

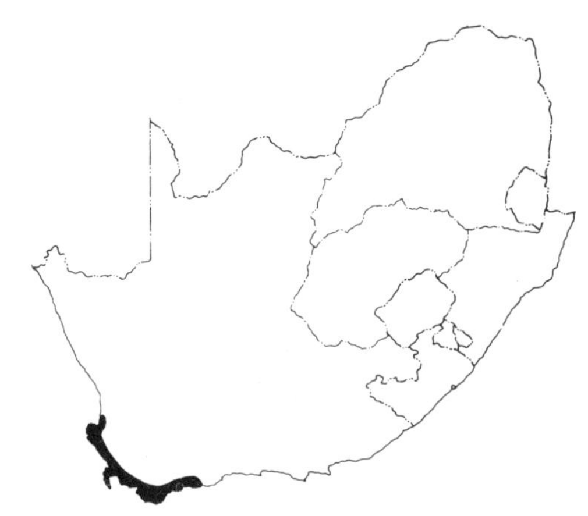

VOICE

A single, very brief cheep, emitted continuously. About one call per second.

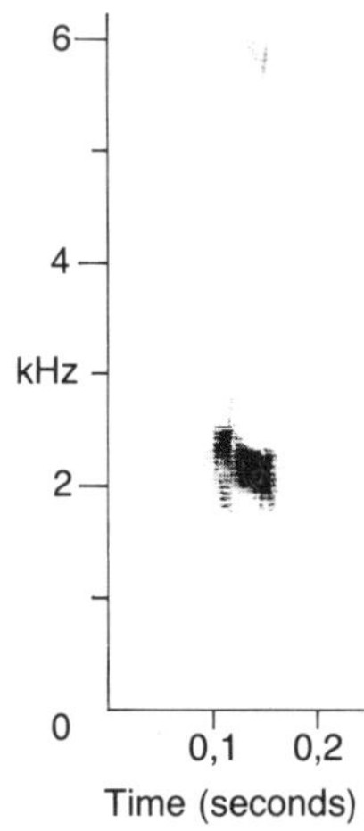

Witsand, Cape, H. H. Braack

- The dorsum is lightly granular. The light grey or tan paravertebral patches tend to fuse into a scalloped band with dark ridged edges — cf. *B. namaquensis*, *B. adspersus* and *B. mossambicus*. A pale vertebral line is common.
- The eye is comparatively large.
- The tympanum is hidden within a conspicuous dark streak running from eye to armpit.

LIFE SIZE
Witsand, Cape

- The venter is slightly granular and light beige coloured with dark flecks which are concentrated on the throat, more so in males. Granulation is heavier on the throat but not noticeably heavier on the hindlimbs — cf. *B. montanus.*

Witsand, Cape

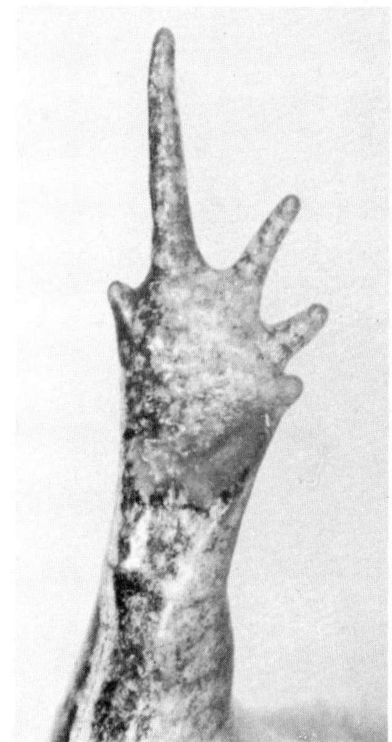

Witsand, Cape

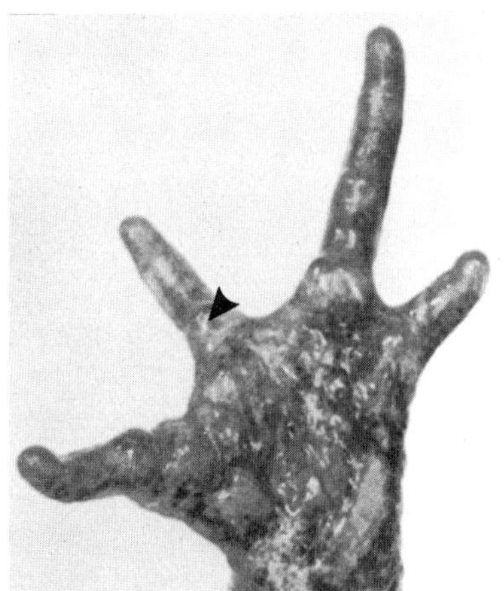

Witsand, Cape

- Palmar tubercles are moderately developed, and the basal subarticular tubercles ▲ are single.

- The inner and outer toes are not noticeably longer than they are wide — cf. species other than *B. montanus*, *B. adspersus* and *B. mossambicus* which are either dorsally or ventrally distinctive.

NAMAQUA RAIN FROG *Breviceps namaquensis* Power 1926

NAMAQUA RAIN FROG *Breviceps namaquensis*

Clanwilliam, Cape
Preserved specimen, Transvaal Museum

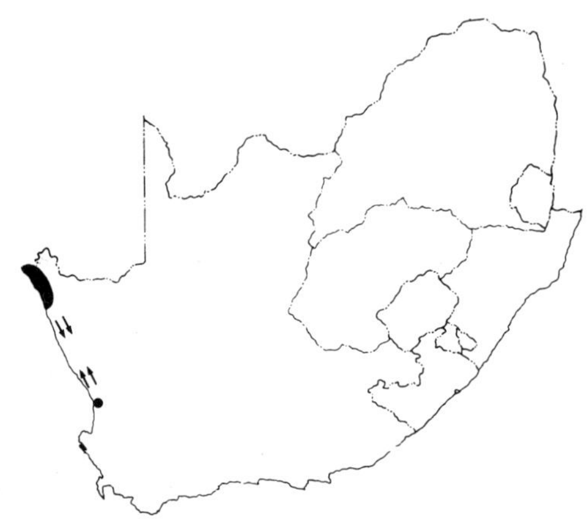

BREEDING HABITAT

Burrows in arid, scrub-covered Namaqualand mountains.

★ The dorsum bears small granules, sparsely distributed. Large, light-coloured paravertebral patches tend to fuse mid-dorsally, and the light ventral coloration extends high on the flanks leaving only a dorso-lateral band of brown ground colour.
★ The eye is large with a pale-coloured iris.
★ The tympanum is hidden.

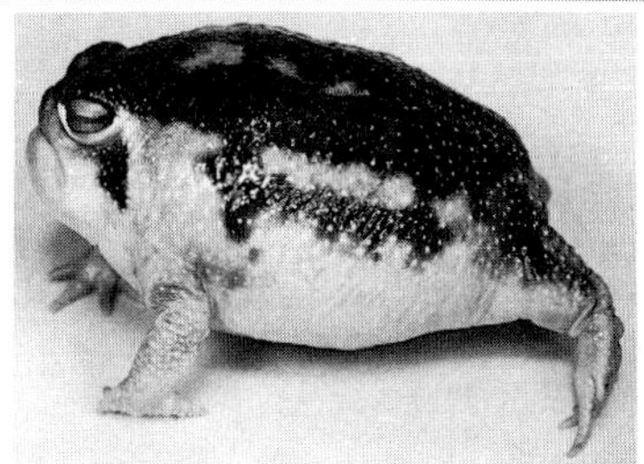

LIFE SIZE Clanwilliam, Cape
Preserved specimen
Transvaal Museum

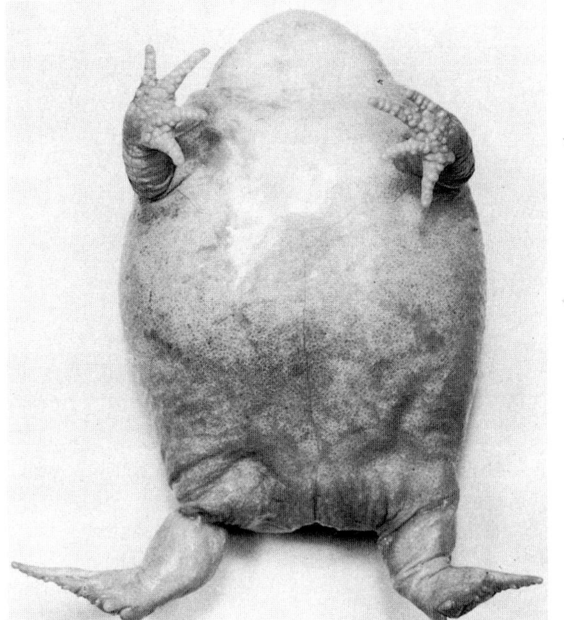

Clanwilliam, Cape
Preserved specimen, Transvaal Museum

★ The venter is uniformly smooth, except for granulation on the throat.

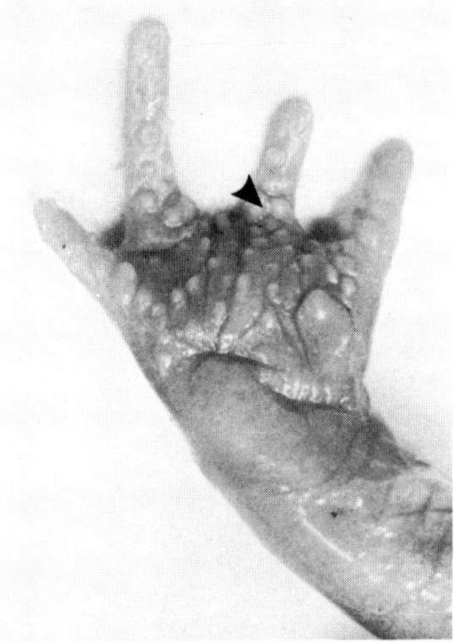

Clanwilliam, Cape
Preserved specimen
Transvaal Museum

★ Palmar tubercles are well developed and the basal subarticular tubercles ▲ are double — cf. other species.

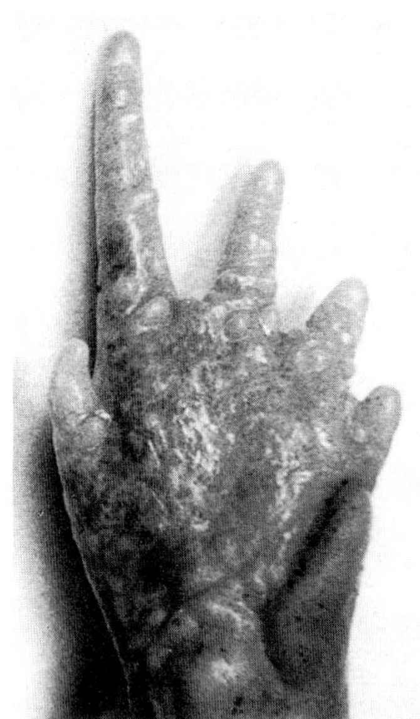

Clanwilliam, Cape
Preserved specimen
Transvaal Museum

★ The inner toe is not noticeably longer than it is wide — cf. species other than *B. sylvestris* and *B. gibbosus*, which are either ventrally distinctive or may be distinguished by the palmar tubercles.

DESERT RAIN FROG *Breviceps macrops* Boulenger 1907

Melkpadda

DESERT RAIN FROG *Breviceps macrops* Port Nolloth, Cape

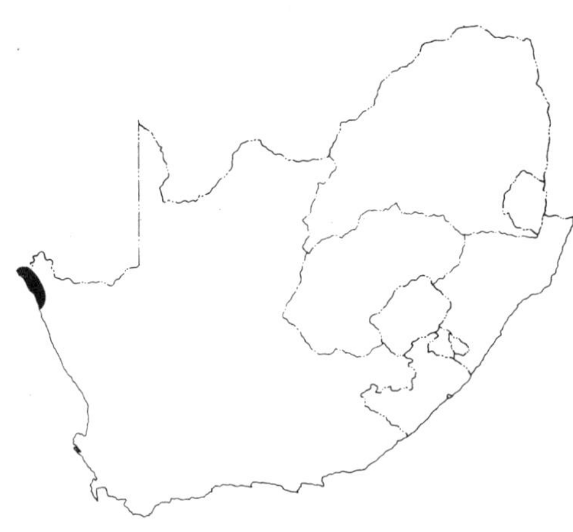

BREEDING HABITAT

Sand dunes and beaches of the Namaqualand coast. At night they range over large areas on the surface of the sand. Desiccation is avoided during the day by burrowing a few centimetres below the surface where the sand is slightly damp.

- ★ The dorsum is smooth, cream, or tan with characteristic chocolate-brown vermiculations, which are heavier in the occipital region.
- ★ The eye is large with a pale-coloured iris.
- ★ The tympanum is hidden.

LIFE SIZE Port Nolloth, Cape

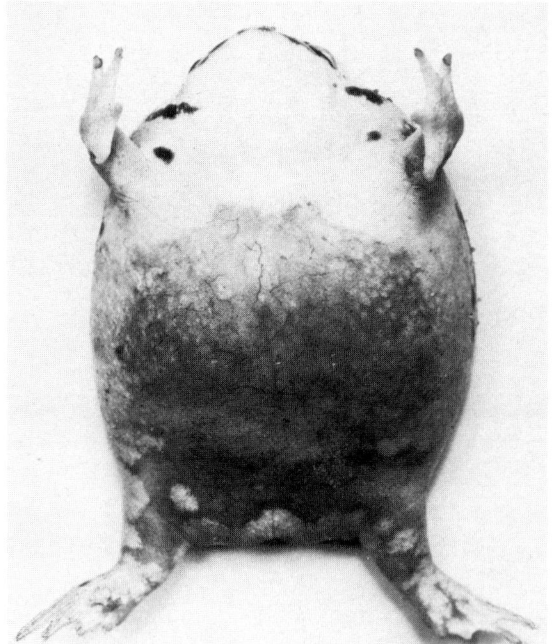

Port Nolloth, Cape

- ★ The venter is smooth and translucent from the level of the forelimbs posteriorly, with dense white pigment elsewhere. The gular region is deeply wrinkled in males.

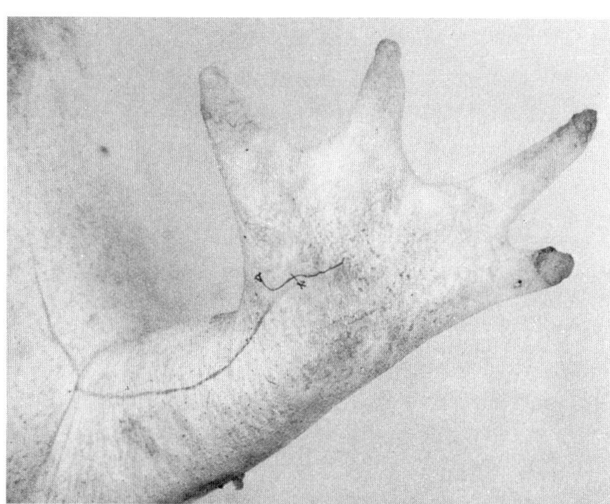

Port Nolloth, Cape

- ★ Palmar tubercles are absent and fingers are fleshily webbed — cf. all other species.

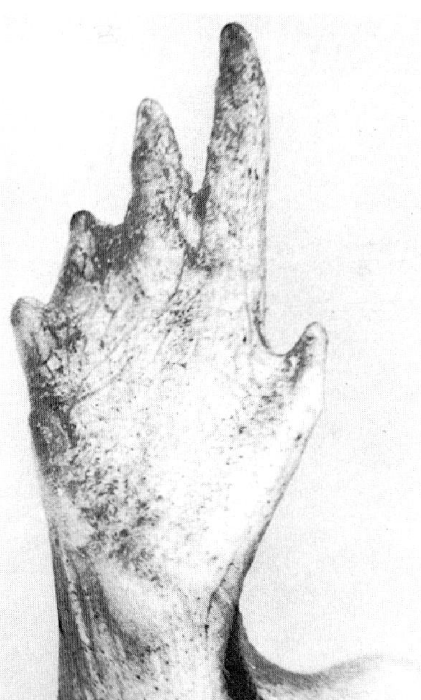

Port Nolloth, Cape

- ★ The feet are very distinctive, being smooth and paddle-like with fleshy webbing between the toes.

BUSHVELD RAIN FROG *Breviceps adspersus** Peters 1882

Common Rain Frog
Blaasop

Subspecies
Breviceps adspersus adspersus Peters
Breviceps adspersus pentheri Werner
See page 260

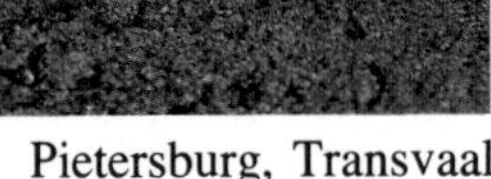

B. a. adspersus Pietersburg, Transvaal
BUSHVELD RAIN FROGS *Breviceps adspersus*

B. a. pentheri Port Elizabeth
R. Boycott

BREEDING HABITAT

Deep burrows (up to 50 cm) in areas of open or lightly wooded savanna where the soil is sandy. Males call both from within the burrows and while walking around at the surface.

VOICE

A short, discordant, creaking chirp, repeated continuously at short intervals. About two or three calls per second.

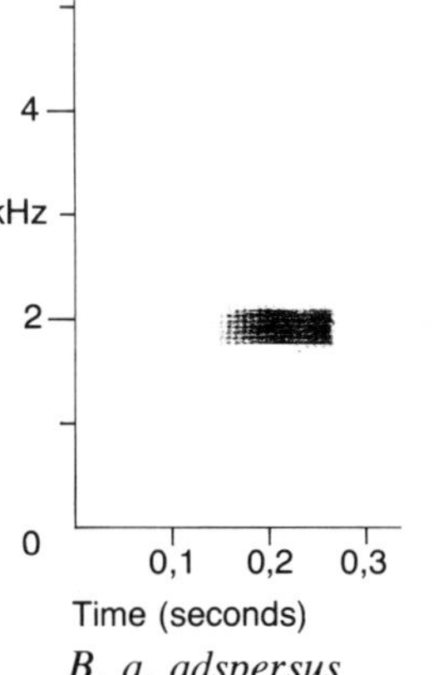

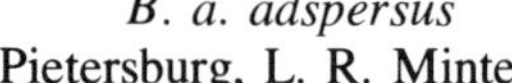

B. a. adspersus
Pietersburg, L. R. Minter

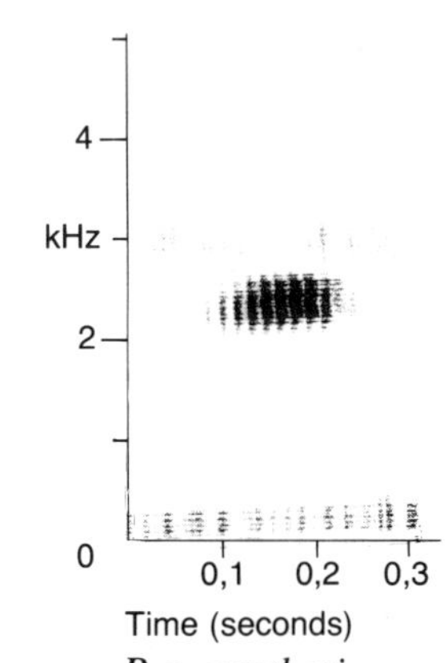

B.a. pentheri
Van Reenen, J. C. Poynton

*In view of the distinct differences between the mating calls of *mossambicus* and *adspersus*, these forms are here considered distinct at the specific level. *B. adspersus* was previously considered by us to be a subspecies of *mossambicus* (Pienaar, Passmore and Carruthers, 1976). Poynton (personal communication) is of the opinion that 'pure' *mossambicus* is not present in southern Mozambique and Rhodesia, and that intergradation of the two species occurs in this region.

★ The dorsal texture and coloration are variable but a dark brown ground colour with lighter yellowish or orange patches is common. The dorsal variability in this species makes identification based on colour or pattern unreliable, especially when comparing it with *B. mossambicus*.

★ The eye is moderately large.

★ The tympanum is hidden within a dark streak running from eye to armpit. The streak is conspicuous except in some specimens from the south and east of the range (*B.a. pentheri*) where it may be obscured by an over-all dark ground colour.

LIFE SIZE
Pietersburg, Transvaal

★ The ventral surface is smooth and white with brown marbling on the throat, and occasionally at the perimeter, but not mid-ventrally, except in some specimens from the south and east of the range (*B. a. pentheri*) — cf. *B. montanus, B. rosei* and *B. mossambicus*. The throat is very dark in males.

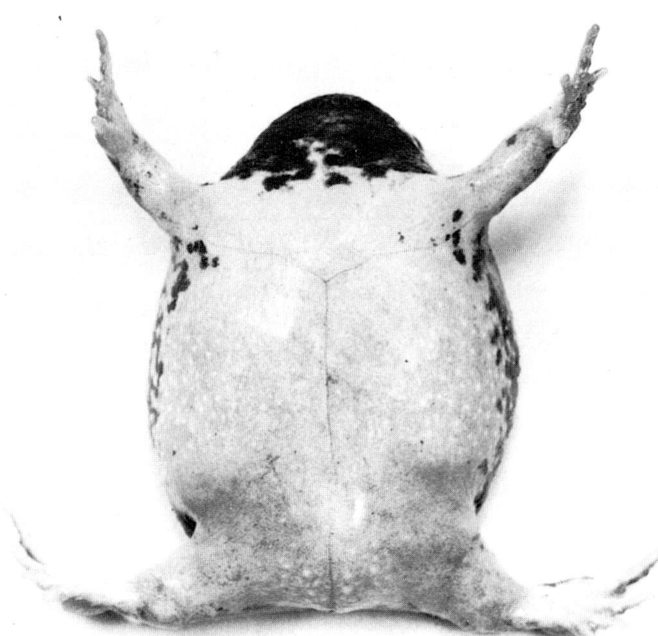

Pietersburg, Transvaal

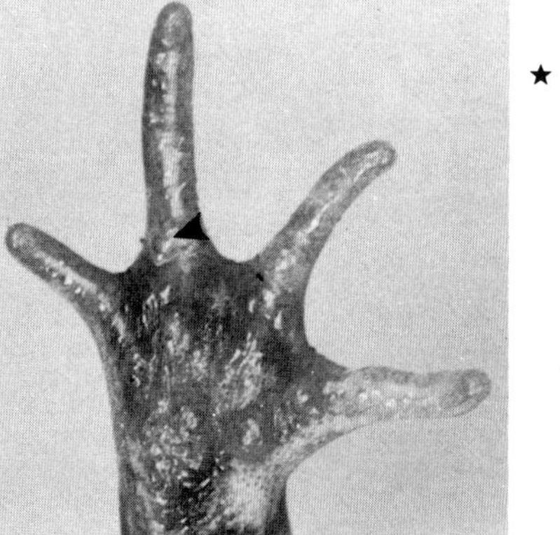

Pietersburg, Transvaal

★ Palmar tubercles are moderately to well developed, and the basal subarticular tubercles ▲ are single — cf. *B. namaquensis*.

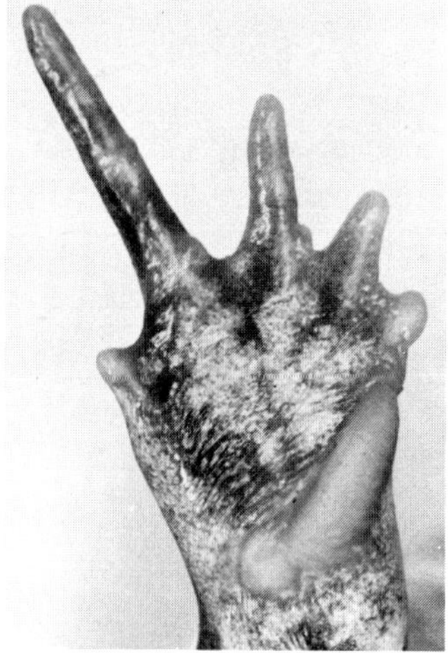

Pietersburg, Transvaal

★ The inner and outer toes are not noticeably longer than they are wide — cf. species other than *B. montanus, B. rosei* and *B. mossambicus*, which are ventrally distinctive, and which can be distinguished by the palmar tubercles.

MOZAMBIQUE RAIN FROG *Breviceps mossambicus** Peters 1854

Flat-faced Frog

MOZAMBIQUE RAIN FROG *B. mossambicus* Malongane, Mozambique

BREEDING HABITAT

"The habitat seems to be open grassland or scrub country" (Stewart, 1967). Males are known to call from the mouths of burrows.

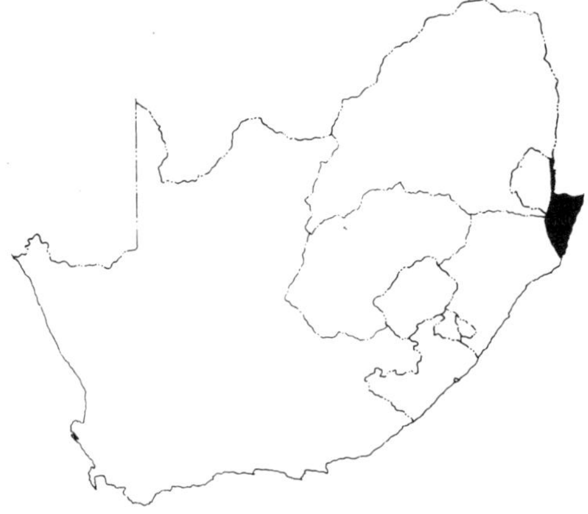

VOICE

A short sparrow-like chirp. About two calls per second.

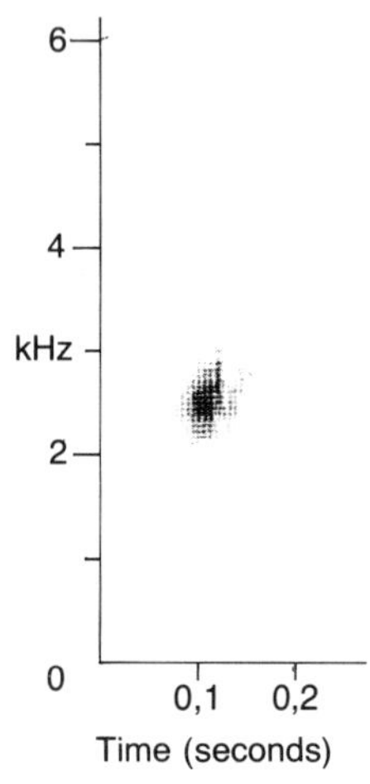

Malongane, Mozambique

*See note under *Breviceps adspersus* page 102

- ★ The dorsal texture and coloration are variable but the ground colour is commonly grey to brown and sometimes pinkish anteriorly. This species cannot be separated from *B. adspersus* on the basis of the dorsum, but can be distinguished from *B. montanus* and *B. rosei*.
- ★ The eye is moderately large.
- ★ The tympanum is hidden within a conspicuous dark streak running from eye to armpit.

LIFE SIZE
Namaacha, Swaziland

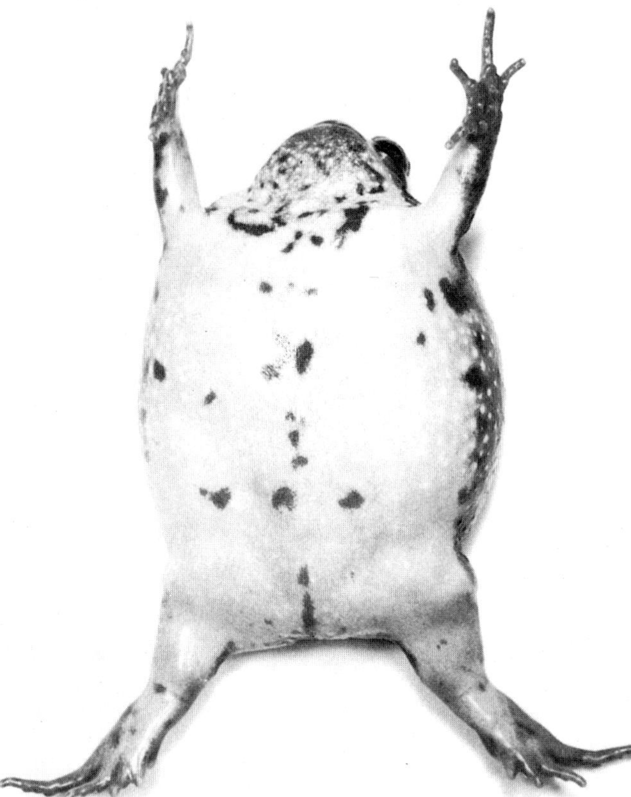

★ The ventral surface is smooth and marbled brown on white anteriorly and mid-ventrally — cf. *B. adspersus*. The throat is very dark in males.

Namaacha, Swaziland

★ Palmar tubercles are moderately to well developed, and the basal subarticular tubercles ▲ are single.

Namaacha, Swaziland

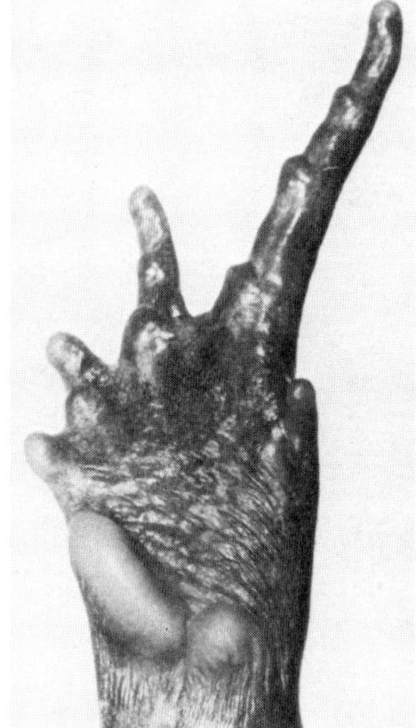

Namaacha, Swaziland

★ The inner and outer toes are not noticeably longer than they are wide — cf. species other than *B. montanus, B. rosei* and *B. adspersus*, which dorsally or ventrally are distinctive.

RUBBER FROGS

Phrynomerus Noble

- ★ The dorsum is dark with conspicuous red or pink markings.
- ★ The pupil is circular.
- ★ Tips of the fingers and toes are expanded.
- ★ Fingers lack webbing.
- ★ Webbing on the toes is either scanty or absent.

Two species occur in South Africa. They are essentially savanna forms, capable of surviving in arid regions, but not confined to such areas.

Both species are of moderate size, with bodies more elongated and depressed than most other frogs. The head is characteristically mobile and capable of some movement in the lateral plane. The eyes are comparatively small and dull with an approximately circular pupil. During walking or running, which is the normal mode of progression, *P. bifasciatus* carries its body high on slender limbs, while *P. annectens* scurries about flat against the ground. The genus is not arboreal in habit, as is suggested by the terminally expanded digits, but is most often encountered at or near ground level. Individuals, however, are sometimes found in more elevated positions on rocks, stumps, or even vertical walls. They have also been reported to burrow. Coloration is striking, and the bright colours are aposematic in function. The skin is smooth and rubbery to the touch, and the skin secretion of at least one of the species, *P. bifasciatus*, is toxic and irritant. Teeth are absent. Ants form a significant part of the diet. Breeding occurs in both temporary rain pools and permanent standing water.

Sexual Dimorphism

The gular region in males is darker than the belly, but it may retain the over-all ventral pattern in darker colour.

Eggs

Oviposition occurs at the surface or beneath it. The eggs are small and laid together with copious amounts of jelly. They are usually attached to, or entangled amongst, vegetation.

Tadpoles

Both species have nektonic filter feeding tadpoles which lack horny mouthparts. They are somewhat similar in behaviour to *Xenopus* tadpoles and are gregarious in the case of *P. annectens*. The tail is well developed and highly motile (Wager, 1965; Channing, 1976).

Distribution

The genus is distributed on the African continent south of the Sahara.

BANDED RUBBER FROG *Phrynomerus bifasciatus* (Smith) 1847

Red-banded Frog

BANDED RUBBER FROG *Phrynomerus bifasciatus* Tshaneni, Swaziland

BREEDING HABITAT

Shallow pans or inundated grass in savanna and acacia veld. Calling males usually remain exposed at the water's edge.

VOICE

A loud melodious trill sustained over one or two seconds. About one call every six seconds.

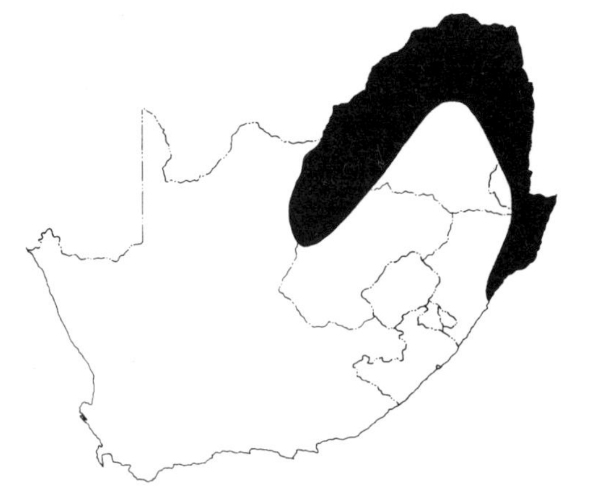

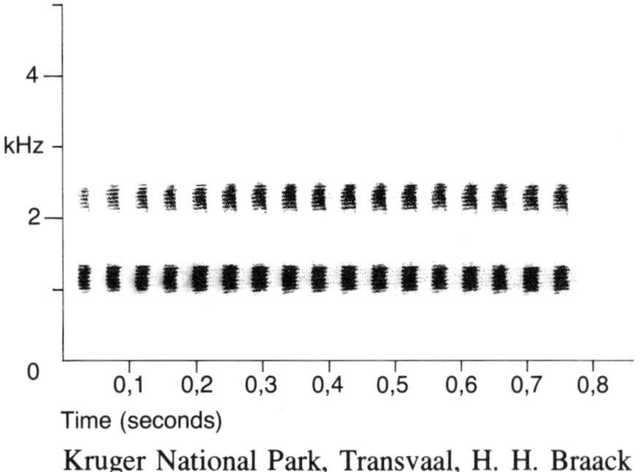

Kruger National Park, Transvaal, H. H. Braack

★ The dorsal skin is smooth. The pattern is fairly consistent although some variation is found in the degree of ventro-lateral mottling and the dorso-lateral stripes are sometimes broken. Lighting conditions and attitude bring about considerable colour changes. The black ground colour can take on a gold sheen and dorsal markings change from deep crimson to almost white.

LIFE SIZE   Naboomspruit, Transvaal

Tshaneni, Swaziland

★ The venter is smooth and grey with distinct white spots. The throat in males is dark with the spots smaller or absent.

★ Webbing is almost absent from the toes.

Tshaneni, Swaziland

MARBLED RUBBER FROG *Phrynomerus annectens* (Werner) 1910

Red Marbled Frog

MARBLED RUBBER FROG *Phrynomerus annectens* Augrabies Falls National Park, N. Cape

BREEDING HABITAT

Temporary pools in depressions in rocky, arid areas. Males call from positions concealed amongst rocks around the pools (Channing, 1976).

VOICE

A loud harsh trill sustained for several seconds.

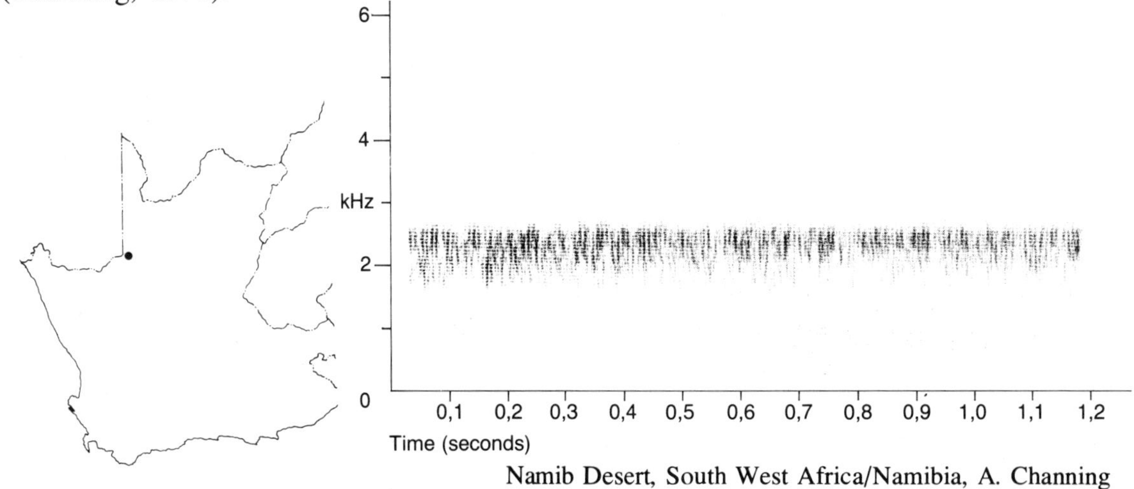

Namib Desert, South West Africa/Namibia, A. Channing

★ The red dorsal patches are variable in shape, but they are never elongated into stripes as in *P. bifasciatus*.

Life Size

Augrabies Falls National Park N. Cape

★ The venter is smooth, pinkish brown and darker under the jaw in males.

Augrabies Falls National Park, N. Cape

★ The toes are slightly webbed at the base.

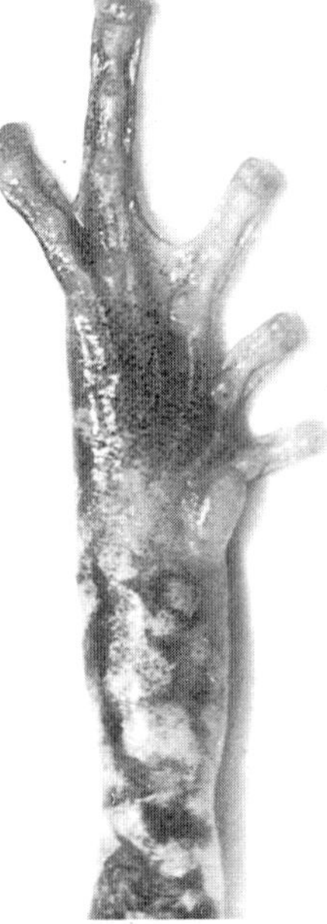

Augrabies Falls National Park N. Cape

BULLFROGS

*Pyxicephalus** Tschudi

- ★ Large tooth-like projections are present on the lower jaw.
- ★ The pupil is horizontal.
- ★ Fingers lack webbing.
- ★ Fleshy webbing is present between toes.
- ★ The inner metatarsal tubercle is massive and flanged.

The genus is monotypic. Generic and specific characteristics are illustrated together in the identification section of the only species, *Pyxicephalus adspersus*.

Bullfrogs are the largest South African frogs, reaching 200 mm in length. They show strong burrowing tendencies and they occur in both wet and dry regions of the country.

The body is stout with a broad, heavy head and a wide gape. The general appearance undergoes noticeable changes with age. Younger specimens (under 100 mm) are stocky and agile, whereas larger ones become flaccid and develop a clumsy gait. The large tubercle on the heel facilitates the backward shuffling movement with which burrowing is accomplished. Bullfrogs are infrequently encountered, even in areas where large populations are known to exist. This gives credence to reports that as many as 10 months of the year may be spent underground. Large-scale emergence occurs during the breeding season, and in some areas moderate sized individuals are more common than really large ones. Sexual maturity is reached well before the maximum size is attained.

Large males are known to defend themselves aggressively if threatened, and they also exhibit aggressive tendencies towards one another at the breeding site. Bullfrogs may derive their name from the loud bovine call they emit if molested. This is not the mating call.

*Most herpetologists appear to regard *Tomopterna* and *Pyxicephalus* as distinct genera, and they are here treated in this way. Morphological and ecological differences between the two are not really extensive, but the smaller species (*Tomopterna*) form a very homogeneous group, within which interspecific differences are small. The differences between these species and *Pyxicephalus* are of *comparatively* much greater magnitude, and in the opinion of the present authors, generic distinction is warranted.

Sexual Dimorphism

The throat in males is deep yellow and uniform cream in females.

Eggs

Numerous heavily pigmented eggs are laid individually in shallow water.

Tadpoles

The benthonic tadpoles are squat, heavy-bodied and gregarious.

Distribution

Pyxicephalus occurs in most of sub-Saharan Africa in both wet and dry conditions, but primarily in open country.

BULLFROG *Pyxicephalus adspersus* Tschudi 1838

Giant Pyxie

SUB-ADULT Tshaneni, Swaziland

ADULT Sandton, Transvaal JUVENILE Sandton, Transvaal

BULL FROGS *Pyxicephalus adspersus*

BREEDING HABITAT

Temporary rain-filled depressions or vleis in open veld. Males call from positions in the shallow water.

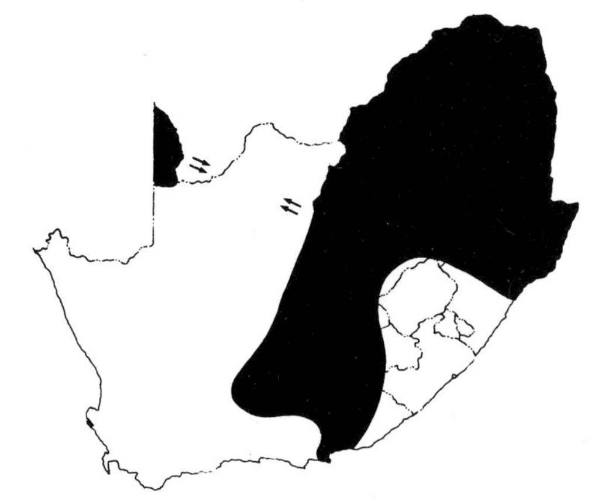

VOICE

Short, low-pitched whooping sounds emitted at irregular intervals.

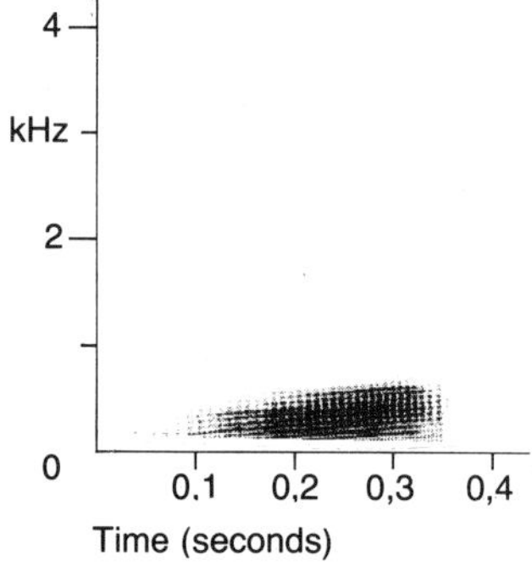

Kruger National Park, H. H. Braack

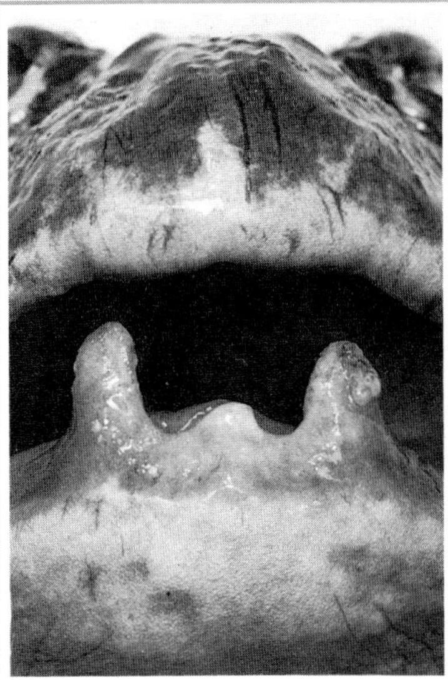

HALF LIFE SIZE Sandton, Transvaal

★ The dorsum bears a number of longitudinal elevated skin folds which are more prominent in larger specimens. Smaller animals are usually spotted and variable in colour, while larger ones are plain, with a dark olive-green dorsum.

★ Three toothlike projections are present in the lower jaw. With age, the outer two become longer and more prominent.

★ The ventral surface is smooth. In large specimens it is cream or pale yellow with bright orange infusions in the axillary region. In small specimens the venter is blueish grey.

Tshaneni, Swaziland

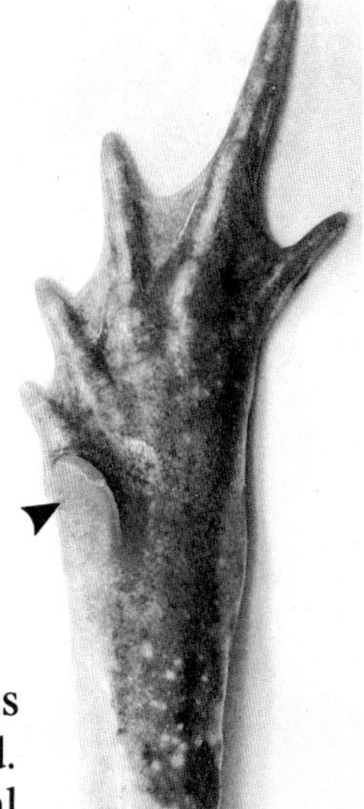

★ The inner metatarsal tubercle ▲ is massively developed and flanged. There is no outer metatarsal tubercle.

Tshaneni, Swaziland

SAND FROGS

*Tomopterna** Duméril and Bibron

- ★ There are no distinctive black and white Y-shaped markings on throat, nor paired external gular sacs in males — cf. *Hildebrandtia*.
- ★ The pupil is horizontal.
- ★ Fingers lack webbing.
- ★ The inner metatarsal tubercle ▲ is massive and flanged.

Five species occur in South Africa. All of these are essentially burrowers and they are successful in the more arid parts of the country, but are not confined to such regions.

Adults are stout, moderate sized frogs, rather toad-like in both form and gait. The head is broad and carries large bulging eyes with horizontal pupils. The limbs are short, and the large inner metatarsal tubercle enables the frog to burrow rapidly into the substrate by way of a 'shuffling' soil-displacing movement of the hindlimbs. The toes are moderately webbed. The dorsal patterning and coloration are cryptic.

Sexual Dimorphism

Some black pigmentation is usually evident along the margins of the lower jaw of both sexes, but in males it is carried well down over the gular region.

*See note under *Pyxicephalus*, page 112

EGGS

Eggs are small and pigmented, with individual jelly capsules which sometimes adhere to one another.

TADPOLES

The tadpoles are heavy-bodied, benthonic and sluggish.

DISTRIBUTION

The genus is confined to sub-Saharan Africa and India.

CAPE SAND FROG

*Tomopterna delalandii** (Tschudi) 1838

Delalande's Frog

Syn: *Pyxicephalus delalandei delalandei* Tschudi

CAPE SAND FROG *Tomopterna delalandii* — Hout Bay, Cape

BREEDING HABITAT

The edges of pans, dams, vleis or lagoons in sandy terrain. Calling males generally conceal themselves under vegetation or in cavities.

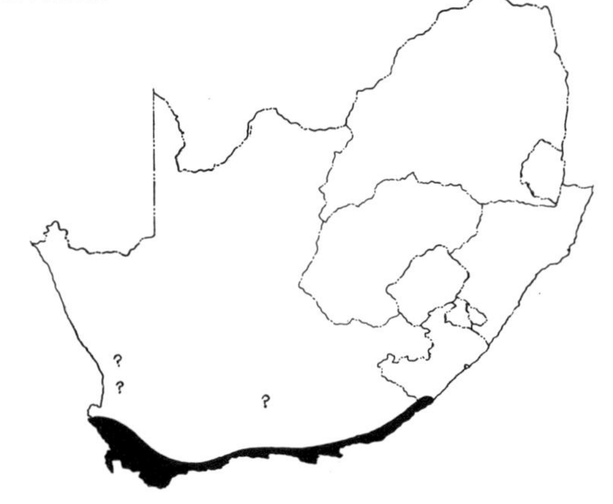

VOICE

Distinct ringing notes emitted at the rate of about six to eight per second.

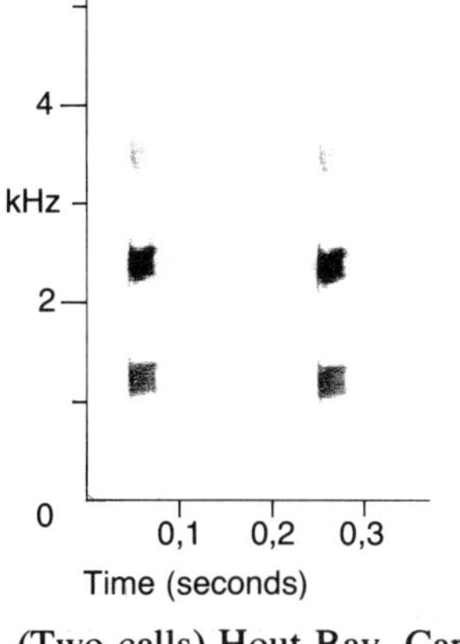

(Two calls) Hout Bay, Cape

*See note under *Tomopterna cryptotis,* page 120

★ The dorsum varies through shades of grey to dark brown. Both vertebral and dorsolateral lines are usually present and sometimes a pale occipital patch ▲ is evident.
★ Glandular elevations below the tympanum ▲ are not completely fused to form a continuous ridge — cf. other species.

LIFE SIZE
Hout Bay, Cape

Bontebok National Park, Cape

★ The ventral skin is smooth and white with grey pigmentation along the jawline and covering much of the gular region in breeding males.
★ Tubercles at the base of the thumb are single — cf. *T. krugerensis*.

★ The outer metatarsal tubercle ▲ is conspicuously elevated — cf. other species.
★ Not more than 3 phalanges of the longest toe are free of webbing ▲ — cf. *T. natalensis*.

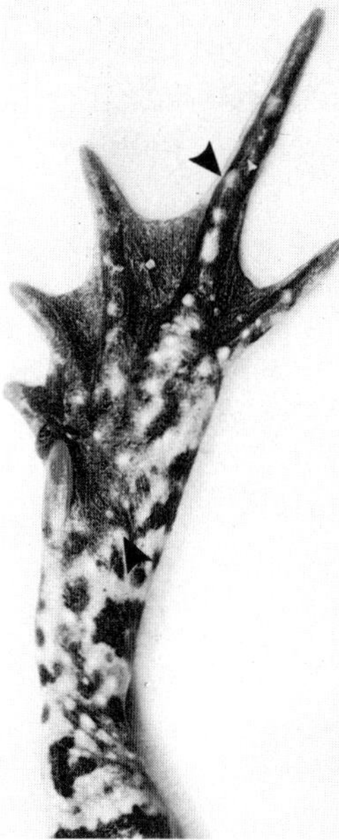

Hout Bay, Cape

TREMOLO SAND FROG

*Tomopterna cryptotis** (Boulenger) 1907

Striped Burrowing Frog
Striped Pyxie

Syn: *Pyxicephalus delalandei cryptotis* (Boulenger)

Tshaneni, Swaziland

Suikerbosrand Nature Reserve, Transvaal

TREMOLO SAND FROGS *Tomopterna cryptotis*

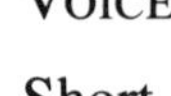

BREEDING HABITAT

Temporary rain pools and vleis in open savanna. Males call from exposed situations on marginal mud or rocks at the water's edge.

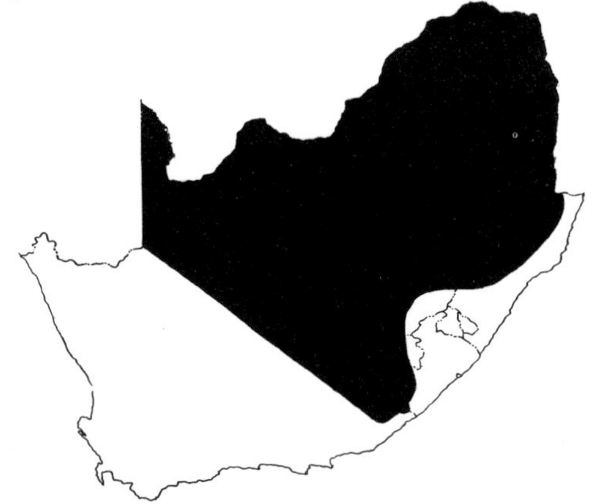

VOICE

Short, clear notes repeated at the rate of about ten or twelve per second.

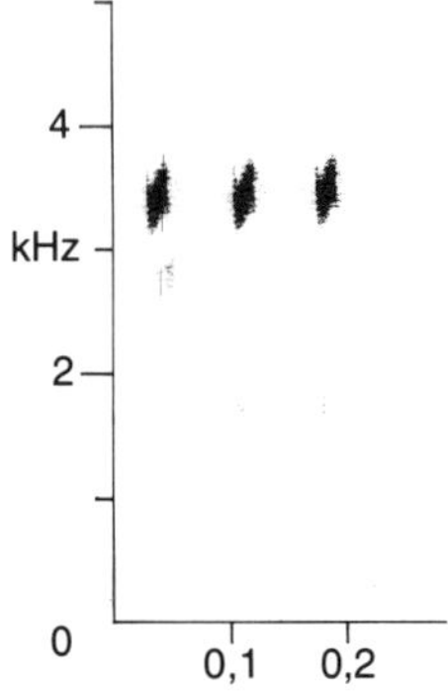

(Three calls) Kruger National Park, H. H. Braack

*This form has previously been regarded as a subspecies of *T. delalandii*. The specific status accorded it here is justified on the basis of differences in the mating calls.

- ★ Dorsal coloration and pattern are variable. The presence of vertebral and dorso-lateral lines is common, as is a light-coloured, occipital patch ▲.
- ★ Glandular elevations below the tympanum are fused into a conspicuous ridge ▲ which is sometimes interrupted — cf. *T. delalandii* and *T. marmorata*.

LIFE SIZE

Punda Milia
Kruger National Park

Sandton, Transvaal

- ★ The ventral skin is smooth and white, with grey pigmentation along the jaw-line and covering much of the gular region in breeding males.
- ★ Tubercles at the base of the thumb are single — cf. *T. krugerensis*.

- ★ The outer metatarsal tubercle ▲ is very small, or absent altogether — cf. *T. natalensis*.
- ★ Not more than 3½ phalanges of the longest toe are free of webbing ▲ — cf. *T. natalensis*.

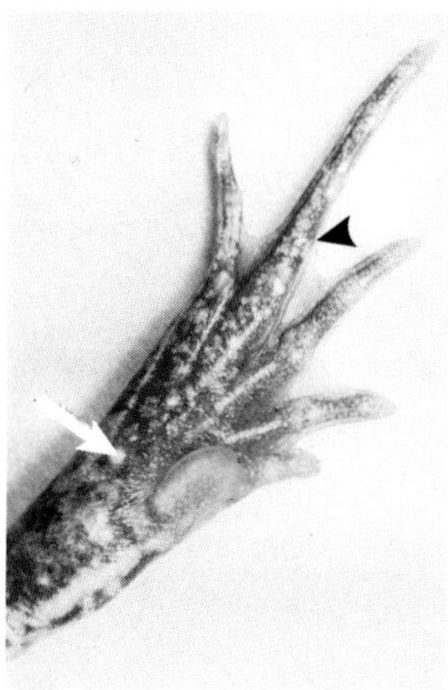

Mountain Zebra National Park, Cape

KNOCKING SAND FROG

Tomopterna krugerensis Passmore and Carruthers 1975

Sandveld Pyxie

KNOCKING SAND FROG *Tomopterna krugerensis* Pafuri, Kruger National Park

BREEDING HABITAT

Pans and vleis in savanna. Males call from partly concealed positions at the water's edge either on the bank or in a few millimetres of water.

VOICE

A percussive, wooden knocking note is repeated at the rate of four or five per second.

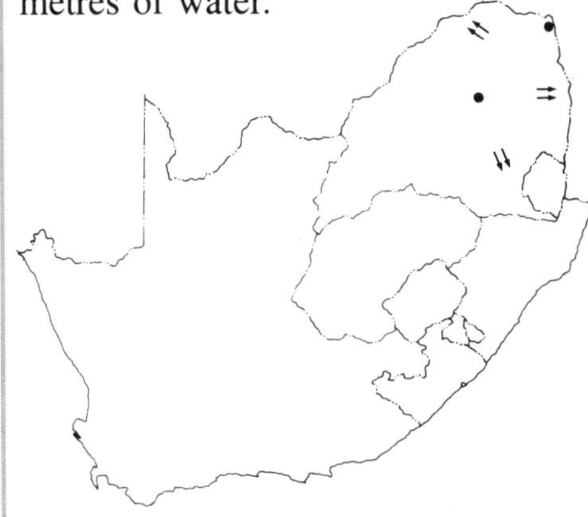

DISTRIBUTION

Prior to 1975, specimens (and hence locality records) might have been referred to *T. cryptotis*. The distribution of both species therefore remains uncertain.

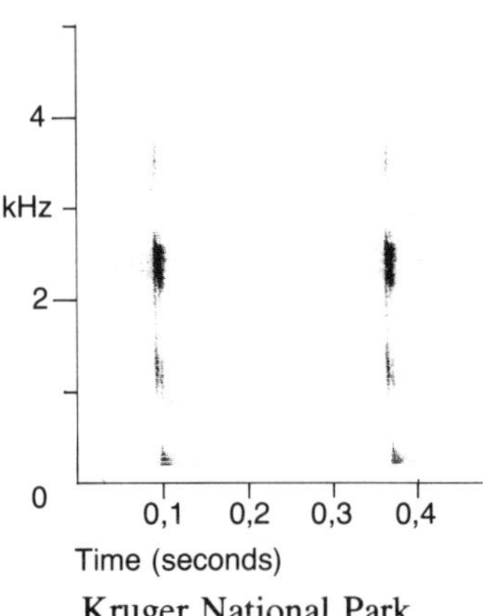

Kruger National Park

★ Dorsal coloration and pattern are variable. Dorsal stripes are usually absent. An indistinct occipital patch ▲ is sometimes discernible but it is not as obvious as it usually is in *T. cryptotis*.

★ Glandular elevations below the tympanum are fused into a conspicuous ridge ▲ which is sometimes interrupted — cf. *T. delalandii* and *T. marmorata*.

LIFE SIZE
Pafuri, Kruger National Park

Pafuri, Kruger National Park

★ The ventral skin is smooth and white, with grey pigmentation along the jawline and covering much of the gular region in breeding males.

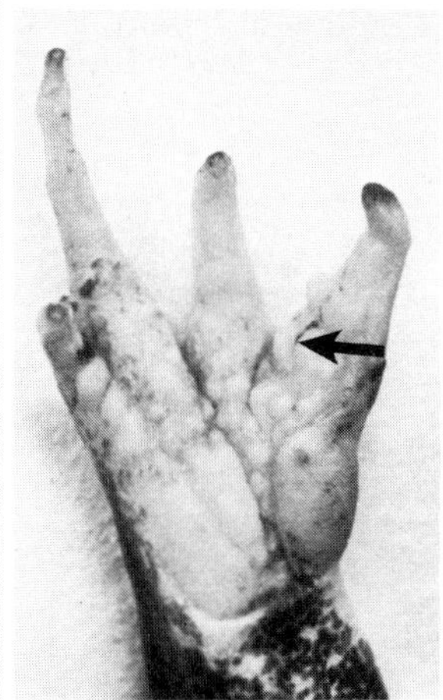

Pafuri, Kruger National Park
Preserved specimen,
Transvaal Museum

★ Tubercles at the base of the thumb are divided or partly divided ▲. Similarly divided subarticular tubercles are often present on the adjacent fingers — cf. other species.

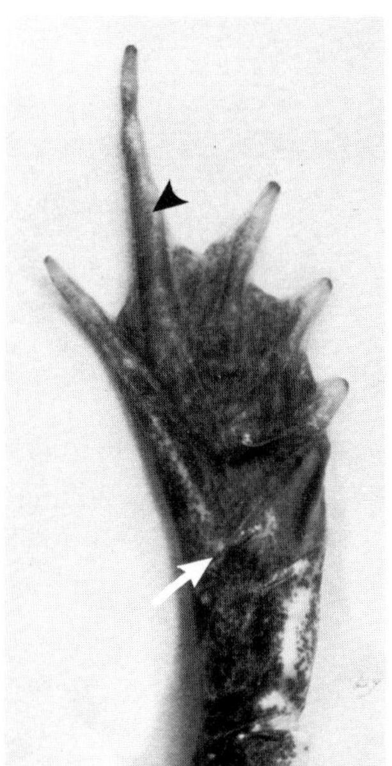

Pafuri, Kruger National Park
Preserved specimen,
Transvaal Museum

★ The outer metatarsal tubercle ▲ is very small or absent altogether — cf. *T. delalandii*.

★ Not more than 3½ phalanges of the longest toe are free of webbing ▲ — cf. *T. natalensis*.

RUSSET-BACKED SAND FROG *Tomopterna marmorata* (Peters) 1854

Marmorate Pyxie
Mozambique Burrowing Frog

Syn: *Pyxicephalus marmoratus* Peters

RUSSET-BACKED SAND FROG *Tomopterna marmorata* Skukuza, Kruger National Park

BREEDING HABITAT

Rivers flowing though sub-tropical savanna. Males call from exposed positions on the sandbanks.

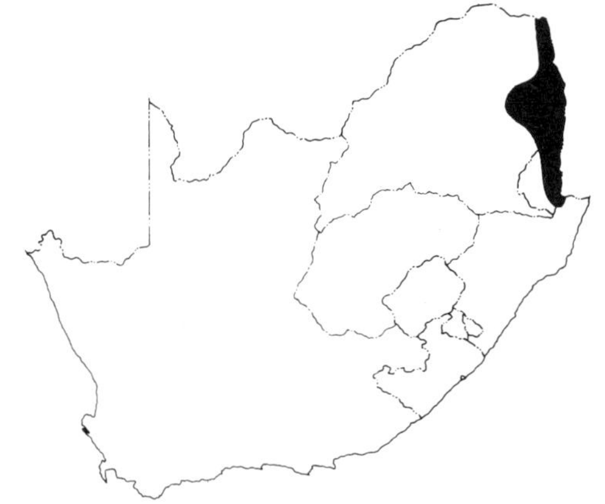

VOICE

A piping note repeated rapidly at a variable rate.

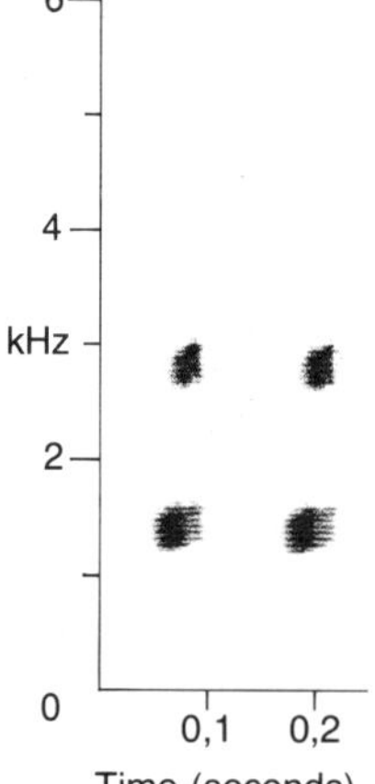

(Two calls) Kruger National Park, H. H. Braack

- ★ The dorsal coloration is marbled russet and lacks conspicuous dark markings, although a pale occipital patch ▲ is generally evident.
- ★ The gland below the tympanum is not as elevated as in the other species.

LIFE SIZE
Skukuza, Kruger National Park

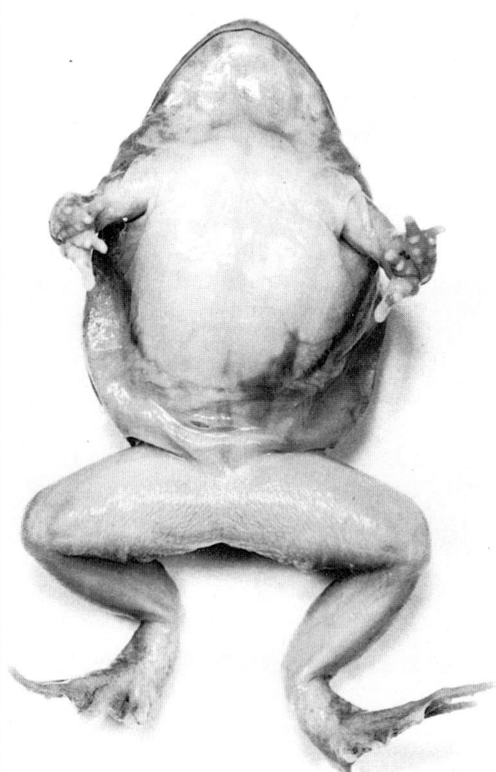

Skukuza, Preserved specimen, KNP Museum

- ★ The ventral skin is smooth and white with grey pigmentation along the jaw-line and covering much of the gular region in breeding males.
- ★ Tubercles at the base of the thumb are single — cf. *T. krugerensis*.

- ★ The outer metatarsal tubercle is absent or extremely small.
- ★ Not more than 3 phalanges of the longest toe are free of webbing ▲ — cf. *T. natalensis*.

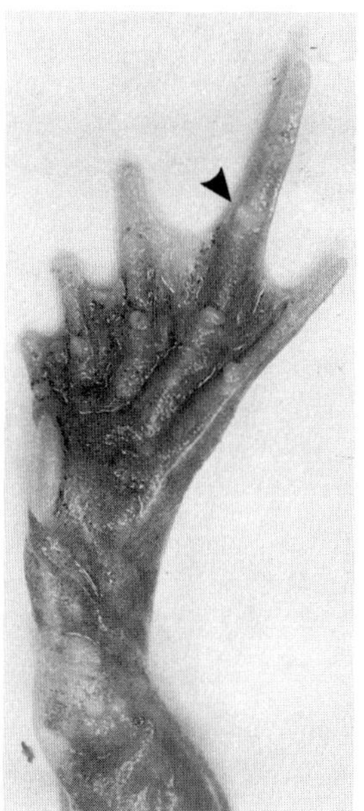

Skukuza, Kruger National Park
Preserved specimen, KNP Museum

NATAL SAND FROG

Tomopterna natalensis (Smith) 1849

Natal Pyxie
Natal Burrowing Frog

Syn: *Pyxicephalus natalensis* Smith

Sandton, Transvaal

Mbabane, Swaziland

NATAL SAND FROGS *Tomopterna natalensis*

BREEDING HABITAT

Permanent streams, furrows or vleis in grassland. The call site is open or partially concealed.

VOICE

Penetrating yelps emitted at a variable rate, sometimes preceded by a gradual build-up of slowly accelerating croaks.

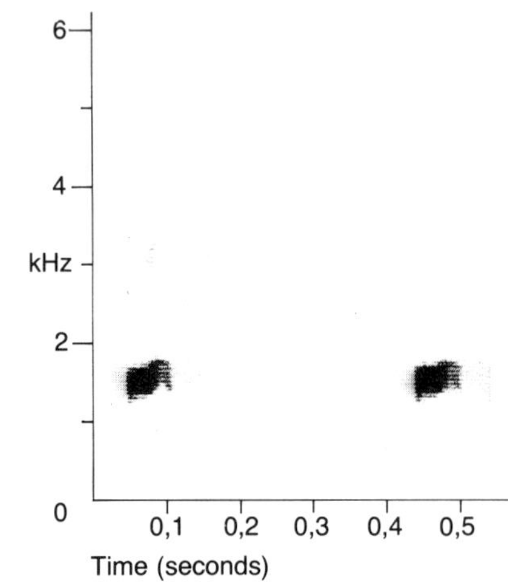

(Two calls) Kruger National Park, H. H. Braack

★ Dorsal pattern and coloration are variable. A pair of small, dark glandular elevations are usually present in the centre of the dorsum.
★ The snout is more pointed than in other members of the genus.
★ Two glandular ridges ▲ one from the eye, and the other from the mouth, converge behind the tympanum.

LIFE SIZE
Sandton, Transvaal

Sandton, Transvaal

★ The ventral skin is smooth and white. In males, the throat is black along the edges.
★ Tubercles at the base of the thumb are single — cf. *T. krugerensis*.

★ The outer metatarsal tubercle ▲ is absent or small.
★ 4, or nearly 4, phalanges of the longest toe are free of webbing ▲ — cf. other species.

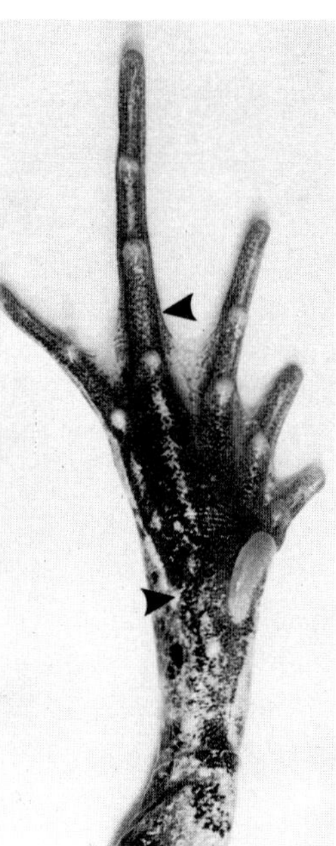
Sandton, Transvaal

RIVER AND STREAM FROGS

*Rana** Linnaeus

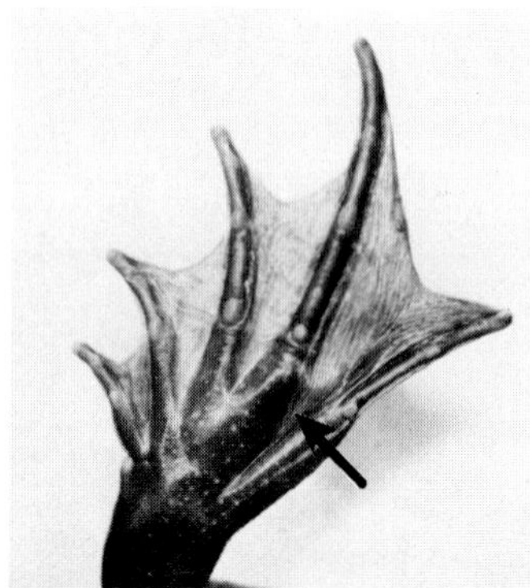

- ★ The dorsal surface lacks six complete skin ridges — cf. *Ptychadena*.
- ★ The pupil is horizontal.
- ★ Fingers lack webbing.
- ★ Toes are webbed.
- ★ Webbing is present between the outer metatarsals ▲.

Eight species occur in South Africa. The genus is widely distributed in the more temperate parts of the country from sea level to very high altitudes.

All the species are moderate to large in size, typically with streamlined bodies and pointed snouts. They generally live in close proximity to water and readily seek refuge in it when disturbed. The hindlimbs are muscular and powerful and most species are accomplished jumpers. The digits are elongated and lack terminal discs. Webbing is present between the toes and metatarsals, providing a large effective surface area to the foot, and facilitating swimming. The elongated digits also aid in clambering through vegetation. Cryptic coloration is common. Breeding occurs in shallow, often flowing, water.

*Some workers place the Stream Frogs in a separate genus, *Strongylopus*.

Sexual Dimorphism

Males in breeding condition have enlarged nuptial pads on the thumbs.

Eggs

Small pigmented eggs are laid, often in large numbers. Each egg is surrounded by a large jelly capsule. Oviposition typically occurs in shallow water in streams, but in *Rana grayii* the eggs are sometimes laid in damp situations out of the water.

Tadpoles

Tadpoles are mostly of the benthonic type, and although capable of rapid swimming, they often lie motionless on the bottom mud. *R. vertebralis* has a stream dwelling tadpole which is adapted by its sucker-like mouth to life in rapidly flowing water (Wager, 1965). The tadpoles have a long larval life and often reach a large size. Over-wintering occurs in some species.

Distribution

This is a very large genus, comprising several hundred described species, many of which may be grouped into the genus *Rana* simply for taxonomic convenience. Representatives occur on all major land masses except Greenland and the Australian region. The genus is particularly well represented in temperate regions.

COMMON RIVER FROG *Rana angolensis* Bocage 1866

Common Rana
Dusky-throated Frog
Angola River Frog

COMMON RIVER FROG *Rana angolensis* Suikerbosrand Nature Reserve, Transvaal

BREEDING HABITAT

Perennial streams or other permanent bodies of water. Calling occurs from the water's edge or from partly submerged positions amongst aquatic vegetation.

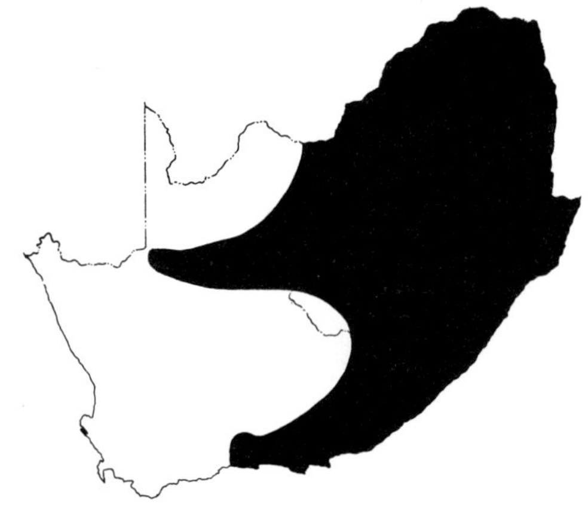

VOICE

Two different calls are commonly heard. One is a short croak. The other is a sharp rattle of one or two seconds' duration. The two calls are often, but not always, sequential.

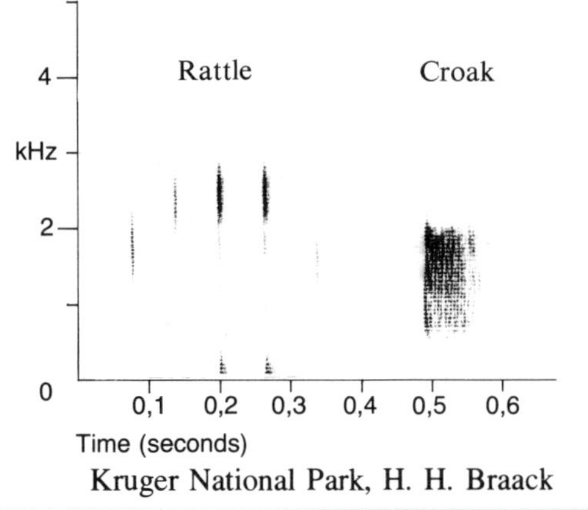

Kruger National Park, H. H. Braack

- ★ The dorsal coloration varies from brown to green. Dark spots and a light vertebral stripe are usually present.
- ★ The jawline tapers sharply from behind the eyes to a fairly acutely pointed snout — cf. *R. fuscigula.*

LIFE SIZE Sandton, Transvaal

Sandton, Transvaal

- ★ The ventral surface is smooth and white, often with mottling on the jaw and throat. Sometimes this mottling extends over the venter.

- ★ The toes are well webbed, but not beyond the last subarticular tubercle of the longest toe ▲ — cf. *R. fuscigula.*

Sandton, Transvaal

CAPE RIVER FROG *Rana fuscigula* Duméril and Bibron 1841

Cape Rana
Dark-throated or
Dusky-throated River Frog

CAPE RIVER FROG *Rana fuscigula* Bontebok National Park, Cape

BREEDING HABITAT

Large still bodies of water or permanent streams and rivers. Males usually call from deep water, supporting themselves on floating vegetation, but on occasions they call from the bank.

VOICE

Two different calls are commonly heard. One is a short, strangled groan or grunt, emitted once or twice a minute with occasional long intervals. The other is a series of taps delivered at the rate of four to six per second, sustained for more than ten seconds.

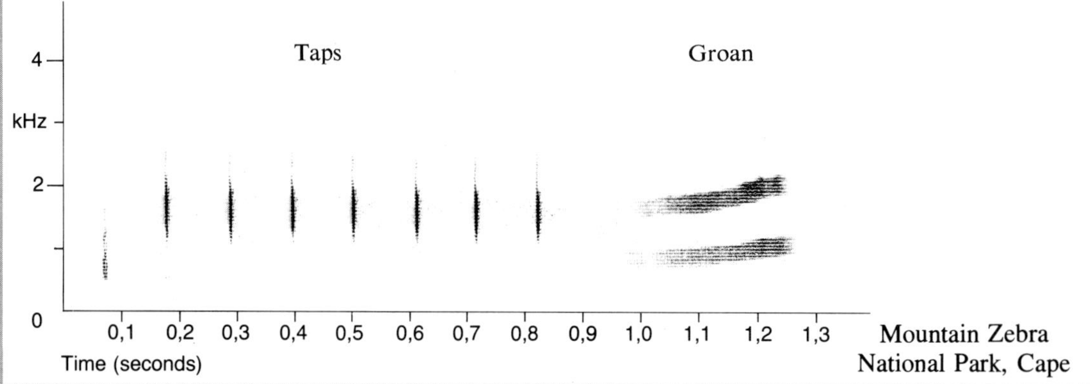

Mountain Zebra National Park, Cape

- ★ The dorsal coloration varies from brown to green. Dark spots and a light vertebral stripe are usually present.
- ★ The jawline tapers gradually from behind the eyes to a slightly rounded snout — cf. *R. angolensis*.

LIFE SIZE   Sandton, Transvaal

Suikerbosrand Nature Reserve, Transvaal

- ★ The ventral surface is smooth and white with dark mottling on the throat, and often over the entire venter.

- ★ Toes are webbed beyond the last subarticular tubercle ▲ of the longest toe — cf. *R. angolensis*.

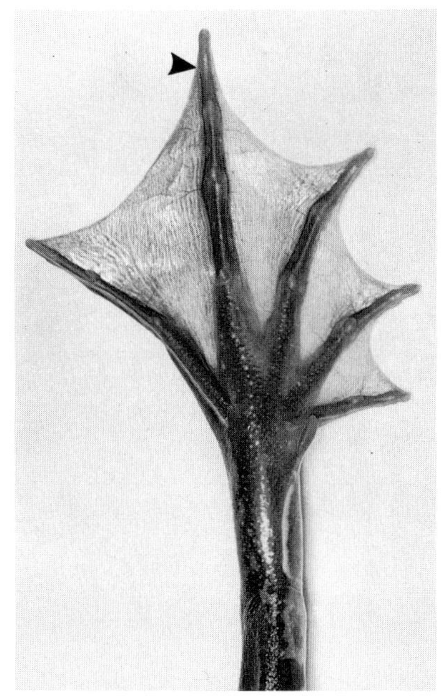

Suikerbosrand Nature Reserve, Transvaal

AQUATIC RIVER FROG *Rana vertebralis* Hewitt 1927

Water Rana

AQUATIC RIVER FROG *Rana vertebralis* Sani Pass, Lesotho

BREEDING HABITAT

Streams in the Drakensberg, including those at very high altitudes. The species is predominantly aquatic.

VOICE

Two different calls are commonly heard. One is a low-pitched stuttering groan. The other is several seconds of hollow knocking, at a rate of about seven per second.

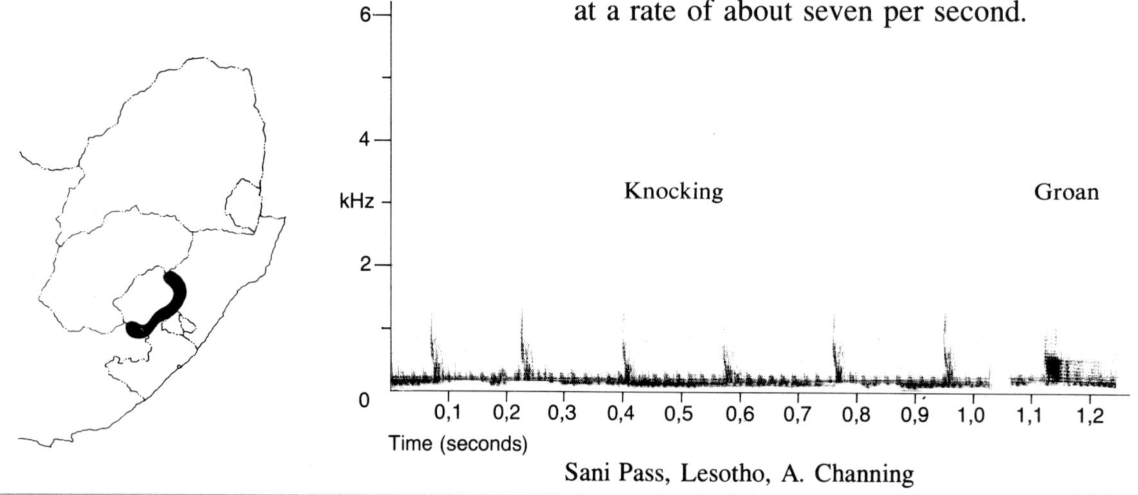

Sani Pass, Lesotho, A. Channing

LIFE SIZE Sani Pass, Lesotho

★ The dorsum is dark mottled greenish grey or brown.
★ The snout is distinctly rounded — cf. *R. angolensis* and *R. fuscigula.*
★ A distinctive umbraculum ▲ is present in the cornea of the eye.

Sani Pass, Lesotho

★ The venter is white with dark vermiculations.

Sani Pass, Lesotho

★ Webbing extends beyond the last subarticular tubercle of the longest toe ▲.

PLAIN STREAM FROG *Rana wageri* Wager 1961

Plain Rana

PLAIN STREAM FROG *Rana wageri* Cathkin Park, Natal

BREEDING HABITAT

Wooded streams in the escarpment and foothills of the Natal and Transvaal Drakensberg. Males call from the edges of streams.

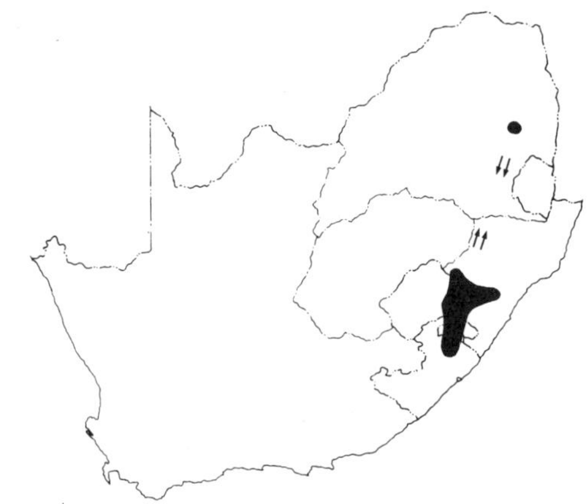

VOICE

A raucous cackle of four or five notes. Repeated at irregular intervals.

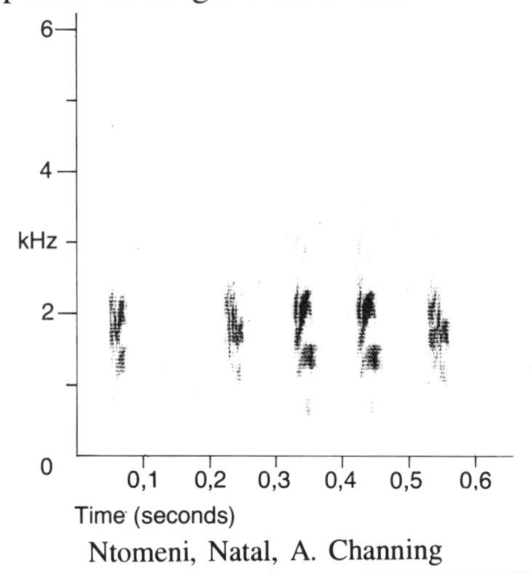

Ntomeni, Natal, A. Channing

- ★ The dorsum varies from cream to brick-red. It is generally free of large dark markings, but dark flecks or stippling are sometimes evident.
- ★ The snout is paler than the rest of the dorsum.

LIFE SIZE Bulwer, Natal

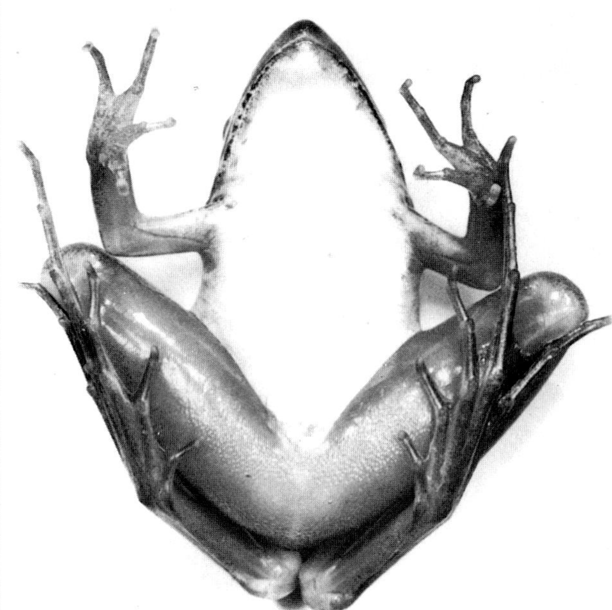

Bulwer, Natal

- ★ The ventral surface is smooth and pure white, occasionally with grey around the jawline.

- ★ The toes are webbed, with up to 3 phalanges of the longest toe ▲ free.

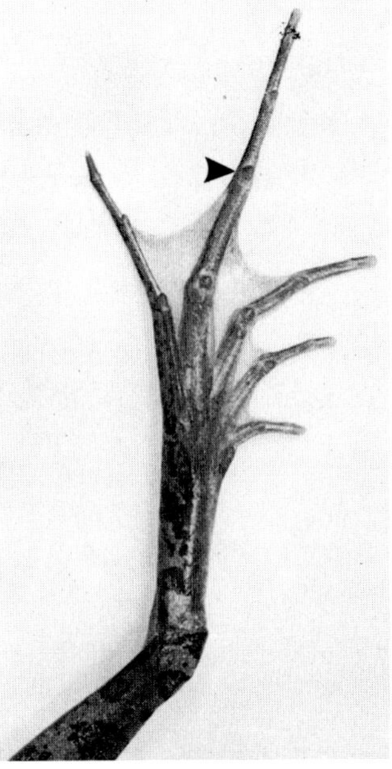

Bulwer, Natal.

CLICKING STREAM FROG *Rana grayii** Smith 1849

Spotted Rana, Gray's Frog
Gray's Grass Frog

Subspecies
The form in South Africa is *Rana grayii grayii* Smith. Other subspecies are recognized elsewhere in Africa.

De Hoek, Transvaal

Tsitsikamma National Park, Cape

Mooi River, Natal

CLICKING STREAM FROGS *Rana grayii*

BREEDING HABITAT

Almost any body of water which is well provided with vegetation. Males usually remain well concealed while calling although exposed ones are sometimes encountered.

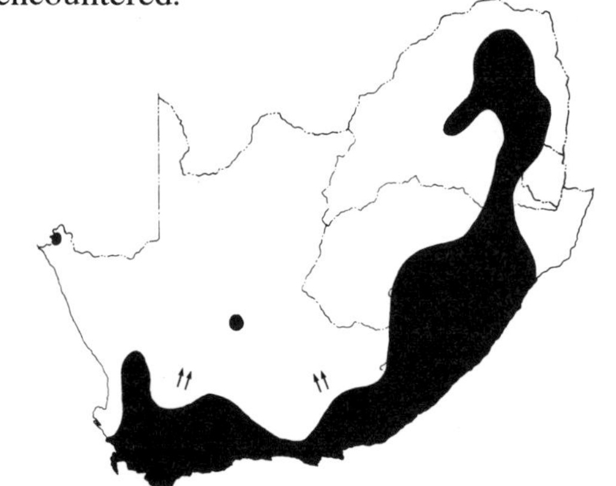

VOICE

A wooden tapping sound emitted with monotonous regularity. Sometimes in choruses the regularity is disrupted by a timbreless chirping.

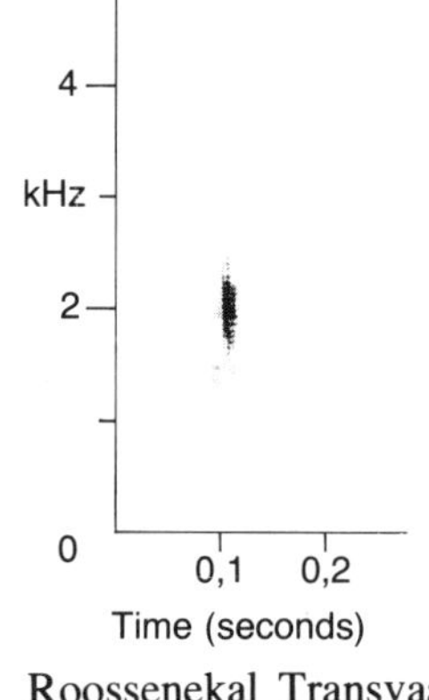

Roossenekal Transvaal

*Poynton (personal communication) has indicated that forest and grassland forms of *R. grayii* may prove to be separable, the mating calls having slight differences in pitch.

- ★ Dorsal coloration is extremely variable. Dark spots are frequently evident on a lighter ground colour and a vertebral line or band of variable width and colour is common.
- ★ The lower leg is barred — cf. *R. fasciata*.
- ★ The toes are long but do not extend beyond the level of the eye when the animal is sitting normally with the heel in line with the vent — cf. *R. fasciata* and *R. montana*.

LIFE SIZE

Roossenekal, Transvaal

Keurbooms River, Cape

- ★ The ventral surface is smooth and white with slight gold pigmentation sometimes evident on the lower jaw of males.

- ★ The toes are slightly webbed, but 4 phalanges of the longest toe are free of webbing ▲.

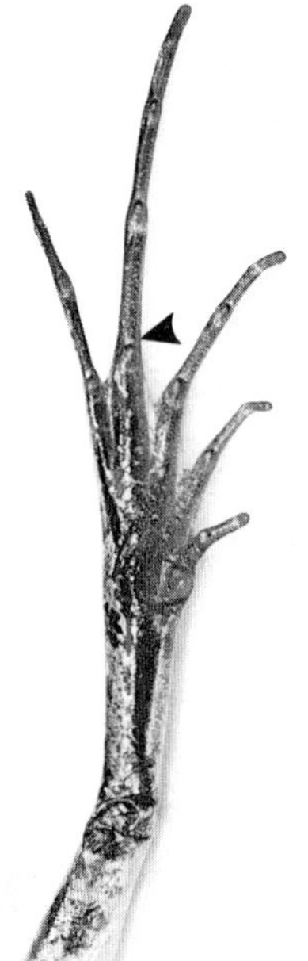

Keurbooms River, Cape

STRIPED STREAM FROG *Rana fasciata* Smith 1849

Striped Rana
Striped Grass Frog
Long-toed Frog

The form in South Africa is *Rana fasciata fasciata* Smith. Other subspecies are recognized elswhere in Africa.

Striped Stream Frog *Rana fasciata* Tsitsikamma National Park, Cape

Breeding Habitat

Grassy margins of streams, pans, dams, seepage or other bodies of water. Males call from slightly elevated positions amongst thick grass adjacent to, or emergent from, the water.

Voice

A sharp piercing 'pip' uttered singly or in a quick series of three or four.

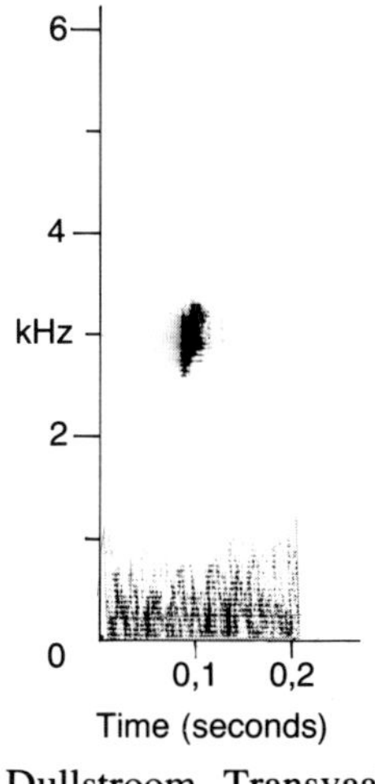

Dullstroom, Transvaal

★ The longitudinal dorsal stripes are conspicuous and characteristic. The dark paravertebral pair are usually continuous — cf. *R. montana*.

★ The lower leg ▲ is striped longitudinally — cf. *R. montana*.

★ The toes are exceptionally long, extending beyond the level of the eye when the animal is sitting normally with the heel in line with the vent — cf. *R. grayii*.

LIFE SIZE
Suikerbosrand Nature Reserve

Bontebok National Park, Cape

★ The ventral surface is smooth and white with the throat yellow in males.

★ The toes are webbed but 3 or 4 phalanges of the longest toe are free of webbing ▲.

Bontebok National Park, Cape

BANDED STREAM FROG

*Rana montana** FitzSimons 1946

Mountain Frog

Syn: *Rana fasciata montana* FitzSimons

BANDED STREAM FROG *Rana montana* Cape Point Nature Reserve, Cape

BREEDING HABITAT

Mountain streams and marshes in the south-western Cape.

VOICE

Short harsh squawks, followed by a rapid cackle.

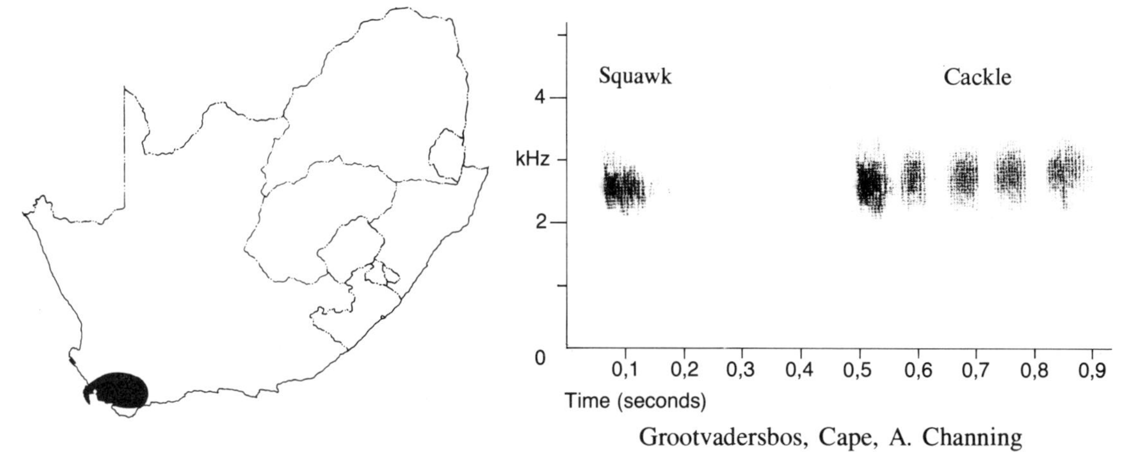

Grootvadersbos, Cape, A. Channing

*This form has previously been regarded as a subspecies of *R. fasciata*. The specific status accorded it here is justified on the basis of differences in the mating calls. These were initially pointed out by Greig, and subsequently confirmed by Channing (personal communication).

★ The longitudinal stripes are often broken or fused into broad paravertebral bands — cf. *R. fasciata*.
★ The lower leg ▲ is barred — cf. *R. fasciata*.
★ The toes are exceptionally long, extending beyond the level of the eye when the animal is sitting normally with the heel in line with the vent — cf. *R. grayii*.

LIFE SIZE
Cape Point Nature Reserve

Cape Point Nature Reserve

★ The ventral surface is smooth and white, with the throat yellow in males.

★ The toes are webbed but 3 or 4 phalanges of the longest toe are free of webbing ▲.

Cape Point Nature Reserve

BERG STREAM FROG — *Rana hymenopus* Boulenger 1920

Drakensberg Rana

BERG STREAM FROG *Rana hymenopus* — Drakensberg Gardens, Natal

BREEDING HABITAT

Streams or seepage in the high altitude riverine grassland of the Natal Drakensberg.

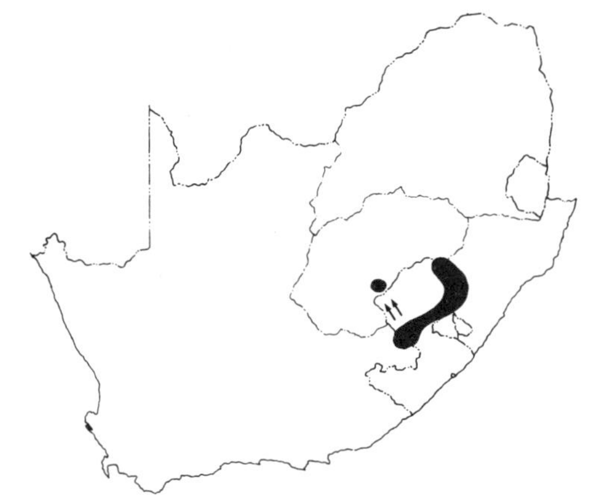

VOICE

A rapid chattering of eight or nine notes interspersed with long pauses.

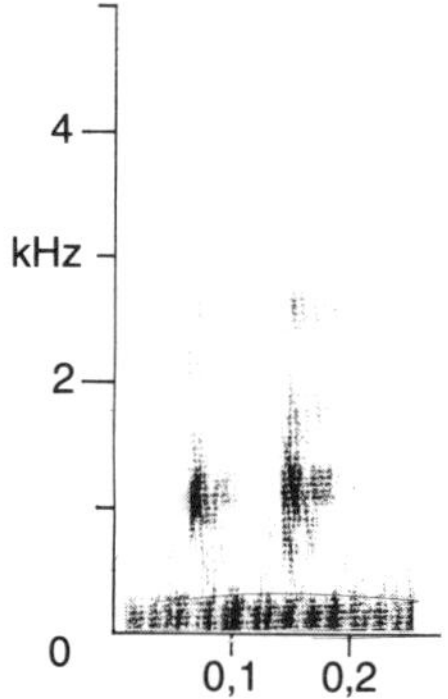

Sani Pass, Lesotho, A. Channing

- ★ The dorsum is variably mottled and grey in colour.
- ★ The snout is very rounded.

LIFE SIZE Mont-aux-Sources, Natal

- ★ The ventral surface is smooth and white, usually with dark spots on the throat.

Barkly East, Cape Preserved specimen, Transvaal Museum

- ★ The extent of the webbing is variable.

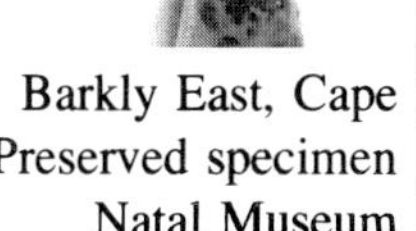

Barkly East, Cape
Preserved specimen
Natal Museum

ORNATE FROGS

Hildebrandtia Nieden

- ★ The throat is dark, with a pair of distinctive white Y-shaped markings — cf. *Tomopterna.*
- ★ Paired lateral vocal sacs are present in males.
- ★ The pupil is horizontal.
- ★ Fingers lack webbing.
- ★ The metatarsals are bound together, not separated by webbing — cf. *Ptychadena, Rana.*
- ★ Toes are webbed.
- ★ The inner metatarsal tubercle is large and flanged.

Only one species occurs in South Africa. Generic and specific characteristics are illustrated together in the description of *Hildebrandtia ornata* below. In South Africa, this species is confined principally to open bushveld and savanna in the Kruger National Park. It is a burrowing form which spends a good deal of time underground and it is usually only encountered after rains.

Because they are infrequently found abroad, not a great deal is known about these frogs. They bear an over-all resemblance to the Sand Frogs, both in their appearance and fossorial habits. Both genera are characterized by squat bodies, short limbs with stubby digits, and a particularly large digging tubercle on the heel. Because of this, it is probable that the same burrowing technique is employed. They are easily distinguished from the Sand Frogs by their dorsal and ventral patterns and by the presence of paired lateral vocal sacs in males. This characteristic is found only in one other South African group, the Grass Frogs. Breeding occurs in the shallow water of vleis and pans.

Sexual Dimorphism

When inoperative, the males' vocal sacs are withdrawn through a pair of gular slits. These are visible on each side of the throat just anterior to the forelimbs.

EGGS

The eggs are small and are laid singly in shallow water (Wager, 1965).

TADPOLES

The tadpoles have characteristically heavy horny jaws, and fat bodies. A large size is attained prior to metamorphosis (Wager, 1965).

DISTRIBUTION

This is a small genus, distributed throughout tropical and sub-tropical Africa.

ORNATE FROG *Hildebrandtia ornata* (Peters) 1878

Hildebrandt's Burrowing Frog

ORNATE FROGS *Hildebrandtia ornata* Skukuza, Kruger National Park

BREEDING HABITAT

Shallow water in pans and vleis in subtropical savanna.

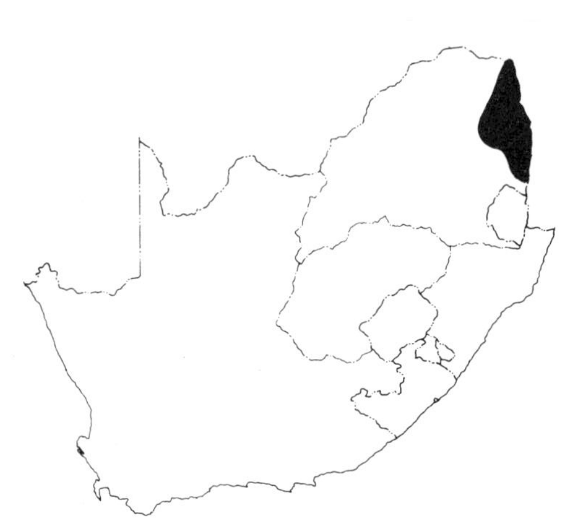

VOICE

Long nasal quacks. About one every two seconds.

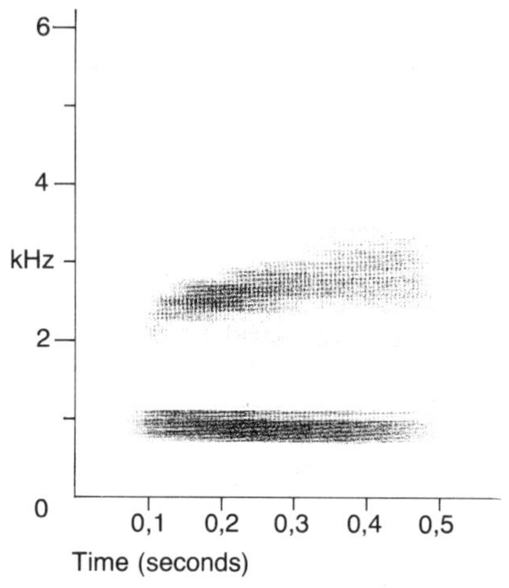

Kruger National Park, Transvaal
H. H. Braack

★ The dorsal pattern and coloration are variable, but always bold and symmetrical.

LIFE SIZE
Skukuza, Kruger National Park

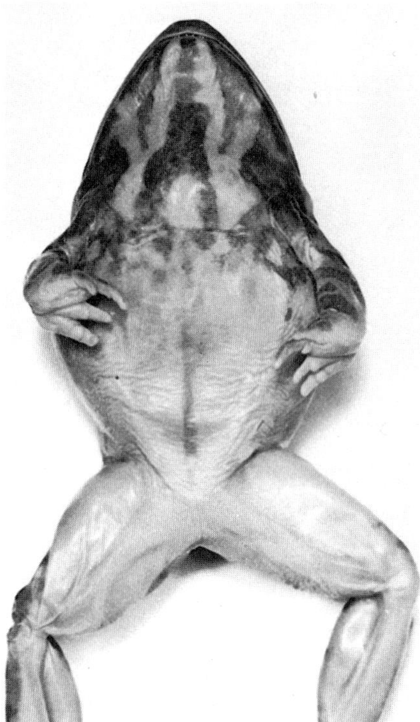

Preserved specimen, Transvaal Museum

Skukuza, Kruger National Park

★ The ventral surface is smooth and white posteriorly. A pair of characteristic white Y-shaped markings are outlined by the dark pigmentation on the throat.
★ Males possess paired lateral vocal sacs which emerge through the conspicuous gular slits during calling.

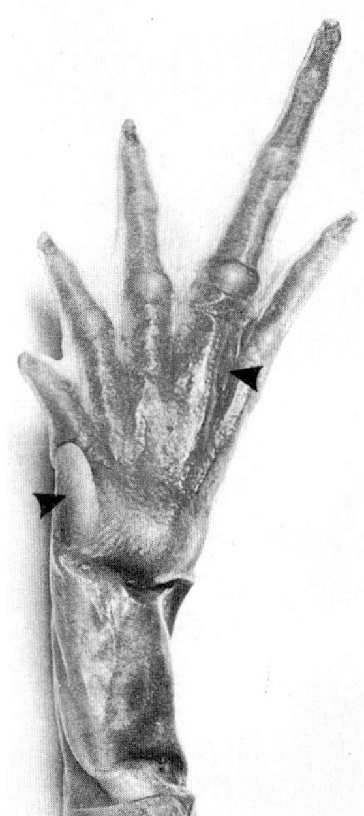

★ Toes are webbed, but the outer metatarsals ▲ are not separated by webbing as in the genera *Rana* and *Ptychadena*.
★ The inner metatarsal tubercle ▲ is large and flanged.

Preserved specimen, Transvaal Museum

GRASS FROGS

Ptychadena Boulenger

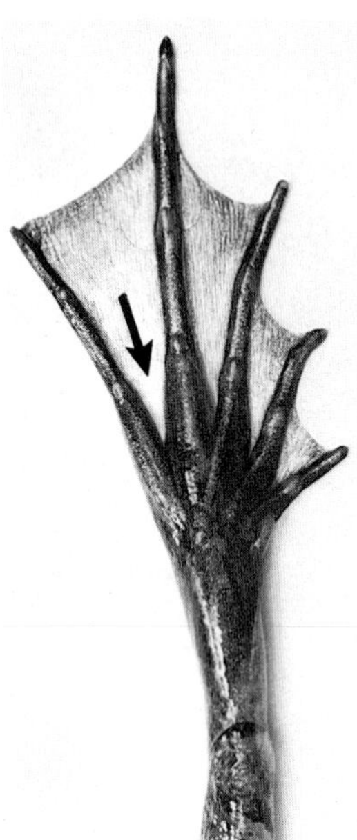

- ★ Six or more parallel dorsal skin ridges ▲ are present — cf. *Rana*.
- ★ Paired gular slits ▲ are present in males.
- ★ The pupil is horizontal.
- ★ Fingers lack webbing.
- ★ Webbing is present between outer metatarsals ▲.
- ★ Toes are webbed.

Six species occur in South Africa, where they are confined to open savanna and thornveld. Most species are found at low elevations, and are particularly common in the low-lying Mozambique Plain in Natal. Morphological species characters are poorly defined.

The genus *Ptychadena* bears close morphological resemblance to the genus *Rana*, but the presence of six or more longitudinal skin ridges and paired external vocal sacs in males distinguishes the Grass Frogs. The body is streamlined, with powerful hindlimbs and pointed snouts. These features facilitate equally efficient movement through water, extended leaps on land, and a creeping progression through dense vegetation. Although common in vleis and swampland, Grass Frogs are secretive in their habits and are easily overlooked by the casual observer. Comparatively little is known of their biology. Breeding occurs principally in the shallow water of vleis and swamps.

Sexual Dimorphism

Males are distinguished by the presence of gular slits through which the vocal sacs emerge when inflated. They are located on either side of the throat just anterior to the axilla.

Eggs

The eggs are small, pigmented, and laid singly in shallow water. The specific gravity of the eggs is very close to that of water. In most species newly-laid eggs float, but may sink shortly thereafter, particularly if the water surface is disturbed.

Tadpoles

Tadpoles are of the standard benthonic type. They are grey or brown in colour.

Distribution

Centred in tropical Africa, the number of species diminishes in the more northern and southern regions of the continent.

SHARP-NOSED GRASS FROG *Ptychadena oxyrhynchus* (Smith) 1849

Sharp-nosed Rana
Ridged Frog

Sharp-nosed Grass Frog *Ptychadena oxyrhynchus* Richards Bay, Natal

Breeding Habitat

Pans, vleis and temporary pools in the tropical lowveld and coastal regions. Males call from exposed positions near the edge of the water.

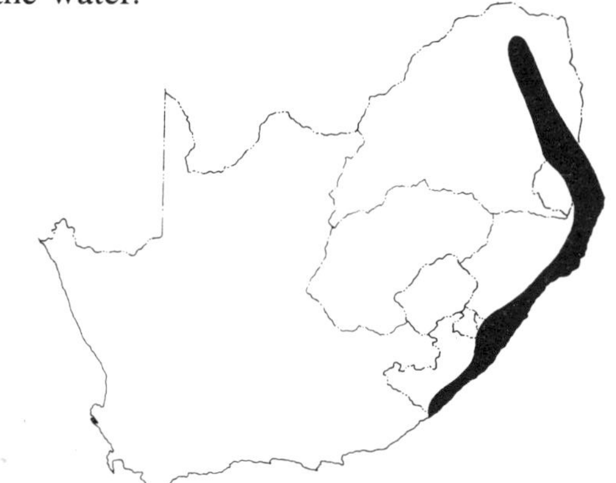

Voice

High-pitched and intense trills. About one call per second.

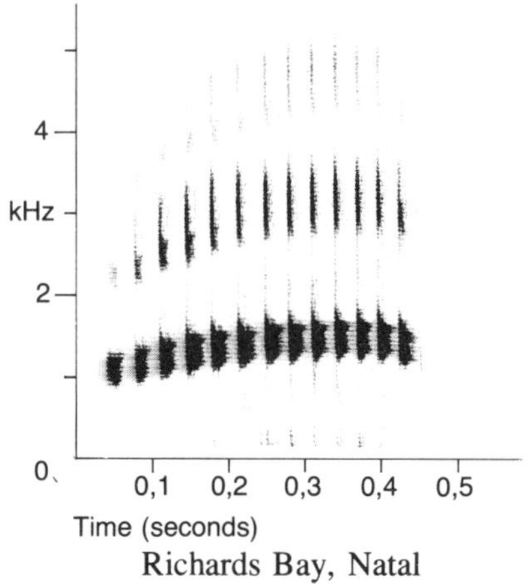

Richards Bay, Natal

- ★ The dorsal pattern usually comprises dark spots superimposed on strongly elevated skin ridges. A vertebral line is absent but the medial skin ridges are sometimes light coloured — cf. other species except *P. anchietae.*
- ★ A pale triangular patch is present on top of the snout. Its projection beyond the nares is greater than the inter-narial distance, and the nares are closer or as close to the eye as they are to the snout tip — cf. *P. anchietae.*
- ★ No light line is present on the upper surface of the lower leg — cf. *P. mascareniensis* and *P. porosissima.*

LIFE SIZE Malongane, Mozambique

KwaMbonambi, Natal

- ★ The venter is smooth and white, except for occasional yellowing in the inguinal region.
- ★ The gular slits when viewed laterally in the male are not parallel to the lower jawline — cf. *P. mascareniensis.*

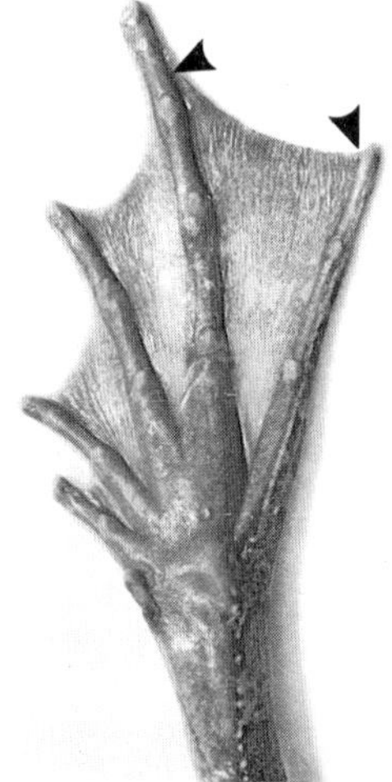

KwaMbonambi, Natal

- ★ The length of the foot is less than the length of the lower leg — cf. *P. mascareniensis* and *P. taenioscelis.*
- ★ Webbing: 1½ to 2 phalanges of the longest toe ▲ and less than 1 phalanx of the 5th toe ▲ are free of webbing.

KwaMbonambi, Natal

- ★ The back of the thigh is mottled and longitudinal lines are not apparent — cf. *P. anchietae* and other species.

PLAIN GRASS FROG

*Ptychadena anchietae** (Bocage) 1867

Northern Rana
Savanna Ridged Frog

Syn: *Ptychadena superciliaris* Poynton (non Günther).

PLAIN GRASS FROG *Ptychadena anchietae* — Pafuri, Kruger National Park

BREEDING HABITAT

Shallow pools, inundated grassland, vleis and dams. Males call from exposed positions near the edge of the water.

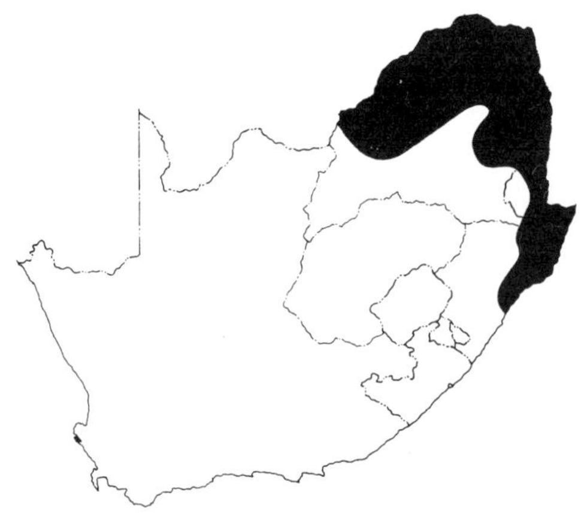

VOICE

A quick high-pitched trill, repeated at a rate of three calls every two seconds. It is similar to that of *P. oxyrhynchus* but of very much shorter duration.

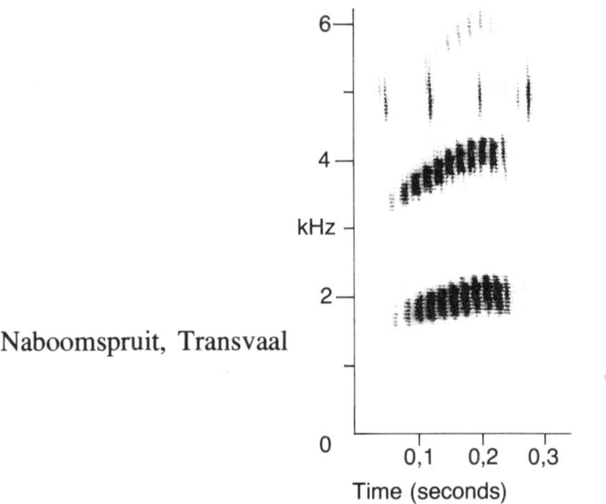

Naboomspruit, Transvaal

*The use of *anchietae* for material previously referred to *superciliaris* by Poynton (1970) follows Perret (1976). *P. superciliaris* is a West African forest form with a different mating call.

- ★ The dorsum is usually fairly plain, occasionally with dark freckling. A vertebral line is absent — cf. other species except *P. oxyrhynchus.*
- ★ A pale triangular patch is present on the top of the snout.
- ★ The snout is pointed but less so than *P. oxyrhynchus*. Its projection beyond the nares is less than the inter-narial distance and the nares are slightly closer to the snout tip than they are to the eye — cf. *P. oxyrhynchus.*
- ★ No light line is present on the upper surface of the lower leg — cf. *P. mascareniensis* and *P. porosissima.*

LIFE SIZE

Naboomspruit, Transvaal

Tshaneni, Swaziland

- ★ The venter is smooth and white, except for occasional yellowing on the lower belly.
- ★ The gular slits when viewed laterally in the male are not parallel to the jawline — cf. *P. mascareniensis.*

Tshaneni, Swaziland

- ★ The length of the foot is less than the length of the lower leg — cf. *P. mascareniensis* and *P. taenioscelis.*
- ★ Webbing: 1½ to 2 phalanges of the longest toe ▲ and less than 1 phalanx of the 5th toe ▲ are free of webbing.

Manzini, Swaziland

- ★ The black markings on the back of the thigh tend to fuse to form longitudinal bands alternating with the yellow — cf. *P. oxyrhynchus.*

MASCARENE GRASS FROG

Ptychadena mascareniensis (Duméril and Bibron) 1841

Broad-banded Rana
Mascarene Ridged Frog

Subspecies
The form in South Africa is *Ptychadena mascareniensis mascareniensis* (Duméril and Bibron). Other subspecies are recognized elsewhere in Africa.

MASCARENE GRASS FROG *Ptychadena mascareniensis* Richards Bay, Natal

BREEDING HABITAT

Coastal pans in the Zululand region and occasionally in roadside ditches. Males call whilst supported on aquatic vegetation or from the bank.

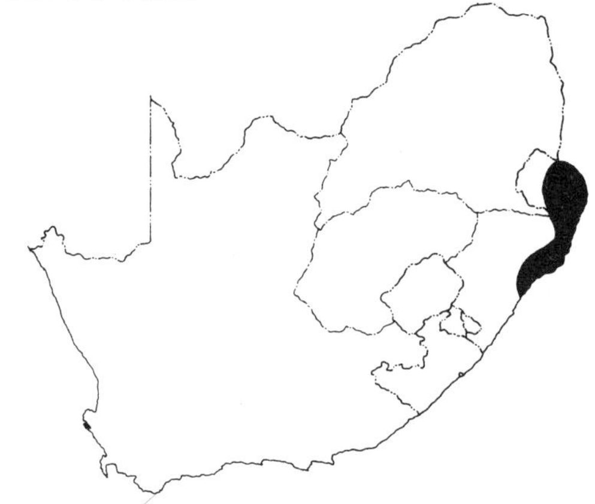

VOICE

Two call types are heard, usually in association with each other. One is a brief nasal bray, emitted at a rate of about two every three seconds, the other a series of clucking sounds.

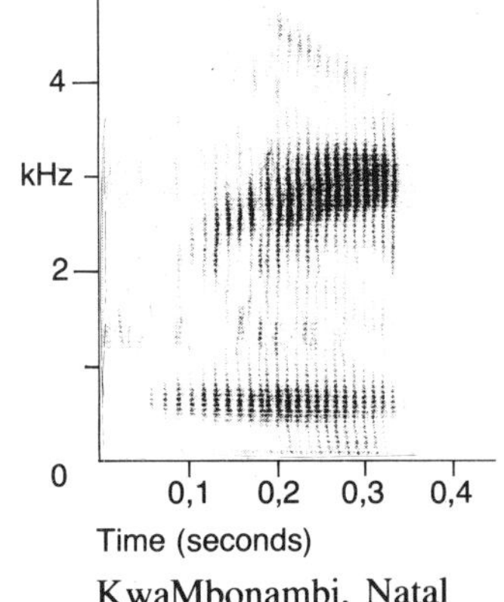

KwaMbonambi, Natal

- ★ The dorsum is generally greenish-brown and a vertebral band is usually present.
- ★ There is no light triangular patch on the snout, save for the anterior extremity of the vertebral band — cf. *P. oxyrhynchus* and *P. anchietae.*
- ★ A light longitudinal line ▲ is present on the upper surface of the lower leg — cf. *P. oxyrhynchus, P. anchietae, P. taenioscelis.*

LIFE SIZE Malongane, Mozambique

KwaMbonambi, Natal

- ★ The venter is smooth and cream except for occasional greenish-yellowing on the lower belly.
- ★ The gular slits when viewed laterally in the male are parallel to the jawline, distinguishing this species from the others.

- ★ The length of the foot is greater than, or equal to, the length of the lower leg — cf. other species except *P. taenioscelis.*
- ★ Webbing: 2 to 2½ phalanges of the longest toe ▲ and 1 or less than 1 phalanx of the 5th toe ▲ are free of webbing.

KwaMbonambi, Natal

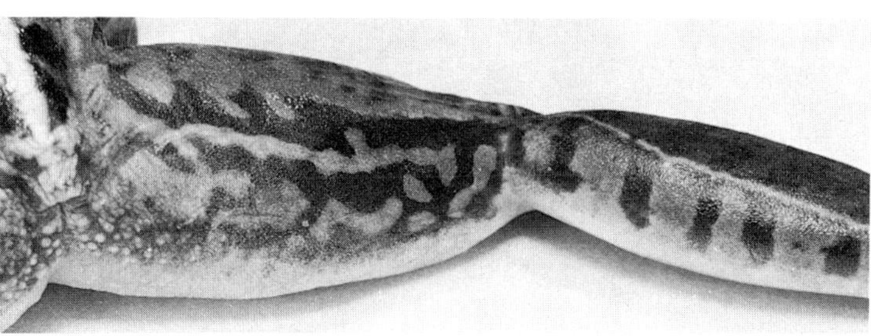

KwaMbonambi, Natal

- ★ On the back of the thigh one, or occasionally two, light coloured lines are continuous through the dark mottling.

STRIPED GRASS FROG *Ptychadena porosissima* (Steindachner) 1867

Three-striped Rana
Grassland Ridged Frog

STRIPED GRASS FROG *Ptychadena porosissima* KwaMbonambi, Natal

BREEDING HABITAT

Marshy areas, and pans in both temperate and sub-tropical regions. Males call from concealed positions in aquatic vegetation and grass.

VOICE

A short low-pitched rasping sound, usually produced in an antiphonal sequence with another nearby caller. About two calls per second.

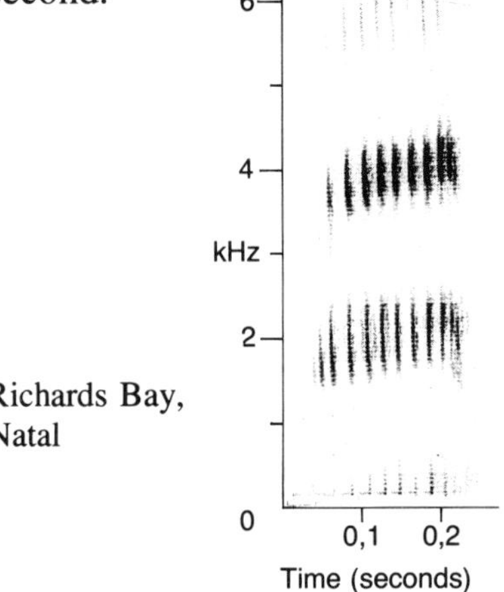

Richards Bay, Natal

- ★ The dorsal pattern is variable, but always includes a vertebral line. Two dorso-lateral skin ridges ▲ are light coloured.
- ★ No light triangular patch is present on the snout, save for the anterior extremity of the vertebral band — cf. *P. oxyrhynchus* and *P. anchietae.*
- ★ A light longitudinal line ▲ is usually present on the upper surface of the lower leg — cf. *P. oxyrhynchus, P. anchietae* and *P. taenioscelis.*

LIFE SIZE
KwaMbonambi, Natal

KwaMbonambi, Natal

- ★ The venter is smooth and white with yellowing on the belly and throat.
- ★ The gular slits when viewed laterally in the male are not parallel to the jawline — cf. *P. mascareniensis.*

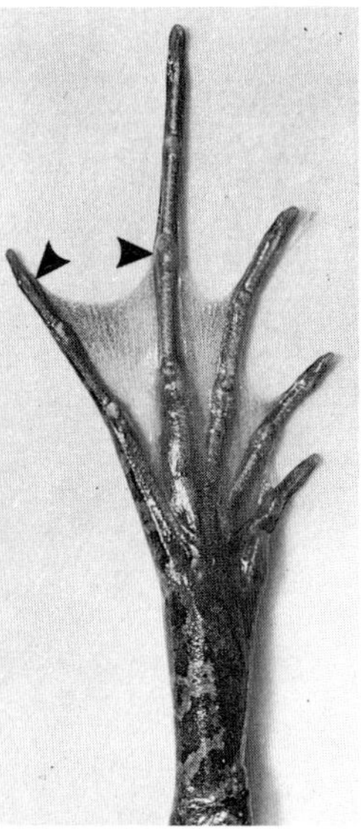

KwaMbonambi, Natal

- ★ The length of the foot is slightly less than the length of the lower leg — cf. *P. mascareniensis* and *P. taenioscelis.*
- ★ Webbing: 3 phalanges of the longest toe ▲, and 1 to 1½ phalanges of the 5th toe ▲ are free of webbing.

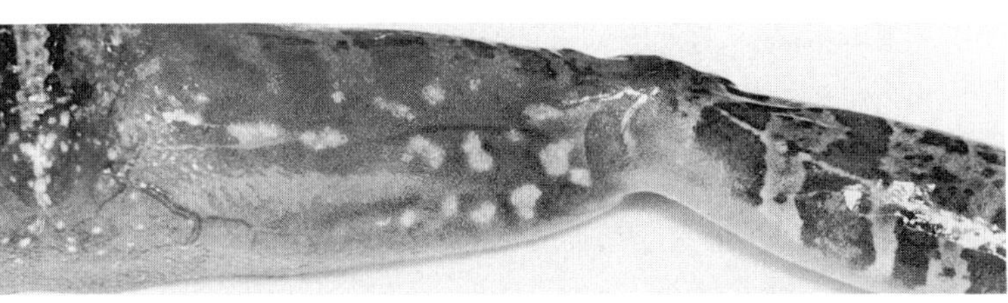

KwaMbonambi, Natal

- ★ The markings on the back of the thigh are usually in the form of light spots separated from each other by the dark mottling, but this spotting is sometimes indistinct.

BROAD BANDED GRASS FROG *Ptychadena mossambica** (Peters) 1854

Mozambique Ridged Frog Syn: *Ptychadena vernayi* (FitzSimons)

BROAD BANDED GRASS FROG *Ptychadena mossambica* Tshaneni, Swaziland

BREEDING HABITAT

Shallow water of vleis, pans and inundated grassland. Males call from concealed positions in the grass.

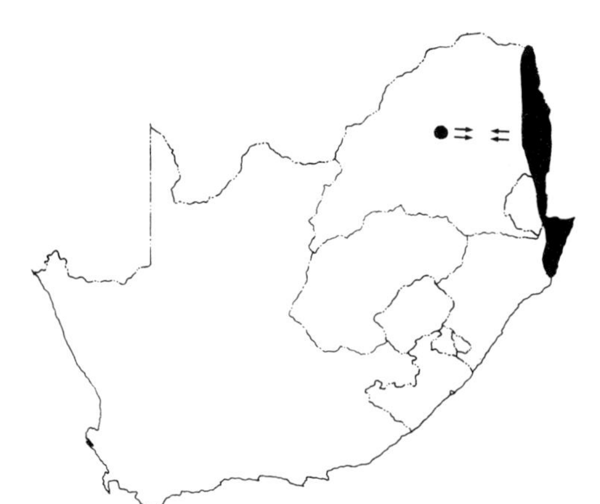

VOICE

A harsh nasal quacking repeated incessantly, at a rate of about two calls per second.

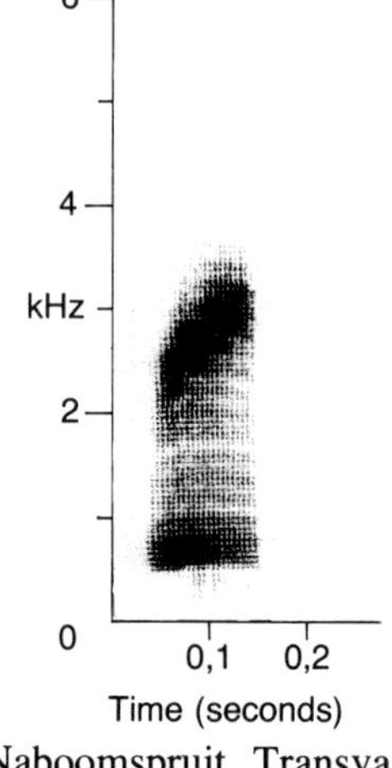

Naboomspruit, Transvaal

*The use of *mossambica* for material previously referred to *vernayi* by Poynton (1964) follows Poynton (1970).

- ★ The dorsal pattern is variable, but always includes a broad light-coloured vertebral band.
- ★ The snout is not paler than the rest of the dorsum as in *P. oxyrhynchus* and *P. anchietae.*
- ★ An irregular light line is occasionally present on the upper surface of the lower leg.

LIFE SIZE
Naboomspruit, Transvaal

- ★ The venter is smooth and white, with slight yellowing on the belly.
- ★ The gular slits when viewed laterally in the male are not parallel to the lower jawline — cf. *P. mascareniensis.*

Tshaneni, Swaziland

- ★ The leg is comparatively short and the length of the foot is decidedly shorter than the length of the lower leg — cf. *P. mascareniensis* and *P. taenioscelis.*
- ★ Webbing: 3, or almost 3, phalanges of the longest toe ▲ and 1 phalanx of the 5th toe ▲ are free of webbing.

Tshaneni, Swaziland

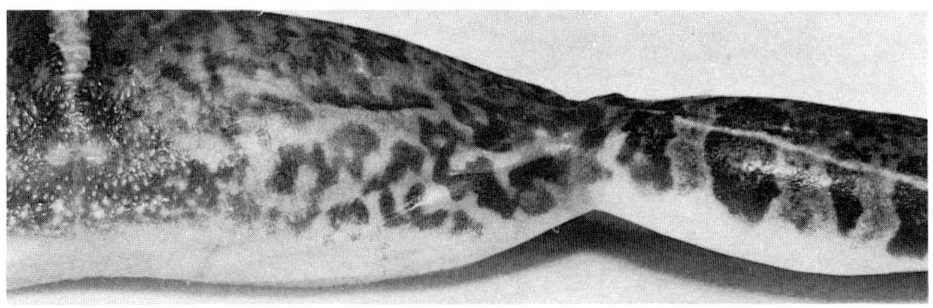

Tshaneni, Swaziland

- ★ The markings on the back of the thigh do not form a consistent pattern; sometimes longitudinal lines are discernible, but usually the mottling is irregular.

DWARF GRASS FROG *Ptychadena taenioscelis* Laurent 1954

Spotted Throated Ridged Frog
Dwarf Rana

DWARF GRASS FROG *Ptychadena taenioscelis* KwaMbonambi, Natal

BREEDING HABITAT

Boggy areas of vleis and seepages with shallow water. Males call from the muddy water margins.

VOICE

A nasal bleat, repeated at a rate of about one call per second.

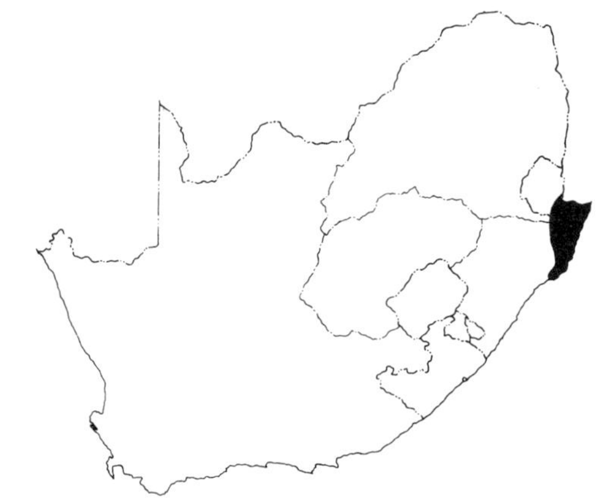

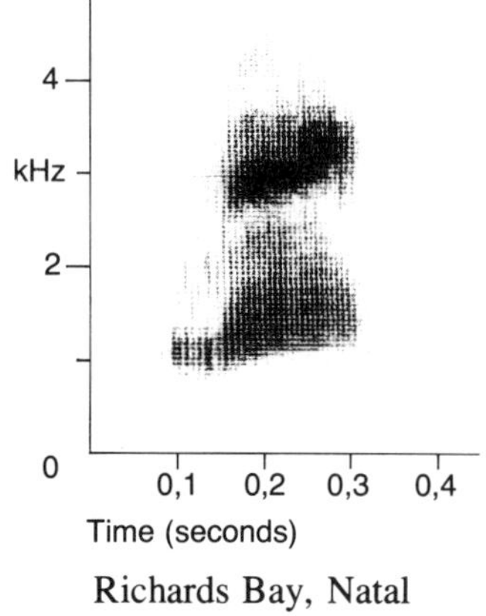

Richards Bay, Natal

★ The dorsal pattern is variable, usually with a dark greenish brown ground colour. A vertebral stripe may be present and the outer dorso-lateral ridges ▲ are usually light coloured.

★ The snout is not paler than the rest of the dorsum — cf. *P. oxyrhynchus* and *P. anchietae.*

★ A light line is absent from the upper surface of lower leg — cf. *P. mascareniensis* and *P. porosissima.*

LIFE SIZE
KwaMbonambi, Natal

KwaMbonambi, Natal

★ The venter is smooth and yellow with slight mottling or spots on the throat.

★ The gular slits when viewed laterally in the male are not usually parallel to the lower jawline but may be in rare cases — cf. *P. mascareniensis.*

★ The length of the foot is slightly greater than the length of the lower leg — cf. all other species except *P. mascareniensis.*

★ Webbing: 3 phalanges of the longest toe ▲, and 1 to 2 phalanges of the 5th toe ▲ are free of webbing.

KwaMbonambi, Natal

KwaMbonambi, Natal

★ The dark markings on the back of the thigh form two or three parallel lines, one of which is continuous, from one thigh to the other below the vent ▲.

PUDDLE FROGS

Phrynobatrachus Günther

- ★ The pupil is horizontal.
- ★ Fingers lack webbing.
- ★ A tarsal tubercle ▲ is present, in addition to inner ▲ and outer ▲ metatarsal tubercles.
- ★ Toes are webbed.

Three species occur in South Africa. They are successful in a variety of wetland habitats including swamps, vleis, small streams and dams. Two of the species are confined to the sub-tropical parts of the country, whilst the third, *P. natalensis,* is successful in both tropical and temperate regions.

The body is squat in over-all appearance, with a comparatively small head and a short pointed snout. The limbs are short, with differing degrees of webbing in the component species. In addition to two metatarsal tubercles, a distinctive tarsal tubercle is present on the 'ankle'. Despite the rather stout appearance of the adults, they are capable of rapid movement and readily seek refuge in the water. The vocal sac is single, subgular in position, and capable of enormous distension during calling. When deflated it forms characteristic lateral folds beneath the lower jaw. Substantial colour pattern polymorphism is evident on the dorsum. Breeding occurs in shallow standing water.

Sexual Dimorphism

The darkly pigmented folded vocal sac is conspicuous on the throat of the male.

Eggs

In the species where eggs have been observed, they are small and pigmented, and float in a single layer on the surface of the water. (*P. acridoides* has not been observed.)

Tadpoles

The tadpoles are small and basically benthonic. The length of the larval period is comparatively short, and metamorphosis occurs after 4-5 weeks (Wager, 1965).

Distribution

The genus is widespread and successful in Africa south of the Sahara.

SNORING PUDDLE FROG *Phrynobatrachus natalensis* (Smith) 1849

Natal Frog
Natal Puddle Frog
Toad Frog

Suikerbosrand Nature Reserve, Transvaal

Pafuri, Kruger National Park

SNORING PUDDLE FROGS *Phrynobatrachus natalensis* De Hoek, Transvaal

BREEDING HABITAT

Pools or marshy areas associated with pans, streams or vleis. Males call from partly concealed positions around the perimeter of shallow water.

VOICE

A rapid snoring. About three calls every two seconds.

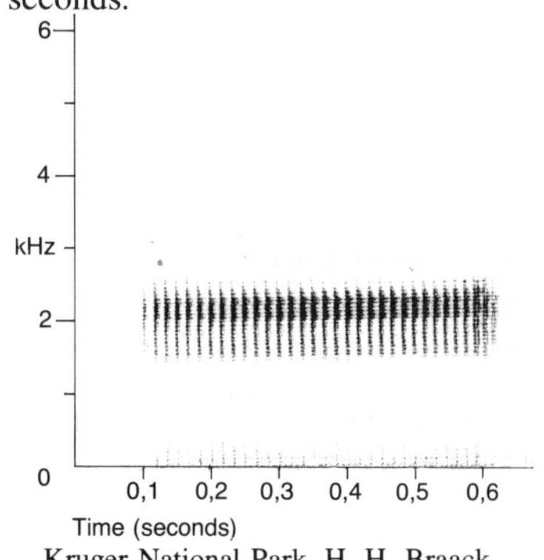

Kruger National Park, H. H. Braack

★ The dorsal coloration and skin texture are both variable, with vertebral stripes or bands often present.

LIFE SIZE
Naboomspruit, Transvaal

KwaMbonambi, Natal

★ The ventral surface is smooth and cream coloured, with occasional flecks. The throat is dark grey in males with the vocal sac folded into a pair of deep lateral creases along the lower jawline ▲.

★ The toes are not expanded into discs, but are sometimes slightly bulbous at the tips — cf. *P. acridoides*.

★ Webbing on the toes is moderate, but at least 2 phalanges of the longest toe are unwebbed ▲ — cf. *P. mababiensis*.

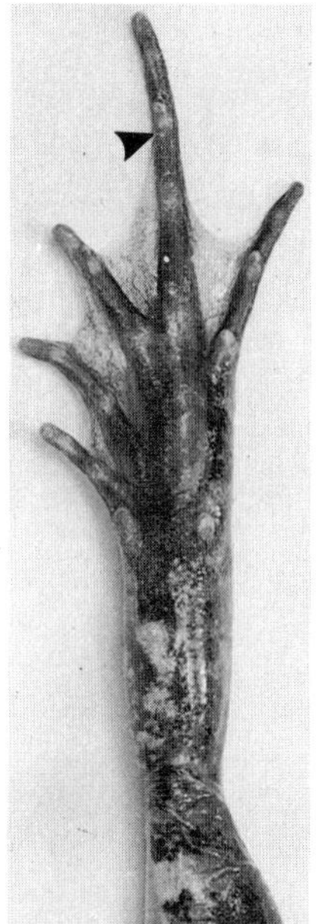

Mbabane, Swaziland

EAST AFRICAN PUDDLE FROG *Phrynobatrachus acridoides* (Cope) 1867

Zanzibar Puddle Frog
Small Puddle Frog

EAST AFRICAN PUDDLE FROG *Phrynobatrachus acridoides* Malongane, Mozambique

BREEDING HABITAT

Swamps and vleis. They are found in "flooded depressions in grassy areas where, resting on the vegetation with their heads out of the water, they call continuously" (Stewart, 1967).

VOICE

A very harsh snore. About one call per second.

The regrettable substitution of this sonagram was necessitated by a printing error.

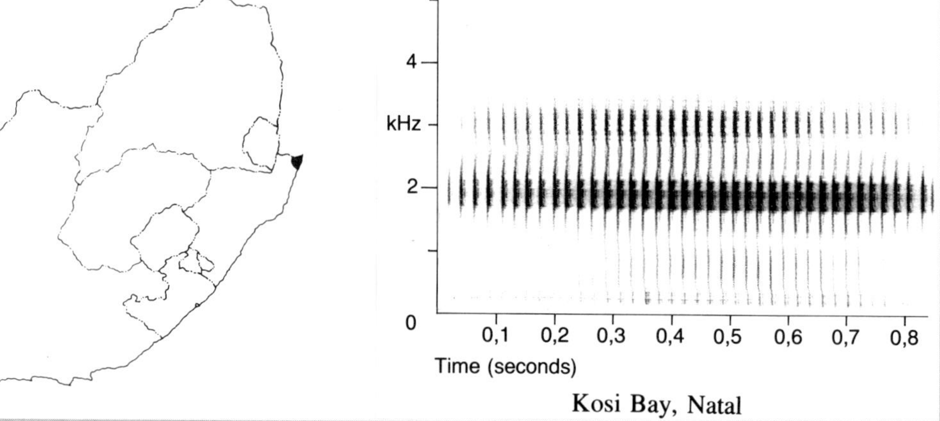

Kosi Bay, Natal

* The dorsal coloration is variable, and a vertebral band is often present. Two longitudinal, and often chevron-shaped glands ▲ are present in the scapular region.

LIFE SIZE
Malongane, Mozambique

Kosi Bay, Natal

* The ventral surface is smooth and mottled grey. The throat is dark in males, and the vocal sac is folded into several lateral creases.

* The toes are terminally expanded into small bulbous swellings ▲ — cf. other species.
* Webbing on the toes is moderate with not more than 2 phalanges of the longest toe unwebbed ▲ — cf. *P. mababiensis.*

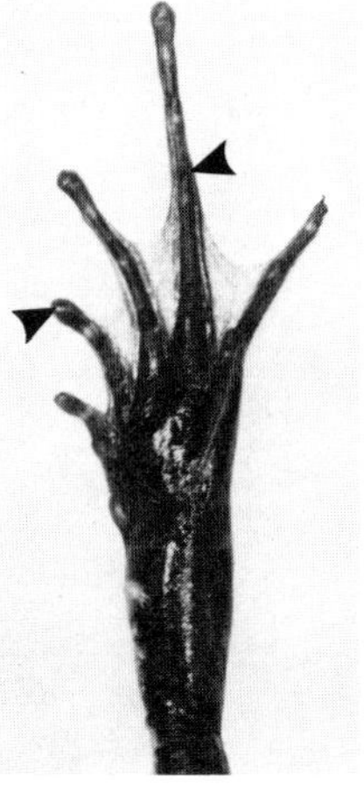

Kosi Bay, Natal

DWARF PUDDLE FROG *Phrynobatrachus mababiensis** FitzSimons 1932

Common Cricket Frog

Syn: *Phrynobatrachus ukingensis mababiensis* FitzSimons

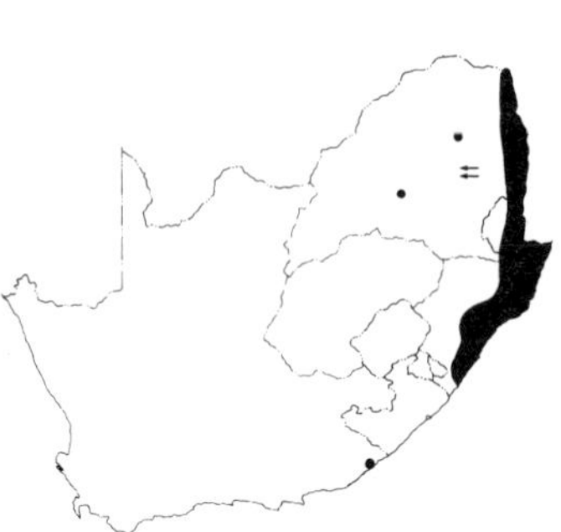

Pafuri, Kruger National Park

DWARF PUDDLE FROG *Phrynobatrachus mababiensis*

BREEDING HABITAT

Any moist, marshy areas in tropical or subtropical regions. Calling males remain concealed amongst the vegetation.

VOICE

An insect-like buzzing and ticking repeated rapidly and sounding continuous when heard in chorus.

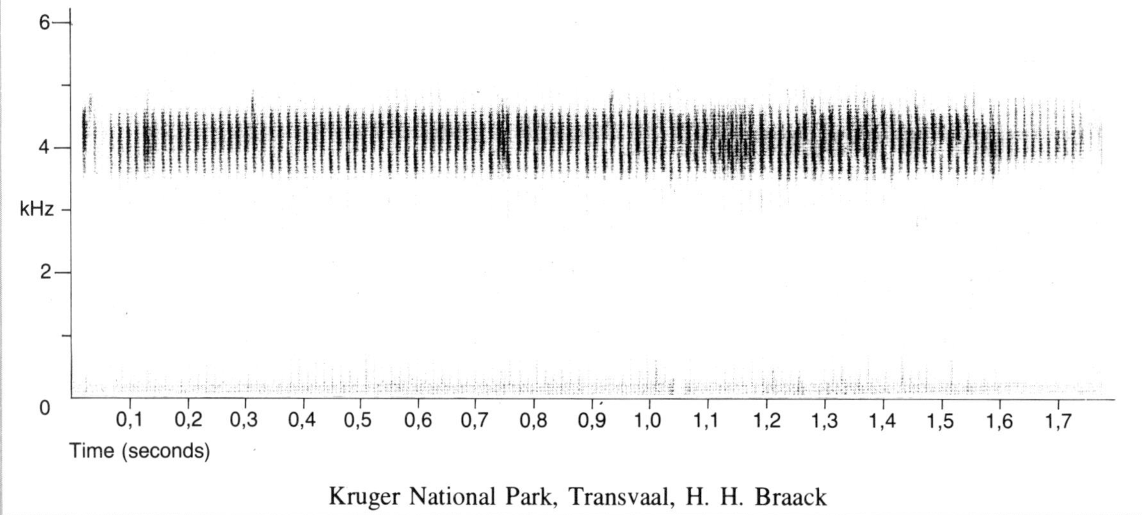

Kruger National Park, Transvaal, H. H. Braack

*Poynton (personal communication) considers this form to be specifically distinct from the forest-dwelling *ukingensis*.

LIFE SIZE

★ The dorsal coloration and skin texture are both variable, with vertebral stripes often present.

Mkuzi, Natal

★ The ventral surface is smooth and speckled, with yellow infusions sometimes evident in the groin. In males the throat is densely speckled and sometimes almost completely black. The vocal sac collapses into irregular folds — cf. *P. natalensis.*

Preserved specimen, Transvaal Museum

★ The toes are not expanded at the tips — cf. *P. acridoides.*

★ Webbing is only just discernible between the toes; at least 3 and usually 4, phalanges of the longest toe are free of webbing ▲.

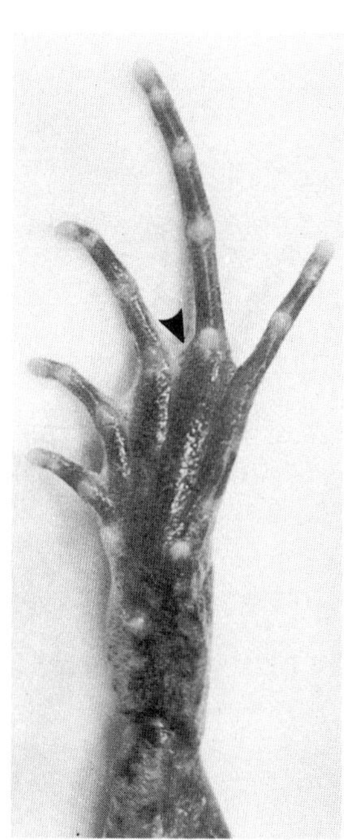

Preserved specimen, Transvaal Museum

KLOOF FROGS

Natalobatrachus Hewitt and Methuen

- ★ A pale triangle is present on the snout.
- ★ The pupil is horizontal.
- ★ Fingers terminate in large, spatulate, triangular discs.
- ★ Fingers lack webbing.
- ★ Discs on the toes are smaller than those on the fingers.
- ★ Toes are slightly webbed.

The genus is monotypic. Generic and specific characteristics are illustrated together in the identification section of the only species, *Natalobatrachus bonebergi*.

Kloof frogs inhabit the dark, rocky stream beds in densely forested ravines. The digits are elongated and expanded terminally into broad discs which enable the frogs to move with spiderlike agility over slippery, sometimes vertical, rock faces. They are capable of long leaps, in addition to being able to swim well under water. The dorsal coloration is cryptic.

Sexual Dimorphism

In males conspicuous nuptial pads are evident on the thumbs.

Eggs

The mode of egg-laying is distinctive. A small number of pigmented eggs are set in a jelly mass on objects overhanging the water. After about 7 days (Wager, 1965) the nest breaks down, and the tadpoles slide into the water below.

TADPOLES

The larval life, begun in the nest, is completed in the water. The tadpoles are capable of active swimming. They are benthonic and light coloured (Wager, 1965).

DISTRIBUTION

Natalobatrachus is confined to the coastal region of Natal and Transkei.

KLOOF FROG

Natalobatrachus bonebergi Hewitt and Methuen 1913

Boneberg's Frog
Gloomy Kloof Frog
Natal Frog

KLOOF FROG *Natalobatrachus bonebergi* — Ngoye Forest, Natal

BREEDING HABITAT

Stream beds and adjacent litter in densely forested kloofs. Males call from exposed positions or whilst hidden in cracks in rocks.

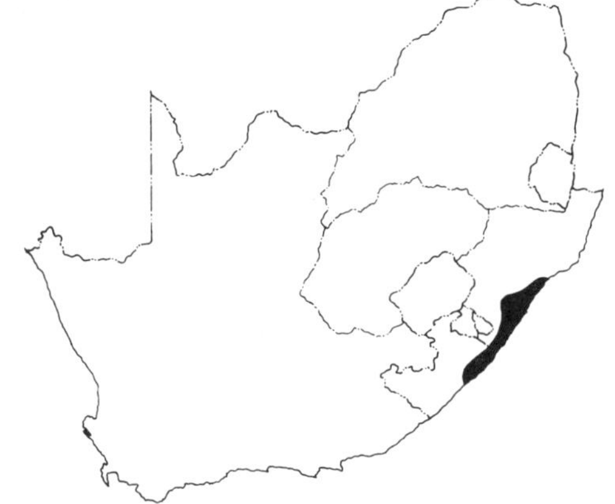

VOICE

A soft click repeated at irregular intervals.

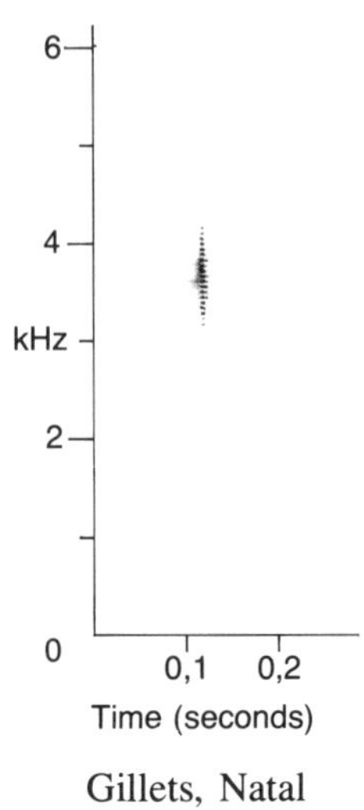

Gillets, Natal

- ★ The dorsal coloration is very variable, ranging from brown to grey. Vertebral stripes are common and are often superimposed on a wider vertebral band.
- ★ The snout is pointed, and bears a pale triangular patch.

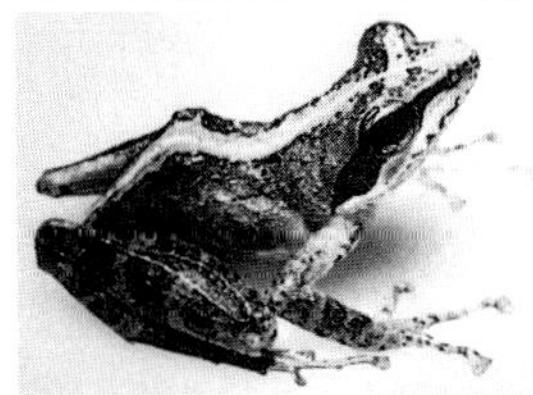

LIFE SIZE
Port St Johns, Transkei

- ★ The ventral surface is cream and usually freckled to some degree.

Ngoye Forest, Natal

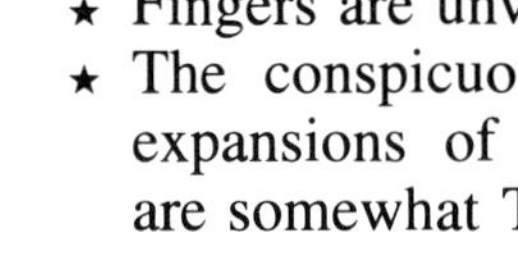

- ★ Fingers are unwebbed.
- ★ The conspicuous terminal expansions of the fingers are somewhat T-shaped.

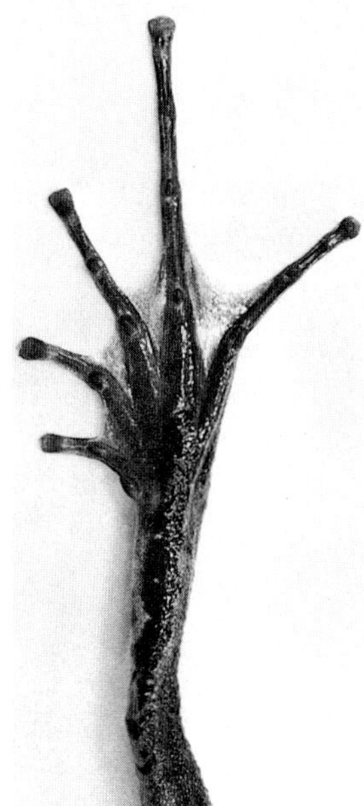

Ngoye Forest, Natal

- ★ The terminal expansions on the toes are not as large as those on the fingers.
- ★ The toes bear a narrow margin of webbing along their length, but webbing between them is not extensive.

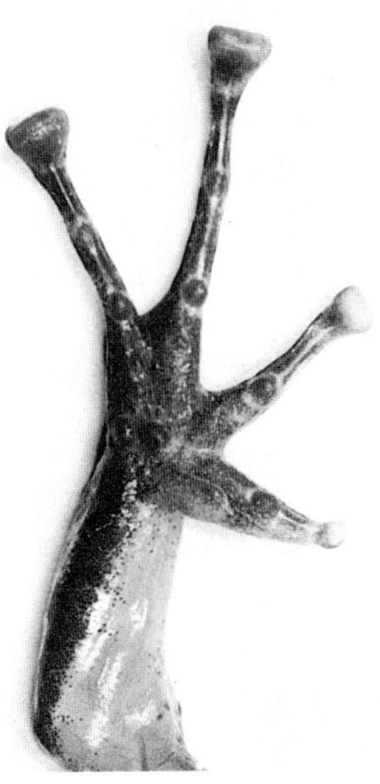

Ngoye Forest, Natal

MICRO FROGS

Microbatrachella Hewitt

- ★ The pupil is horizontal.
- ★ The ventral surface is smooth and black and white mottled.
- ★ Fingers lack webbing.
- ★ Webbing is present between toes and metatarsals — cf. *Cacosternum, Arthroleptella*.
- ★ The shank is less than half the body length — cf. *Rana, Ptychadena*.

The genus is monotypic and the generic and specific characteristics are illustrated together in the identification section of the only species, *Microbatrachella capensis*.

The Micro Frog is the smallest South African species, and it is very similar to the Cacos. Apart from skeletal characters, they are distinguishable only by the webbed toes of the former. They are polymorphic for dorsal pattern and colour, but most individuals display a dark ground colour with a pale vertebral stripe. The males have a disproportionately large subgular vocal sac.

Sexual Dimorphism

In females, the belly coloration extends anteriorly onto the throat. In mature males, the throat is plain yellowish-brown in colour.

Eggs

The eggs are small and pigmented. Each is surrounded by an individual jelly capsule and they are attached in clusters of about 20 to vegetation below the surface (Rose, 1962).

TADPOLES

The tadpoles are small and benthonic.

DISTRIBUTION

Microbatrachella is confined to the coastal flats between the Cape Peninsula and Hermanus.

MICRO FROG *Microbatrachella capensis* (Boulenger) 1910

MICRO FROGS *Microbatrachella capensis* Kleinmond, Cape

BREEDING HABITAT

Vleis and shallow pans in the fynbos and duneveld on the Cape Flats and along the southern seaboard to Hermanus. Males call from half-submerged positions among the marginal vegetation.

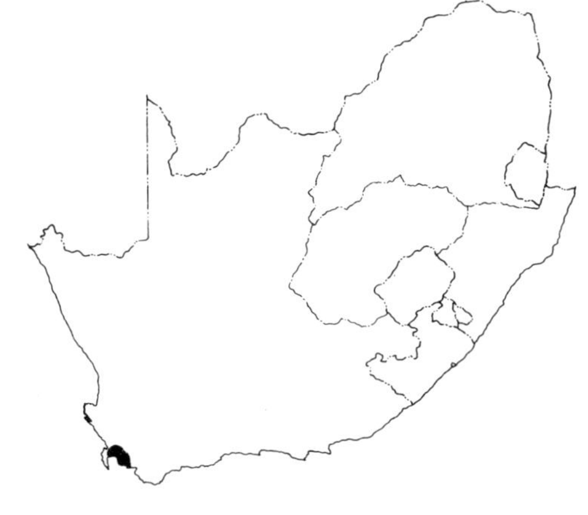

VOICE

A series of low-pitched scratches. About one per second.

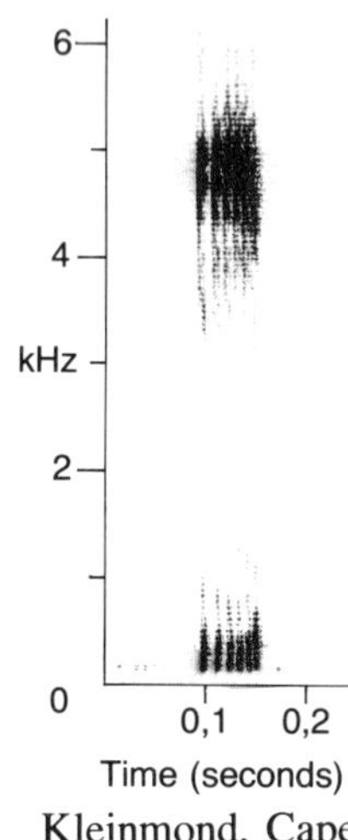

Kleinmond, Cape

Life Size

- ★ The dorsal coloration and pattern are variable, and vertebral stripes are common.
- ★ The shank ▲ is less than half the body length — cf. all species of *Rana* and *Ptychadena*.

Kleinmond, Cape

Kleinmond, Cape

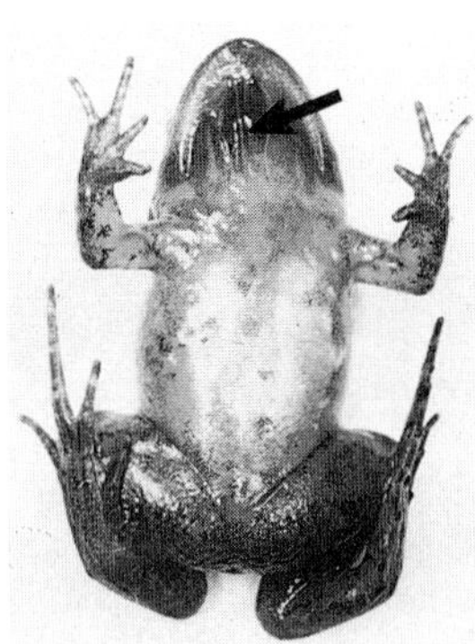

Kleinmond, Cape

Kleinmond, Cape

- ★ The ventral surface is smooth. Black and white mottling is displayed to a very variable degree, being almost absent in some specimens. The gular region ▲ is pale brown and free of mottling in males.

- ★ The toes are webbed, but with at least 2 or 3 phalanges of the longest toe ▲ free of webbing.

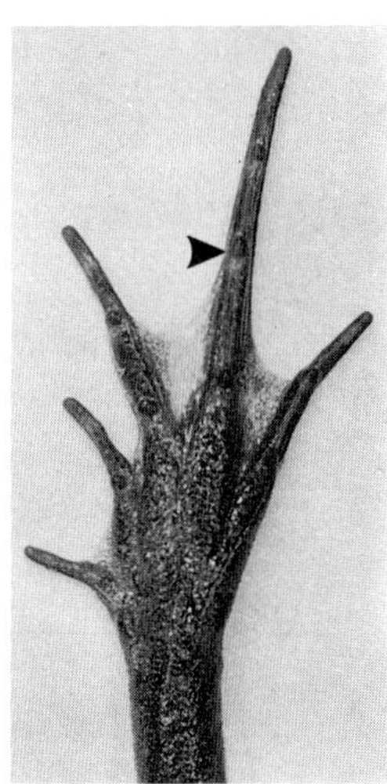

Kleinmond, Cape

CACOS

Cacosternum Boulenger

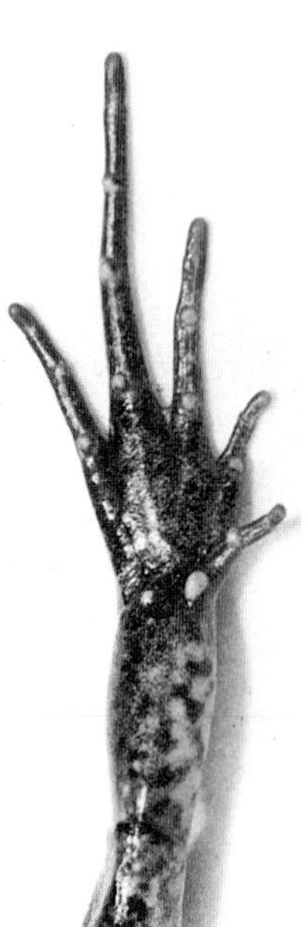

- ★ The pupil is horizontal.
- ★ Dark spots are present on an otherwise smooth white ventral surface.
- ★ Fingers lack webbing.
- ★ Toes lack webbing.

Four species occur in South Africa. Cacos inhabit inundated grasslands, vleis and small streams and they are often extremely abundant. The genus is well represented in both temperate and sub-tropical regions of the country.

Cacos are small, with rather elongated bodies and small heads. The limbs are slender, with long unwebbed digits. They are active frogs, capable of rapid movements both in and out of the water. They are particularly adept at clinging to, and clambering amongst, vegetation, and are often difficult to locate by day. The dorsal coloration is cryptic and provides very effective concealment against their natural surroundings. Substantial colour pattern polymorphism occurs in *C. boettgeri* and to some degree in *C. nanum*. Dark spots are present on the ventral surface and these are characteristic of the genus.

Sexual Dimorphism

Dimorphism differs between species. In *C. boettgeri*, the dark ventral spots are absent from the gular region in males, whereas in *C. nanum* they become more intense. The males of *C. capense* are darkly pigmented under the jaw. No external morphological differences have been recorded for *C. namaquense*.

Eggs

The eggs are small, pigmented, and with individual jelly capsules. They are attached in clusters to submerged vegetation. The clusters are generally small and often closely located (Wager, 1965).

Tadpoles

The tadpoles are small and benthonic. The larval life is extremely short in those species where these aspects of the life cycle have been observed.

Distribution

This is a small genus, occurring principally in southern Africa, with a few isolated populations to the north.

COMMON CACO *Cacosternum boettgeri* (Boulenger) 1882

Common Dainty Frog
Boettger's Dainty Frog
Boettger's Froglet

Suikerbosrand Nature Reserve, Transvaal

Bontebok National Park, Cape

Mooi River, Natal

Naboomspruit, Transvaal

COMMON CACOS *Cacosternum boettgeri*

BREEDING HABITAT

Any marshy area, vlei, inundated grassland or shallow pan. Males call from positions at the base of vegetation in, or adjacent to, very shallow water.

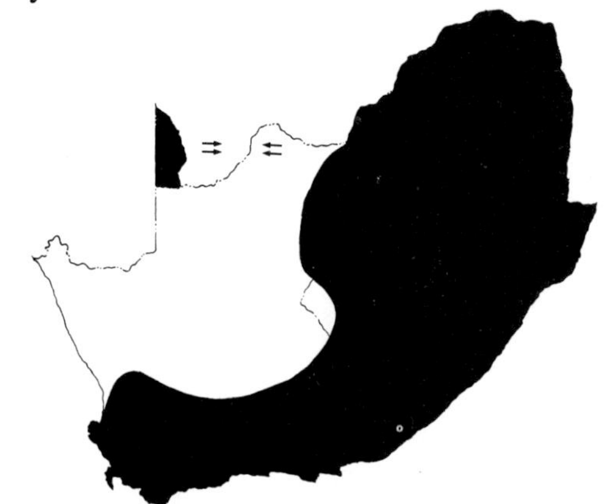

VOICE

About eight high-pitched explosive ticks are rapidly repeated in less than a second.

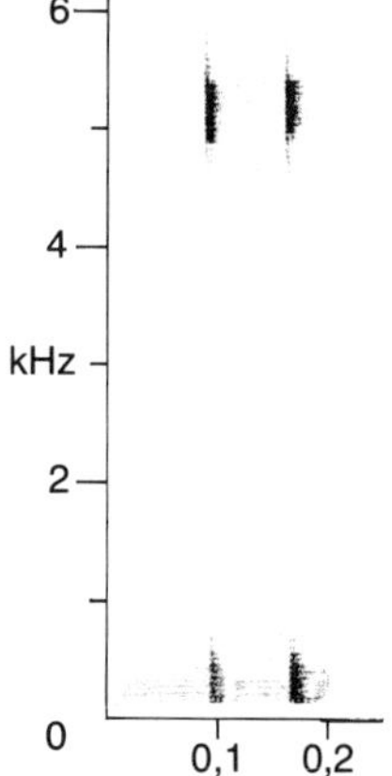

(Two calls) Kruger National Park H. H. Braack

LIFE SIZE

Suikerbosrand Nature Reserve, Transvaal

★ Both the dorsal coloration and pattern show considerable variation. Colours range from dark brown to emerald green and a variety of vertebral stripes, bands or dots may be present.

Mooi River, Natal

Mooi River, Natal

★ The ventral surface is smooth and white with indistinctly outlined grey or black spots. The throat in males is orange-brown and lacks spots. The throat in females is faintly spotted.

★ The subarticular tubercles ▲ on the hands are less prominent than in *C. nanum*.

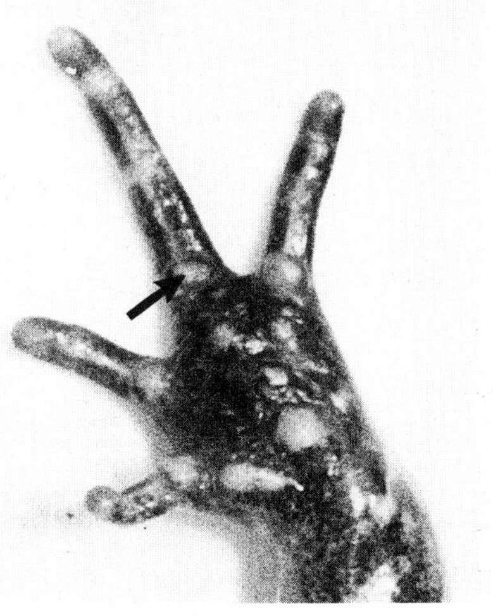

Suikerbosrand Nature Reserve, Transvaal

BRONZE CACO

Cacosternum nanum Boulenger 1887

Dainty Frog

Subspecies
Cacosternum nanum nanum Boulenger
Cacosternum nanum parvum Poynton
See page 260

C. n. nanum Bontebok National Park, Cape

C. n. nanum Tsitsikamma National Park, Cape

BRONZE CACOS *Cacosternum nanum*

BREEDING HABITAT

The marshy areas associated with small streams and vleis. Calling males remain well concealed amongst the vegetation.

VOICE

A short, creaking chirrup repeated at a rate of three or four per second.

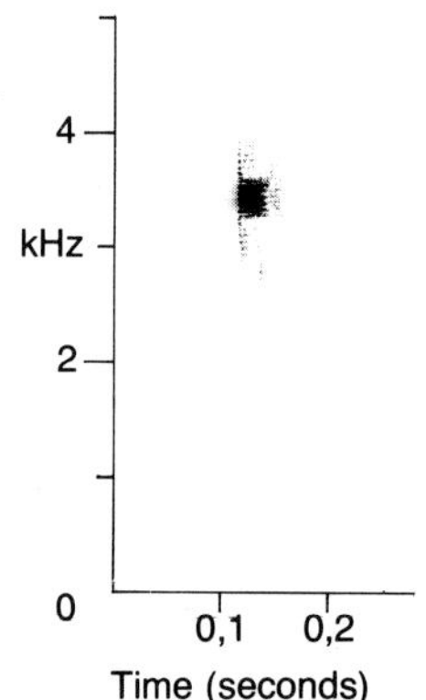

Inanda Game Park, Natal

` LIFE SIZE

Mooi River, Natal

★ The dorsum ranges in colour through various shades of brown. A vertebral stripe and dark dorso-lateral spots are common.

Bontebok National Park, Cape

Tsitsikamma National Park, Cape

Drakensberg Gardens, Natal

★ The ventral surface is smooth and white with many black spots concentrated anteriorly. In males the spots tend to fuse together on the throat leaving at most a trace of white. This tendency is particularly marked in specimens from the Drakensberg ▲ (*C. n. parvum*).

★ The subarticular tubercles ▲ on the hands are more prominent than in *C. boettgeri*.

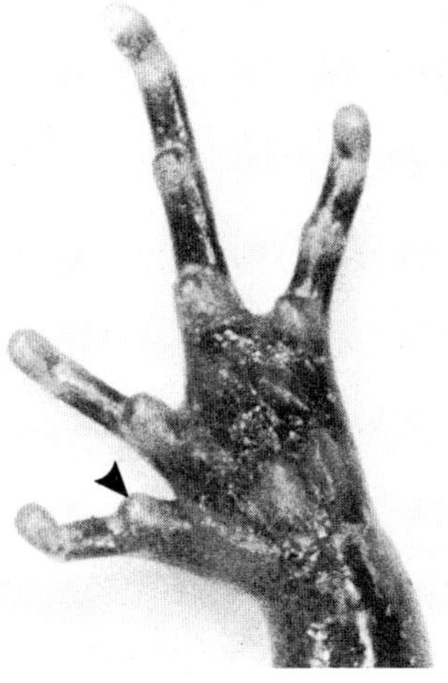

Keurbooms River, Cape

NAMAQUA CACO — *Cacosternum namaquense* Werner 1910

Namaqua Froglet

NAMAQUA CACO *Cacosternum namaquense* — Kamieskroon, N. Cape

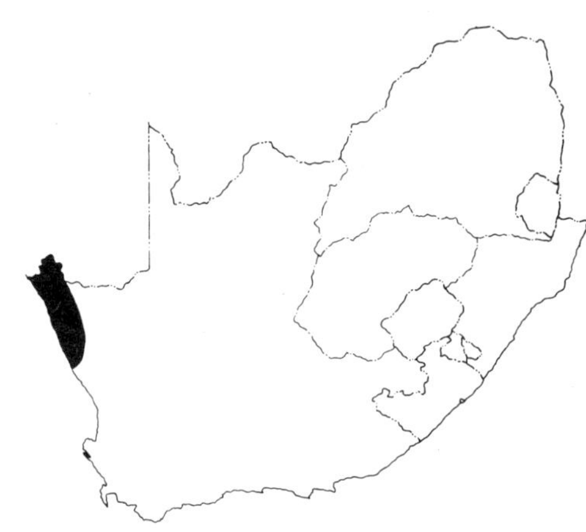

BREEDING HABITAT

Temporary watercourses and pans in Namaqualand.

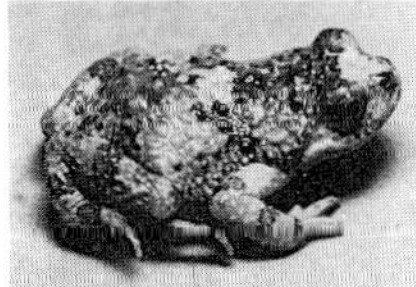

LIFE SIZE

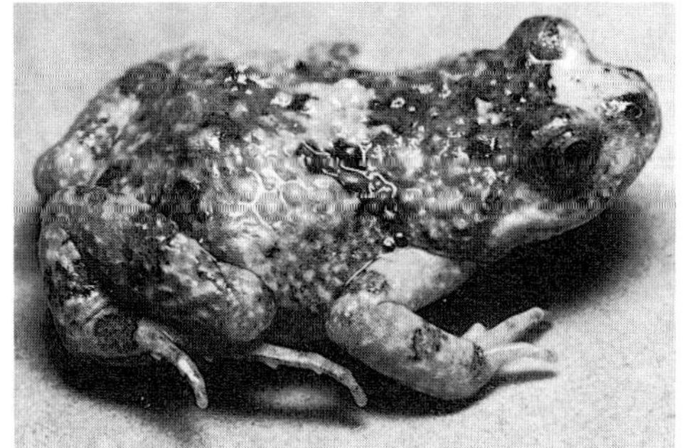

★ The dorsum is mottled grey or brown with a distinct pale triangle on the head.

Kamieskroon, N. Cape

Kamieskroon, N. Cape

★ The ventral surface is smooth. Bold dark ventral spots are usually larger in the middle, becoming smaller at the perimeter and tending to pale and fuse into a mottle along the jawline.

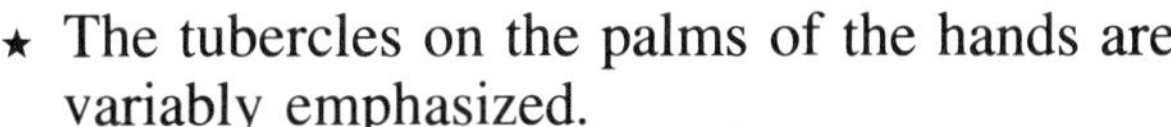

★ The tubercles on the palms of the hands are variably emphasized.

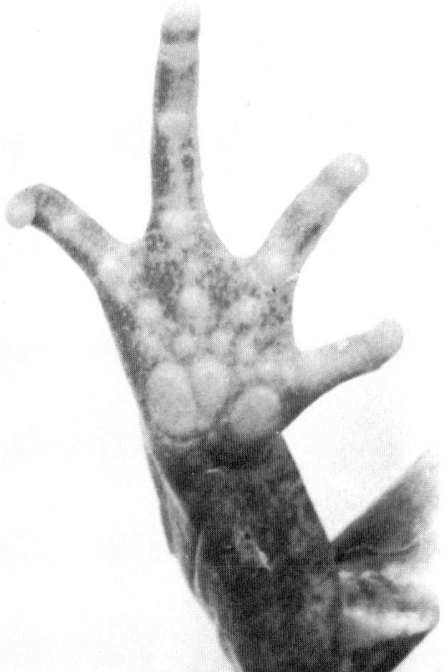

Lüderitz, SWA/Namibia
Preserved specimen, Transvaal Museum

CAPE CACO *Cacosternum capense* Hewitt 1925

Cross-marked Frog

CAPE CACO *Cacosternum capense* Durbanville, Cape

BREEDING HABITAT

Vleis and depressions amongst the dunes and fynbos of the Western Cape.

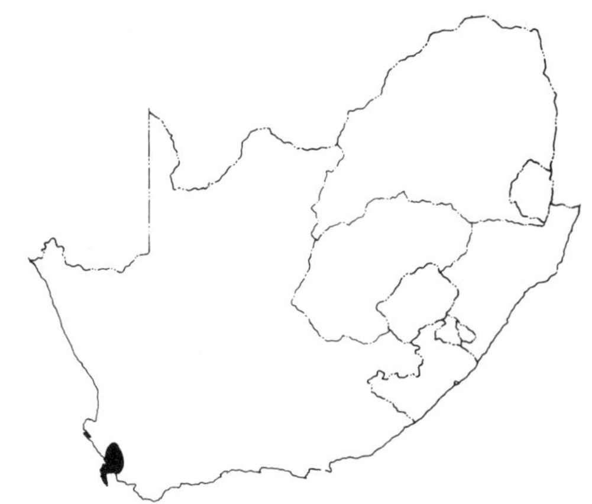

VOICE

A harsh creak uttered repeatedly. About two per second.

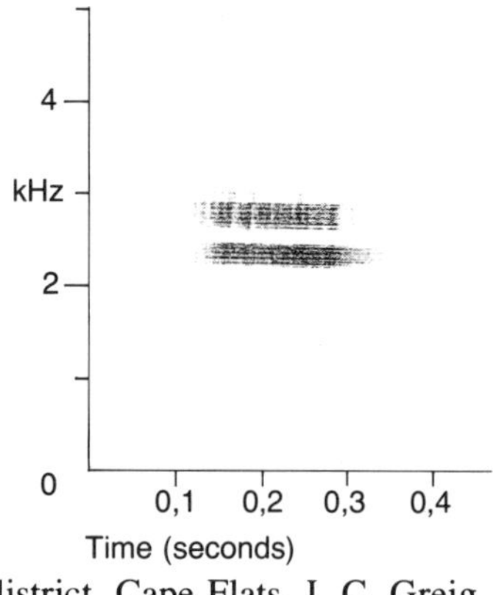

Faure district, Cape Flats, J. C. Greig

★ One pair of distinctive large egg-shaped glands is present in the sacral region and another is present on the flanks.

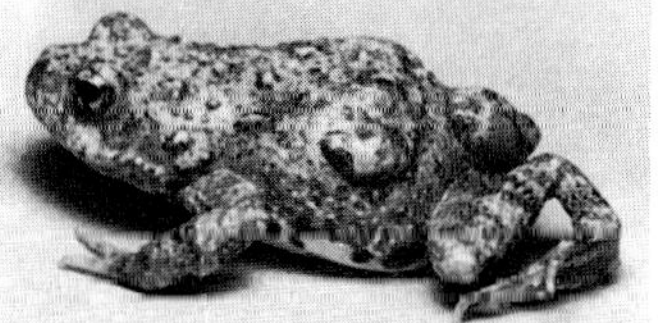

LIFE SIZE Durbanville, Cape

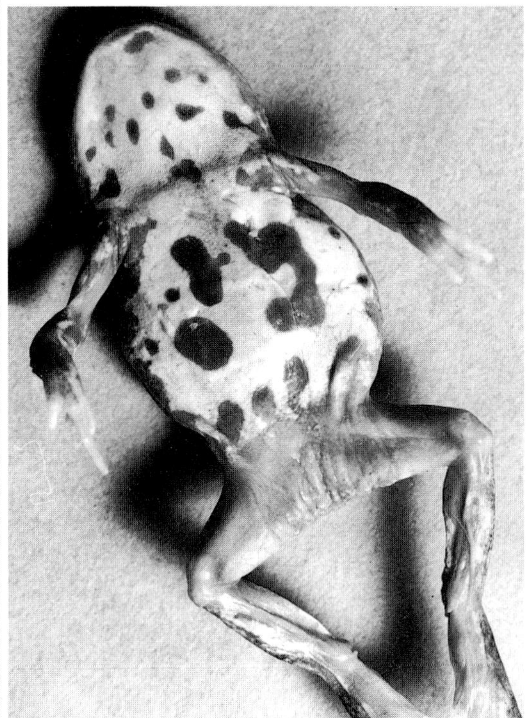

Preserved specimen, Durbanville, Cape

★ The venter is smooth with irregularly shaped dark patches which tend to become smaller peripherally. The throat in males is dark.

★ Tubercles on the palms of the hands are inconspicuous.

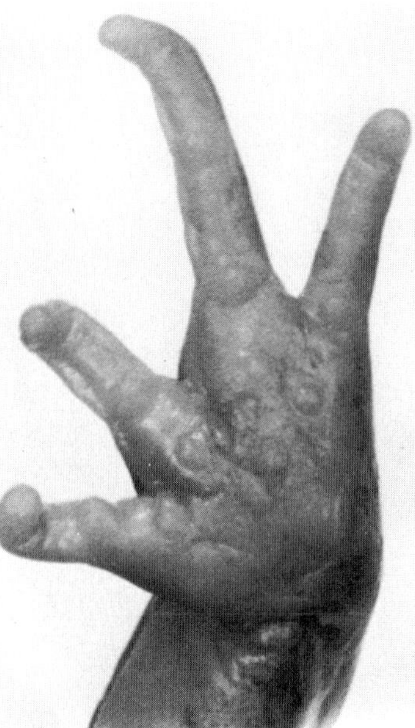

Preserved specimen
Transvaal Museum

CHIRPING FROGS

Arthroleptella Hewitt

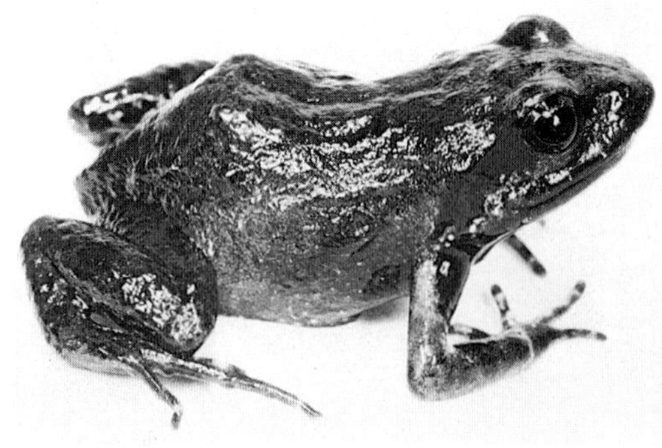

- ★ The pupil is horizontal.
- ★ The ventral surface is smooth and marbled — cf. *Cacosternum*.
- ★ Fingers lack webbing.
- ★ Toes lack webbing.

There are two species with widely separated ranges: *A. lightfooti* is confined to the southern Cape where it is found in abundance in wooded and open areas. *A. hewitti* occurs in riverine bush in Natal.

Adults are small frogs which closely resemble the Cacos. In breeding however, they are terrestrially adapted, with no free-swimming tadpole stage. Polymorphism is extensive for dorsal and ventral coloration and in the Natal species there is considerable variation in size between different populations.

Sexual Dimorphism

The collapsed vocal sac is readily identifiable in males.

Eggs

A few large unpigmented eggs are laid amongst damp vegetation or in shallow nests in wet mud. Each egg is surrounded by an individual jelly capsule (Wager, 1965).

Tadpoles

On emergence from the egg jelly, the tadpoles squirm about on the wet mud or amongst damp vegetation. The larvae have feeble toothless mouths and do not feed. They metamorphose rapidly and the resulting froglets are minute (Wager, 1965).

Distribution

A. lightfooti is confined to the south-western Cape, and *A. hewitti* occurs at moderate to high elevations in Natal. Both species live in the vicinity of streams or hillside seepage.

CAPE CHIRPING FROG *Arthroleptella lightfooti* (Boulenger) 1910

Cape Chirping Frogs *Arthroleptella lightfooti* Constantia Nek, Cape

Breeding Habitat

Wet mossy areas associated with mountain streams and hillside seepages in the south western Cape. Calling males remain well concealed in cavities in the mud or moss.

Voice

A rapidly pulsed insect-like chirp produced at irregular intervals.

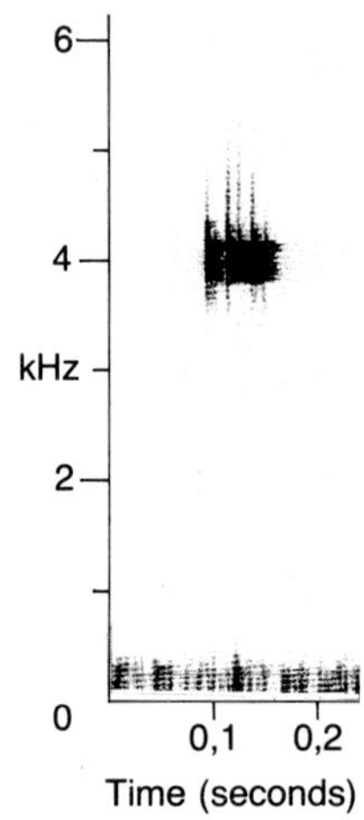

Table Mountain, Cape

Life Size

★ The dorsum ranges from light brown through dark brown to black with the majority of animals giving an over-all dark impression.

Constantia Nek, Cape

★ The ventral surface varies from plain white to dark brown or black anteriorly, with dark stippling or marbling against a white ground colour posteriorly. The gular region is black in males ▲ with fine white stippling anteriorly.

Constantia Nek, Cape

★ The outer metatarsal tubercle ▲ is well developed — cf. *A. hewitti.*

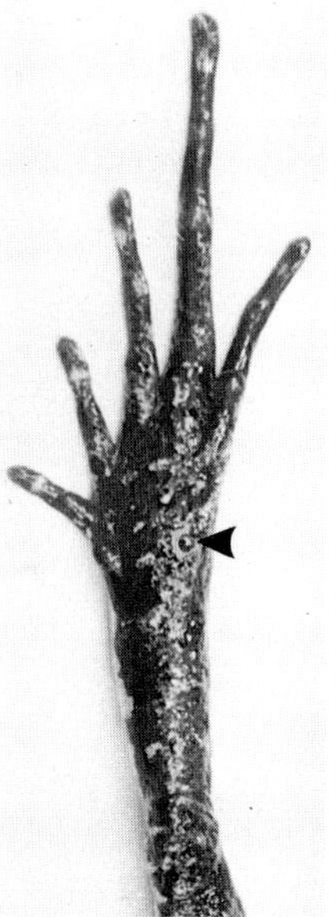

Constantia Nek, Cape

NATAL CHIRPING FROG *Arthroleptella hewitti* FitzSimons 1947

Nkandhla Forest, Natal

Drakensberg Gardens, Natal

Nkandhla Forest, Natal

NATAL CHIRPING FROGS *Arthroleptella hewitti*

BREEDING HABITAT

Wet, mossy embankments near waterfalls and rapids in the riverine bush of the Natal Drakensberg and midlands. Males call from concealed positions in the moss.

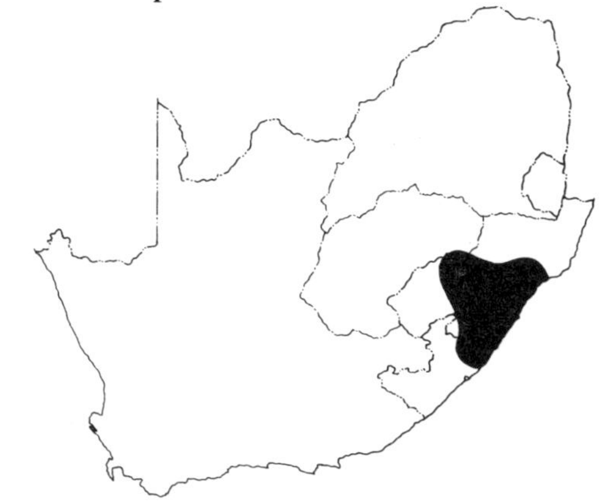

VOICE

Short piping notes repeated quickly. About four to six per second.

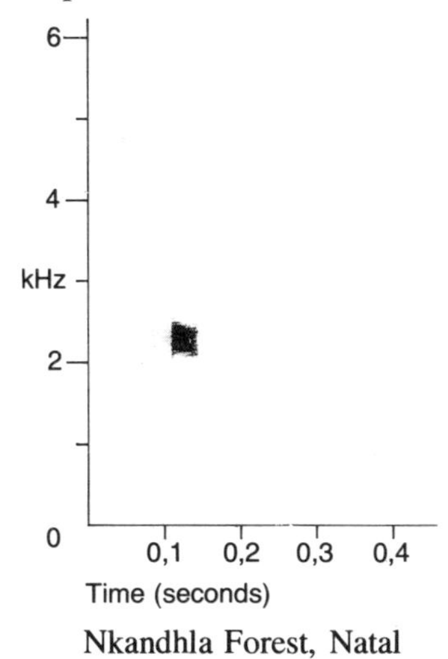

Nkandhla Forest, Natal

★ The size of adults and the dorsal coloration are very variable.
★ A well defined black stripe runs from the snout tip to the axilla.

LIFE SIZE
Nkandhla Forest, Natal

Nkandhla Forest, Natal

★ The ventral surface is smooth with darker mottles or speckles. The gular region is flesh coloured in males.

★ The outer metatarsal tubercle ▲ is inconspicuous or absent — cf. *A. lightfooti*.

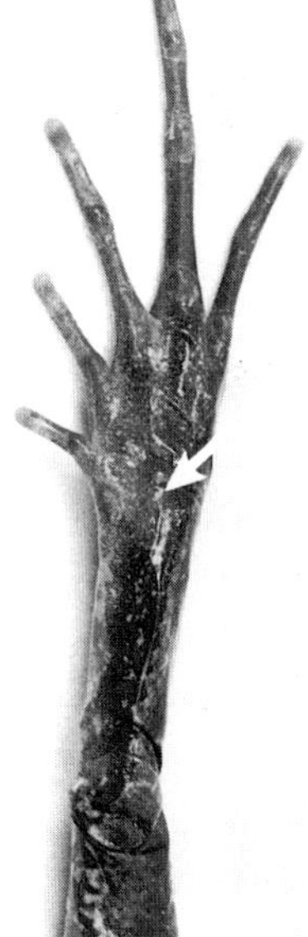

Preserved specimen
Nkandhla Forest, Natal

HOGSBACK FROGS

Anhydrophryne Hewitt

- ★ Males have a calloused snout.
- ★ The pupil is horizontal.
- ★ The ventral surface is smooth and mottled — cf. *Cacosternum*.
- ★ Fingers lack webbing.
- ★ Toes lack webbing.

The genus is monotypic. Generic and specific characteristics are illustrated together in the identification section of the only species, *Anhydrophryne rattrayi*. It occurs in moist situations in forest and shows distinct terrestrial breeding adaptations.

The adults are small bodied inhabitants of the litter of the forest floor. Webbing is absent, and the limbs are slender with long digits. The various dorsal patterns are extremely cryptic in the leaf-litter environment. Males have a calloused snout tip which is utilized in the nest excavation. The larval stage is suppressed and eggs are laid out of water.

Sexual Dimorphism

Males have a calloused snout tip.

Eggs

About 20 large unpigmented eggs are laid in underground nests on the forest floor (Rose, 1962).

Tadpoles

No free-swimming larval stage is present, and metamorphosis takes place within the egg capsule. In less than 4 weeks after laying, the young froglets emerge from the nest (Wager, 1965).

Distribution

Anhydrophryne is confined to the forests of the Amatola range of the eastern Cape.

HOGSBACK FROG *Anhydrophryne rattrayi* Hewitt 1919

Rattray's Forest Frog

HOGSBACK FROGS *Anhydrophryne rattrayi* Hogsback, Cape

BREEDING HABITAT

Nests are found in boggy areas on the forest floor. Calling males are generally concealed amongst moss or leaf litter.

VOICE

Clear, melodious cheeps repeated at a rate of about four per second, for several seconds.

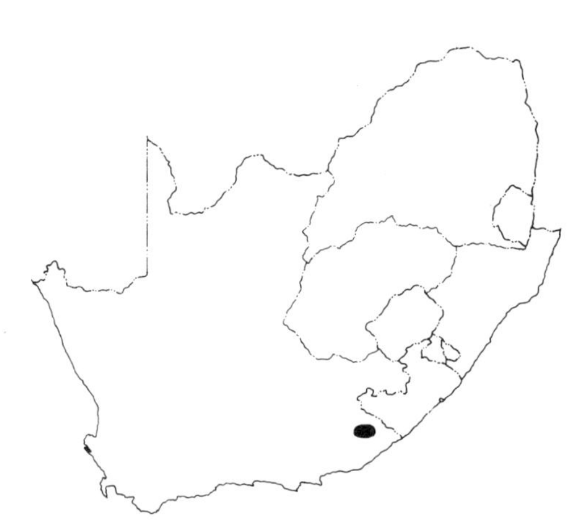

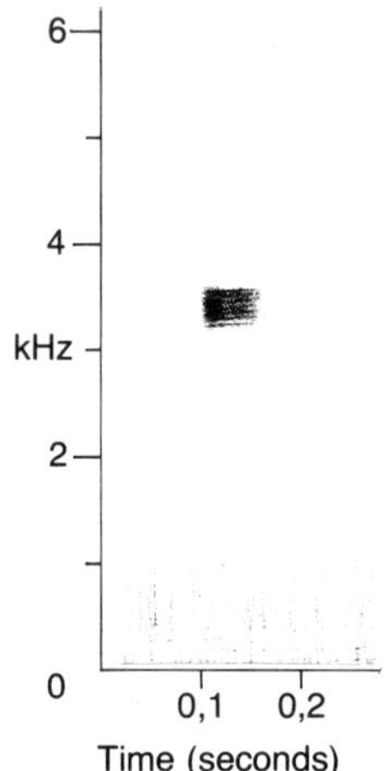

Hogsback Mountains, Cape

Life Size

* ★ The dorsal coloration varies from almost black to bright copper. A thin vertebral line is common, and the dark eye-stripe is always present.
* ★ The male snout is calloused, and usually whitish.

Hogsback, Cape

Hogsback, Cape

* ★ The ventral surface is smooth and white with a variable degree of dark mottling.

* ★ Toes lack webbing and subarticular tubercles are poorly developed.

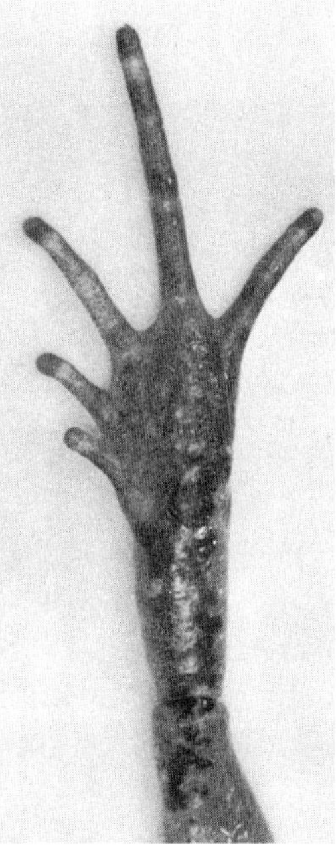

Hogsback, Cape

FOAM NEST FROGS

Chiromantis Peters

- ★ The pupil is horizontal.
- ★ The fingers bear terminal discs.
- ★ Fingers are webbed.
- ★ Toes are webbed.

Only one species occurs in South Africa. Generic and specific characteristics are illustrated together in the description of *Chiromantis xerampelina* below. It is confined to the warmer parts at low altitudes. It is distinctly arboreal, and shows a number of conspicuous adaptations to tree dwelling.

Foam Nest Frogs are large and slender with long, thin limbs. The fingers and toes are elongated and bear terminal discs which assist in the maintenance of purchase on leaves and branches. Furthermore, the two inner fingers are opposable to the outer two, thus enabling an effective grasp which is important in the precarious arboreal environment. The extensively webbed feet provide for efficient swimming. The frogs readily take refuge in the water if disturbed. The dorsal coloration is very effective in concealing the animal against a variety of different backgrounds, especially the bark of trees. Individuals frequently bask in bright sunlight, whereupon they become chalky white. The adults are uricotelic.

Sexual Dimorphism

Whitish nuptial pads are evident on the first and second fingers of the males.

Eggs

Eggs are laid in foam nests attached to branches of trees, leaves, reeds or rocks overhanging the water at varying heights. The eggs are unpigmented. Amplexus is axillary, and the legs of the pair are interlocked and slowly moved up and down, either together or alternately. The oviducal secretion forms a ball of stiff white foam in which the eggs are distributed as they are laid. A single foam nest is often co-operatively constructed by the simultaneous activity of several amplectant pairs and unpaired males. Taylor has reported the later addition of more foam to the nest.

TADPOLES

The developing embryos remain in the nest for about five days, after which they drop into the water below as the nest structure breaks down. The larval period is then completed in the water. The tadpoles are dark coloured, and of the benthonic type (Wager, 1965).

DISTRIBUTION

Chiromantis is a small African genus which is distributed throughout the tropics.

FOAM NEST FROG *Chiromantis xerampelina* Peters 1854

Grey Tree Frog
Southern Foam Nest Tree Frog
Great African Grey Tree Frog

FOAM NEST FROG *Chiromantis xerampelina* Tshaneni, Swaziland

BREEDING HABITAT

Trees and other elevated positions overhanging pans and rivers in tropical lowveld wooded savanna. Males call from exposed positions on branches and other vantage points.

VOICE

Subdued discordant croaks and squeaks, emitted irregularly.

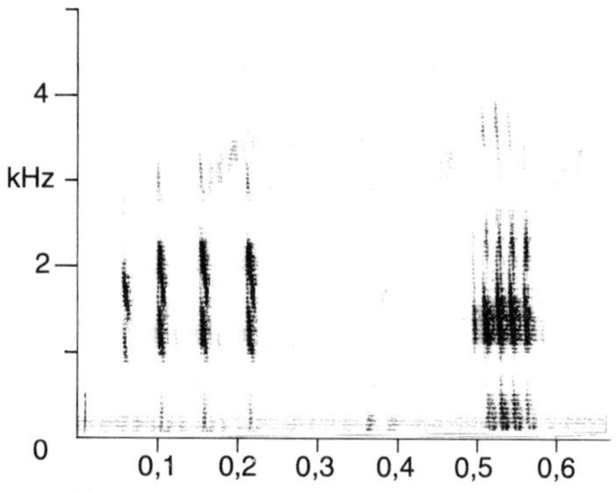

(Two different call types recorded from the same male)
Kruger National Park, Transvaal

★ The dorsal ground colour is generally grey or tan, with a variable number of darker markings. The skin is capable of colour change between dark grey and pure white.

LIFE SIZE Skukuza, Kruger National Park

Tshaneni, Swaziland

★ The ventral surface is granular. The belly is pinkish, and the pectoral fold and throat are white with a variable extent of grey freckling.

Tshaneni, Swaziland

★ The fingers are slightly webbed with large terminal discs. One pair is opposable to the other, and is considerably larger.

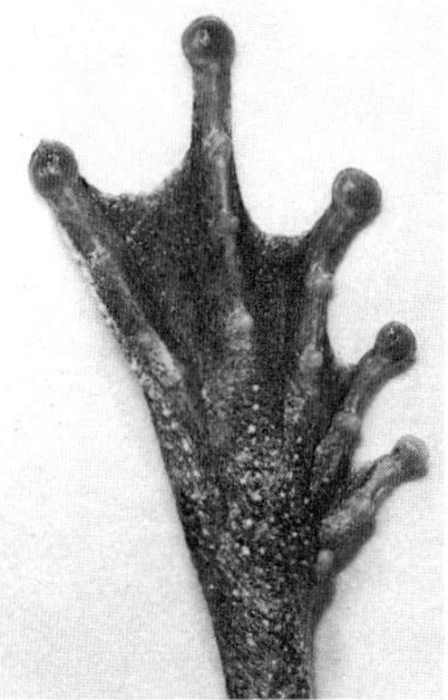

Tshaneni, Swaziland

★ The toes possess terminal discs and are extensively webbed.

SQUEAKERS

Arthroleptis Smith

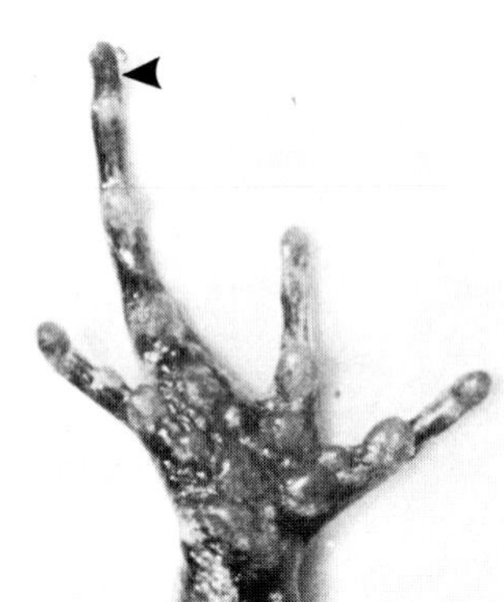

- ★ The dorsum bears characteristic diamond shapes in an 'hourglass' pattern.
- ★ The ventral surface is granular.
- ★ The 3rd finger ▲ is elongated.
- ★ Fingers lack webbing.
- ★ Toes lack webbing.
- ★ There is only one metatarsal tubercle, the inner.

Two species occur in South Africa. They are mainly coastal in distribution, occurring in moist situations in forest and treeveld. Breeding is adapted to a terrestrial mode of life.

Squeakers are small squat frogs, with short legs and long digits. Subarticular tubercles are prominent. The head is broad and carries a wide mouth. The dorsal coloration is cryptic in the dappled lighting of the forest. Diamond-shaped markings forming an 'hourglass' pattern, and an interorbital triangle are distinctive. Males call incessantly, during both the day and night, and the sounds are high pitched and insect-like.

Sexual Dimorphism

The throat is darkly pigmented in males.

EGGS

The eggs are unpigmented. They are laid away from water in nests amongst decaying vegetation. Each egg is enclosed in a stiff jelly capsule (Wager, 1965).

TADPOLES

No free living larval stage occurs, and metamorphosis takes place within the egg capsule. Young froglets emerge from the capsules about 4 weeks after laying (Wager, 1965).

DISTRIBUTION

The genus is distributed in wooded regions of tropical and sub-tropical Africa.

BUSH SQUEAKER *Arthroleptis wahlbergi* Smith 1849

Port St Johns, Transkei

Eshowe, Natal

BUSH SQUEAKERS *Arthroleptis wahlbergi*

BREEDING HABITAT

Litter and low vegetation of coastal and midland bush in Natal and Transkei. Calling males remain well concealed.

VOICE

Long, thin, mournful squeaks repeated continuously. About one call per second.

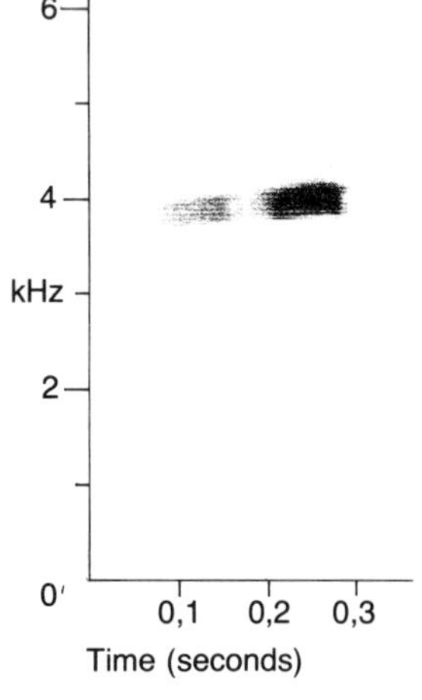

Inanda Game Park, Natal

★ The dorsal coloration is variable, but the pattern of diamond shapes is always evident, even if sometimes very faint.

LIFE SIZE
Eshowe, Natal

Eshowe, Natal

★ The ventral surface is finely granular. It is white with grey freckling. The throat is smooth and dark in males.

★ The inner metatarsal tubercle ▲ is inconspicuous — cf. *A. stenodactylus*.

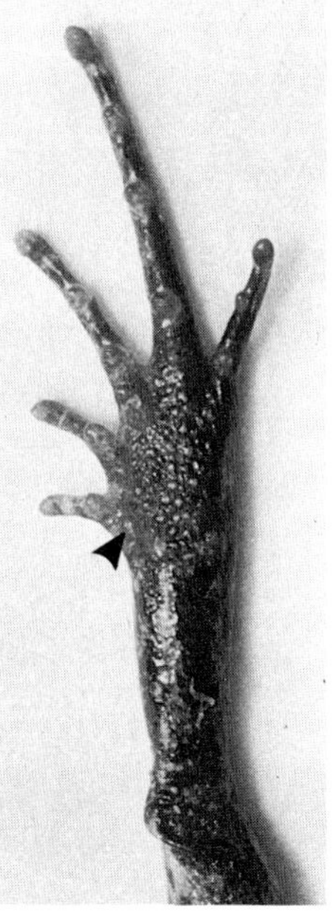

Eshowe, Natal

SHOVEL-FOOTED SQUEAKER *Arthroleptis stenodactylus* Pfeffer 1893

Dune Squeaker
Common Squeaker
Savanna Squeaking Frog

SHOVEL-FOOTED SQUEAKER *Arthroleptis stenodactylus* Pafuri, Kruger National Park

BREEDING HABITAT

Coastal dune forest at Cape Vidal and in acacia bushveld in the Kruger National Park. Males conceal themselves amongst dry leaves when calling.

VOICE

Brief and high-pitched chirp-like sounds are emitted in a series, at a rate of about two per second.

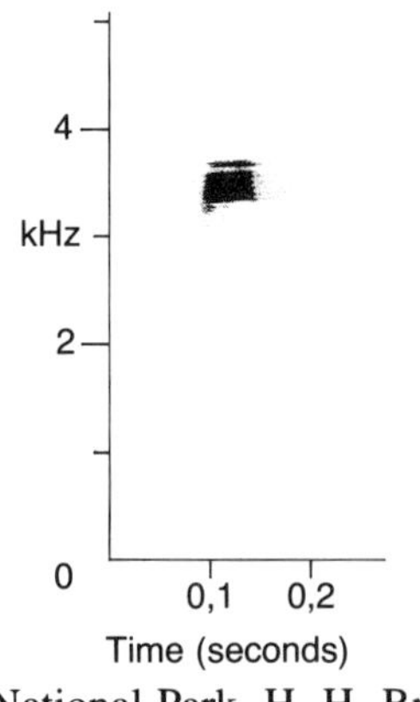

Kruger National Park, H. H. Braack

★ The dorsal coloration is variable but the pattern of diamond shapes is generally evident.

LIFE SIZE
Pafuri, Kruger National Park

Mount Selinda, Rhodesia
Preserved specimen, Transvaal Museum

★ The ventral surface is granular and white with grey flecks, particularly across the chest. The throat is flesh-coloured and smooth in males.

★ The inner metatarsal tubercle ▲ is massive — cf. *A. wahlbergi*.

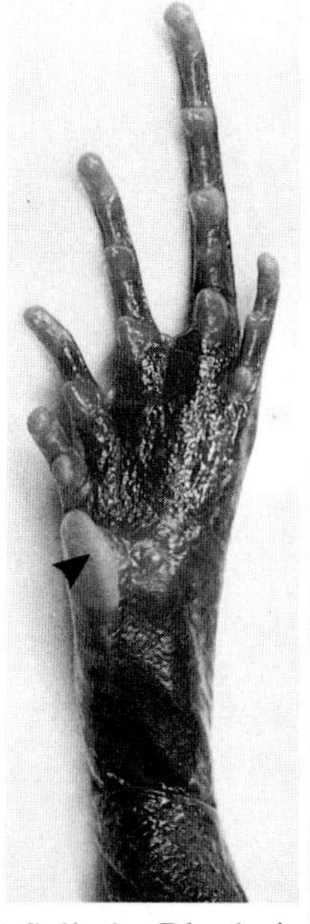

Mount Selinda, Rhodesia
Preserved specimen
Transvaal Museum

SHOVEL-NOSED FROGS

Hemisus Günther

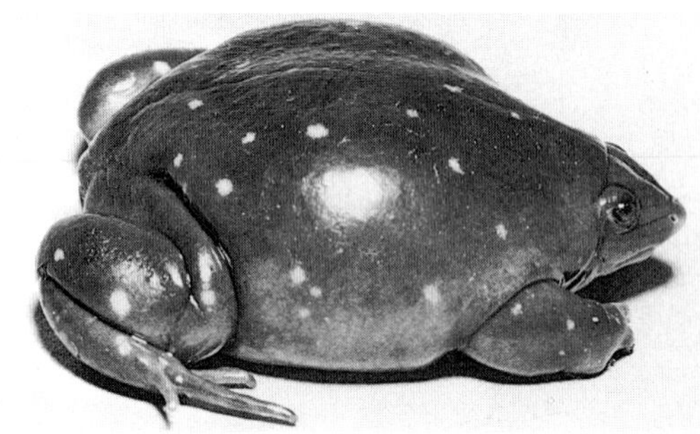

- ★ The head is small and the snout is pointed.
- ★ There is a transverse fold across the top of the head.
- ★ The snout is hardened for digging.
- ★ The lower jaw recedes.
- ★ The eyes are small.
- ★ The pupil is vertical.
- ★ The fingers lack webbing.

Two species occur in South Africa. Poynton (personal communication) reports the presence of a third species of *Hemisus* in South Africa. This tropical form, *H. guiniensis*, is represented in this region by a single specimen collected from north of the Soutpansberg. No treatment of this species has been attempted. Shovel-nosed frogs are burrowers which inhabit open country and are found in the vicinity of pools and vleis. Although locally abundant in some areas, they are seldom seen above ground. Breeding shows terrestrial tendencies.

The Shovel-nosed Frogs are unmistakable, being squat, depressed and somewhat bloated in general appearance. Unlike most other burrowing forms, they tunnel head-first, pushing the spade-like snout into the earth, and moving the head up and down. Several adaptations to this manner of burrowing are noticeable. The tip of the snout is sharp-edged and hardened. The head is narrow and pointed with small, unobtrusive eyes and a receding lower jaw. The limbs and digits are stout: during the burrowing operation the soil is clawed away with the forelimbs, while the hindlimbs push the animal forward. The inner metartarsal tubercle is well developed, probably providing improved purchase. Despite their subterranean adaptations, these frogs are able to move rapidly on the surface.

Sexual Dimorphism

The throat is darkly pigmented in males.

Eggs

Large, unpigmented eggs, surrounded by thick jelly capsules, are laid in subterranean nests near to the water. These are excavated by the female who remains with the brood (Wager, 1965).

Tadpoles

After 10-12 days, tadpoles emerge from the egg capsules. The female is reported to tunnel to the nearby water. The tadpoles are thus afforded access to the water in which larval development is completed (Wager, 1965).

Distribution

The genus occurs in tropical and sub-tropical Africa.

MOTTLED SHOVEL-NOSED FROG *Hemisus marmoratum* (Peters) 1854

Mottled Burrowing Frog
Pig-nosed Frog

MOTTLED SHOVEL-NOSED FROG *Hemisus marmoratum* Tshaneni, Swaziland

BREEDING HABITAT

Tropical and sub-tropical pans, especially where there are exposed mudbanks. Calling males establish themselves on the mud, usually in small holes or depressions.

VOICE

A repetitive incessant buzzing lasting several seconds.

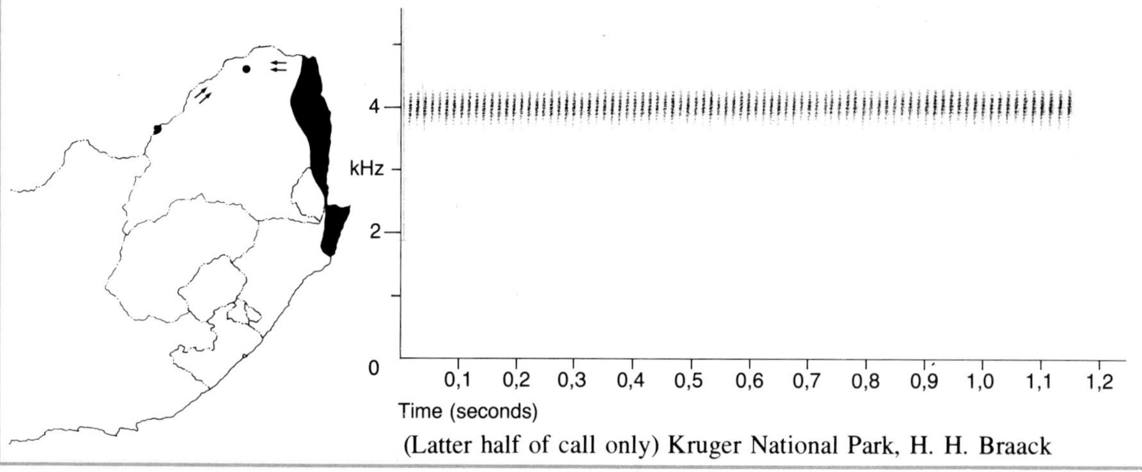

(Latter half of call only) Kruger National Park, H. H. Braack

★ The dorsum is mottled grey or brown.

LIFE SIZE
Tshaneni, Swaziland

Tshaneni, Swaziland

★ The ventral surface is smooth and pinkish-white. The gular region is darkly pigmented in males.

★ The toes are slightly webbed at the base — cf. *H. guttatum*.

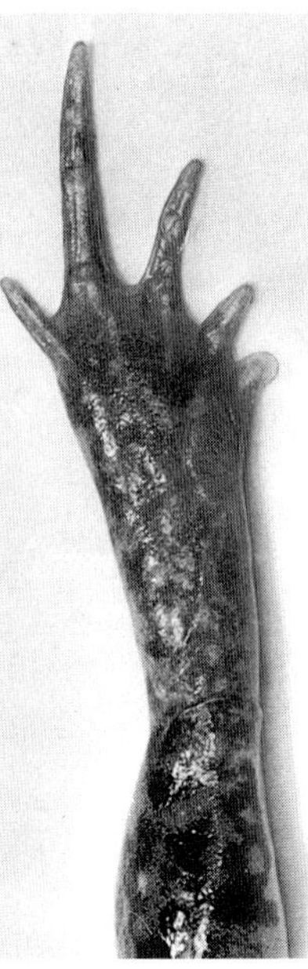

Tshaneni, Swaziland

SPOTTED SHOVEL-NOSED FROG *Hemisus guttatum* (Rapp) 1842

Spotted Burrowing Frog

SPOTTED SHOVEL-NOSED FROG *Hemisus guttatum* Durban, Natal

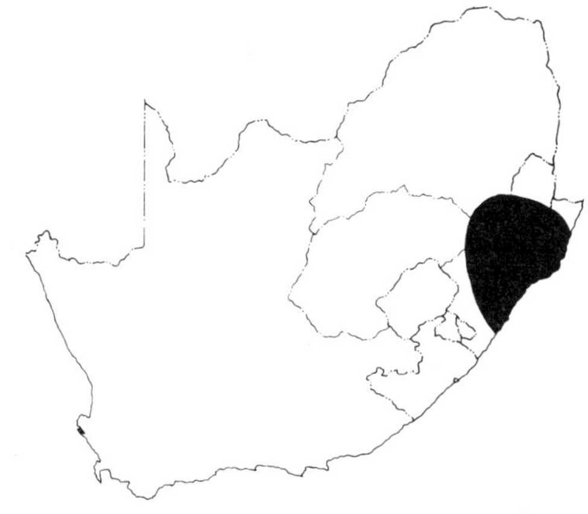

BREEDING HABITAT

Burrows in loamy banks adjacent to pans.

★ The dorsal coloration comprises distinctive yellow dots on an over-all brown ground colour. There is little variation.

LIFE SIZE Durban, Natal

Mtunzini, Natal

★ The ventral surface is smooth and white and the gular region is dark in males.

★ The toes lack webbing — cf. *H. marmoratum*.

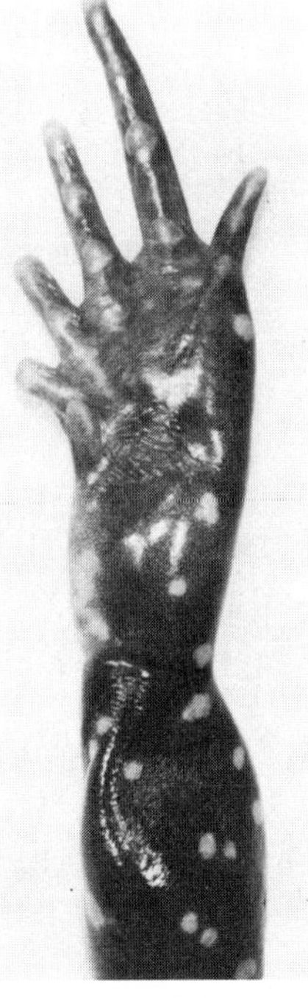

Mtunzini, Natal

TREE FROGS

Leptopelis Günther

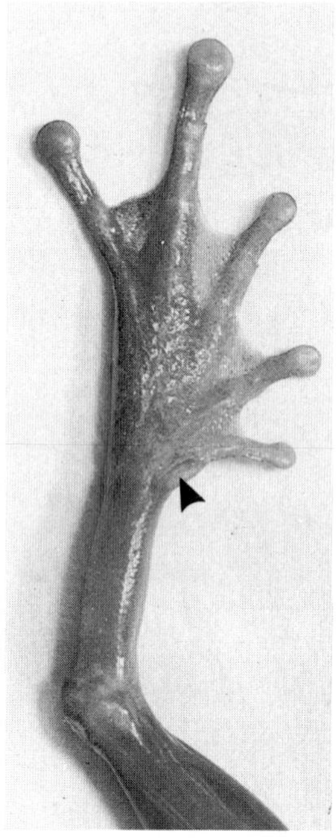

- ★ The tympanum is conspicuous — cf. *Afrixalus*.
- ★ The eyes are large.
- ★ The pupil is vertical.
- ★ Fingers and toes bear terminal discs, although diminutive in *L. xenodactylus*.
- ★ Fingers are slightly webbed, except in *Leptopelis sp*.
- ★ Toes are webbed.
- ★ The inner metatarsal tubercle ▲ is well developed — cf. *Kassina*.

The term 'tree frog' should be regarded as no more than a loose reference to the tendency for members of this genus to climb amongst vegetation. Three species occur in South Africa, each utilizing a very different habitat: *Leptopelis sp.* occurs in semi-tropical bushveld and forest where it is as much a burrowing form as an arboreal one; *L. natalensis* is largely associated with Natal coastal forest, and *L. xenodactylus* which also burrows, is confined to temperate marshlands on the south-eastern escarpment.

Tree frogs are medium sized with broad heads and large, bulging eyes. They exhibit great agility when climbing, and the limbs are long and slender, with the digits terminating in discs. Although the size of these varies between species, they are in all cases extremely adhesive, a single disc providing sufficient grasp for an animal when leaping amongst leaves or grass stems.

The inner metatarsal tubercle is well developed, particularly in *Leptopelis sp*., suggesting a burrowing function.

Sexual Dimorphism

No sexual dimorphism has been reported, other than that males are smaller than females.

Eggs

Of the three species, only the life history of *L. natalensis* is recorded. The eggs are large and very lightly pigmented. They are deposited out of water in damp surroundings on the surface (Wager, 1965).

Tadpoles

After about 2 weeks, the tadpoles emerge from the egg capsules and wriggle towards the water. They are large, with long tails and are benthonic and rather sluggish in habit (Wager, 1965).

Distribution

This is a comparatively large genus occurring in sub-Saharan Africa. Several central and west African species are not arboreal in nature.

FOREST TREE FROG *Leptopelis natalensis* (Smith) 1849

Raucous Tree Frog

Port St Johns, Transkei

Richards Bay, Natal

Eshowe, Natal

FOREST TREE FROGS *Leptopelis natalensis*

BREEDING HABITAT

Riverine bush and swamp along the Natal coast. Males usually call from exposed positions in the foliage of trees and bushes, often close to and overhanging water.

VOICE

A loud monosyllabic quack, often emitted twice in quick succession, interspaced by very long intervals. Sometimes preceded by a softer buzzing.

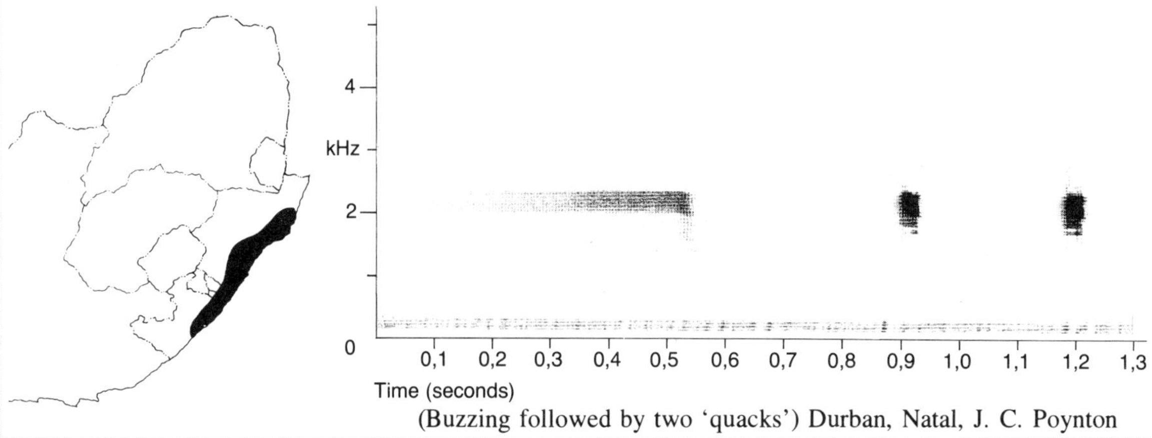

(Buzzing followed by two 'quacks') Durban, Natal, J. C. Poynton

★ The dorsum is slightly granular and the pattern varies from plain green or cream to mottled with brown patches. Markings are never grouped into an inverted horseshoe — cf. *Leptopelis sp*.

LIFE SIZE

Eshowe, Natal

Eshowe, Natal

★ The ventral surface is granular and cream coloured with the underside of the limbs yellowish.

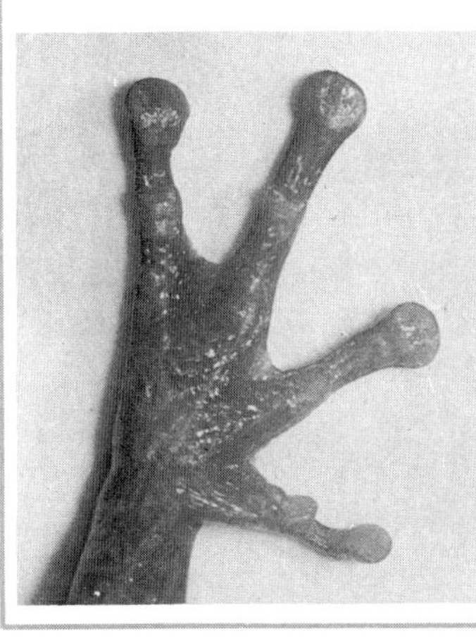

★ Terminal discs on fingers and toes are noticeably larger than those of the other two species.

★ Webbing between the toes is more extensive than that of the other two species.

★ The inner metatarsal tubercle ▲ is present, but smaller than those of the other two species.

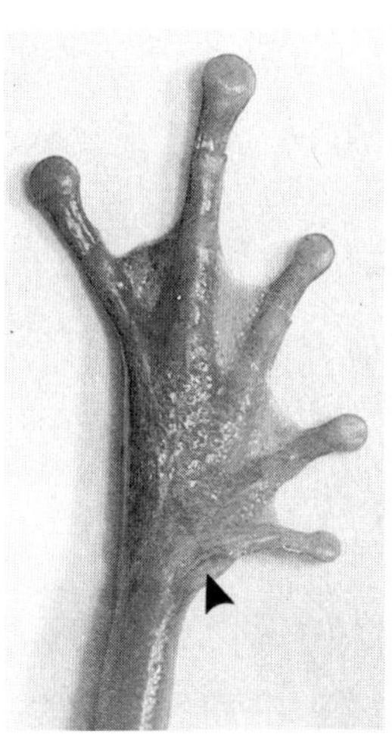

Eshowe, Natal

BROWN-BACKED TREE FROG *Leptopelis sp.**

Syn: *Leptopelis concolor* Poynton (non Ahl)
Leptopelis viridis cinnamomeus Poynton (non Bocage)

ADULT Tshaneni, Swaziland SUB-ADULT Skukuza, Kruger National Park
BROWN-BACKED TREE FROGS *Leptopelis sp.*

BREEDING HABITAT

Wooded savanna in the vicinity of streams and pans. Males call from elevated positions in trees and bushes, sometimes several hundred metres from standing water.

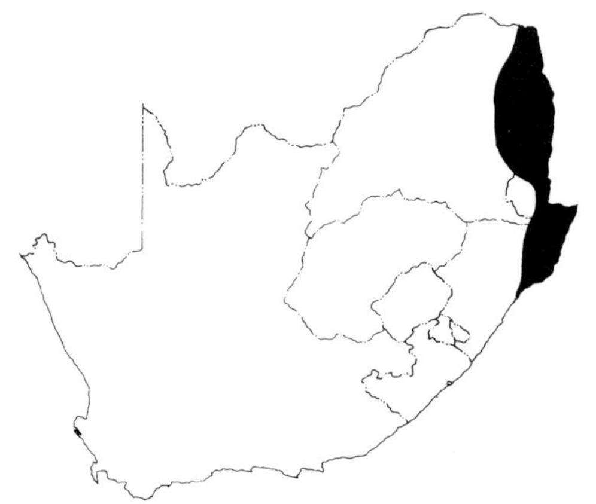

VOICE

A loud, two syllabled quack, emitted at long intervals and sometimes preceded by a buzzing.

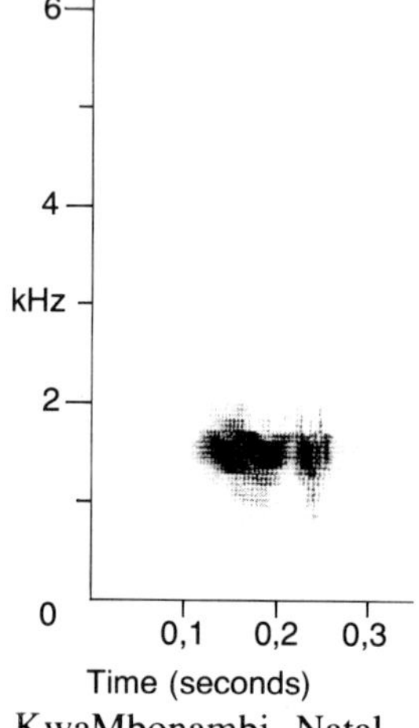

KwaMbonambi, Natal

*This form has previously been referred both to *concolor* Ahl and to *cinnamomeus* (Bocage). Perret (1976) and Poynton (personal communication) have indicated however that it is referable to neither of these. Its status will shortly be clarified.

★ The dorsum is coarsely granular and the coloration in adults is tan with a variable degree of darker brown in an approximately horseshoe shape — cf. *L. natalensis*. In sub-adults the dorsum is plain green.

LIFE SIZE Tshaneni, Swaziland

Tshaneni, Swaziland

★ The ventral surface is granular and fawn coloured with darker stippling on the throat.

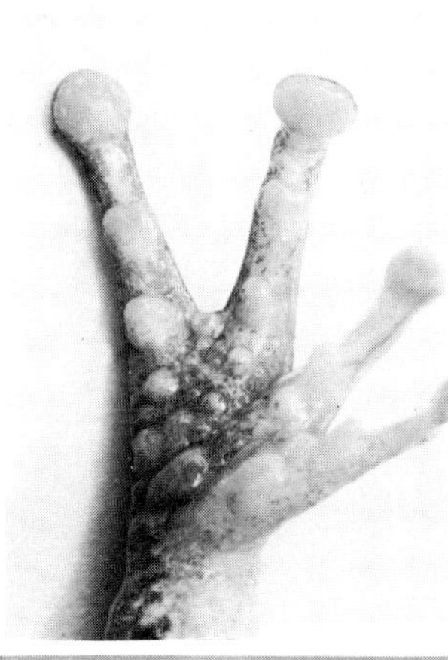

★ Terminal discs on the fingers and toes are smaller than in *L. natalensis* but larger than in *L. xenodactylus*.
★ Fingers are unwebbed and there is very little webbing between the toes — cf. *L. natalensis*.
★ The inner metatarsal tubercle ▲ is large and flanged — cf. *L. natalensis*.

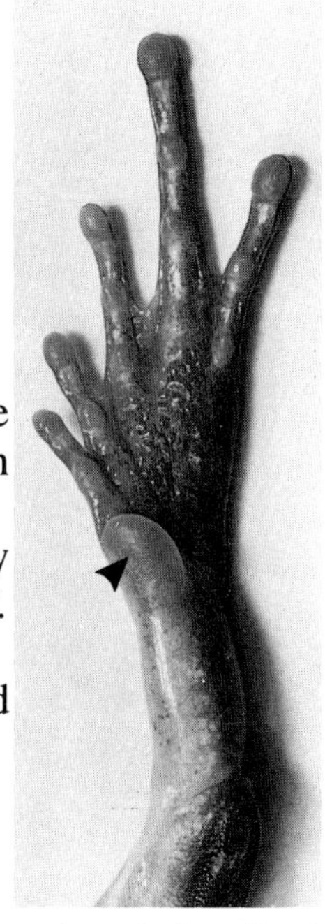

Tshaneni, Swaziland

LONG-TOED TREE FROG *Leptopelis xenodactylus* Poynton 1963

LONG-TOED TREE FROG *Leptopelis xenodactylus* Franklin, Natal

BREEDING HABITAT

Upland marshes in the foothills of the Natal Drakensberg. Males call from well concealed locations at the base of grass tussocks and from burrows in the marsh.

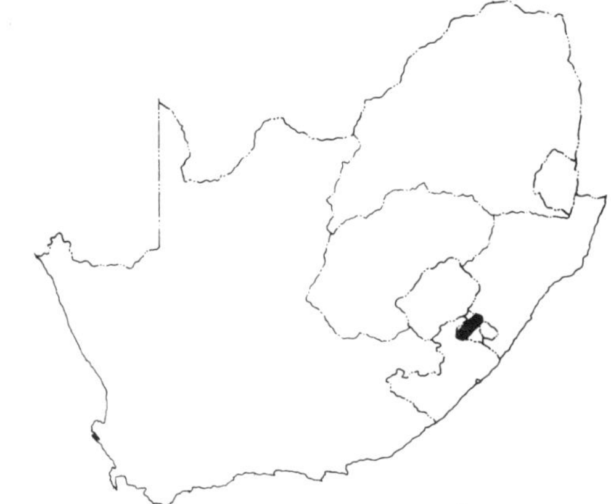

VOICE

One or two deep, brief croaks, separated by long intervals. Sometimes preceded by a very soft buzzing.

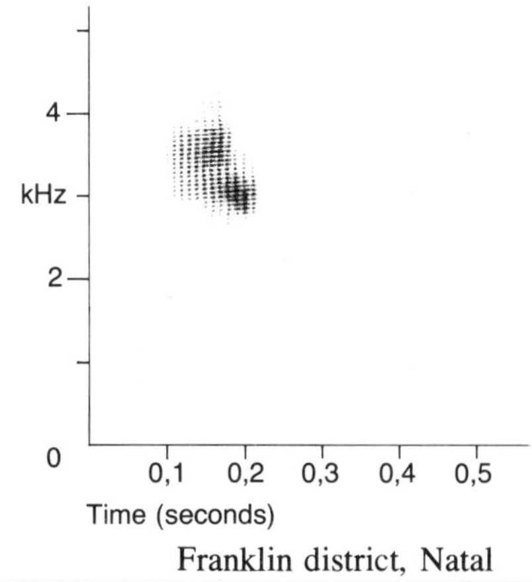

Franklin district, Natal

★ The dorsum is granular and unpatterned green.

LIFE SIZE Franklin, Natal

Franklin, Natal

★ The ventral surface is granular and creamy white.

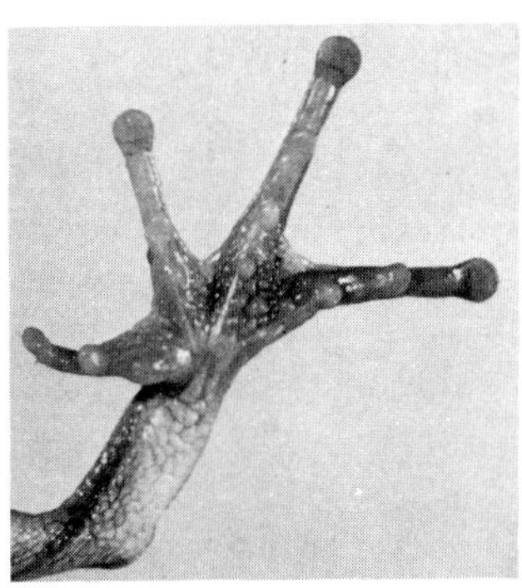

Franklin, Natal
D. E. van Dijk

★ The fingers, and particularly the toes, are noticeably longer than those of either of the other two species.

★ Webbing between the toes is less extensive than that of *L. natalensis* but more so than that of *Leptopelis sp.*

★ The inner metatarsal tubercle ▲ is moderately sized and flanged.

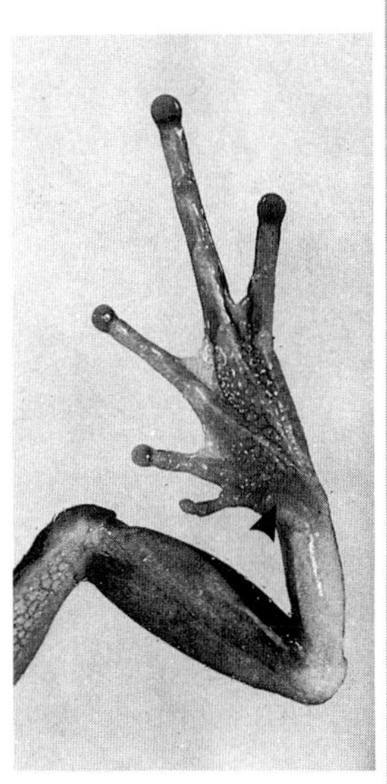

Franklin, Natal
D. E. van Dijk

KASSINAS

Kassina Girard

- ⋆ The pupil is vertical.
- ⋆ Fingers lack webbing.
- ⋆ Toes are slightly webbed.
- ⋆ The inner metatarsal tubercle is poorly developed — cf. *Leptopelis*.

Three species occur in South Africa. They are typically savanna dwellers, with one species, *K. maculata*, predominantly aquatic, and the others more terrestrial. *K. maculata* is confined to low lying sub-tropical regions, while *K. senegalensis* and *K. wealii* are more widely distributed and tolerant of more temperate conditions.

Kassinas are moderately sized frogs which are slow-moving, usually preferring walking in favour of hopping. The body is elongated and the limbs slender, with long digits. These carry terminal expansions only in the case of *K. maculata*, but all species do at times display climbing tendencies. However, they are most often encountered at ground level. The dorsal coloration is strikingly bold, yet cryptic in its natural environment. The vocal sac is subgular and in two species, *K. maculata* and *K. senegalensis*, it appears paired when fully inflated.

Sexual Dimorphism

The collapsed vocal sac, with its central gular disc, is conspicuous in males of all species (see specific illustrations).

Eggs

Small pigmented eggs are laid in water and attached to submerged vegetation. Each egg is surrounded by an individual jelly capsule, but successive eggs may adhere to one another in small clusters.

Tadpoles

The tadpoles are nektonic and compressed with deep, distinctive fins.

Distribution

This is a small genus, but one in which the component species are widely distributed and successful through sub-Saharan Africa.

RED-LEGGED KASSINA *Kassina maculata** (Duméril) 1853

Vlei Frog
Brown-spotted Tree Frog
Red-legged Pan Frog

Syn: *Hylambates maculatus* Duméril

RED-LEGGED KASSINA *Kassina maculata* Sordwana Bay, Natal

BREEDING HABITAT

Well vegetated pans in the tropical and sub-tropical lowveld. Males call from partly submerged positions amongst surface weed in deep water.

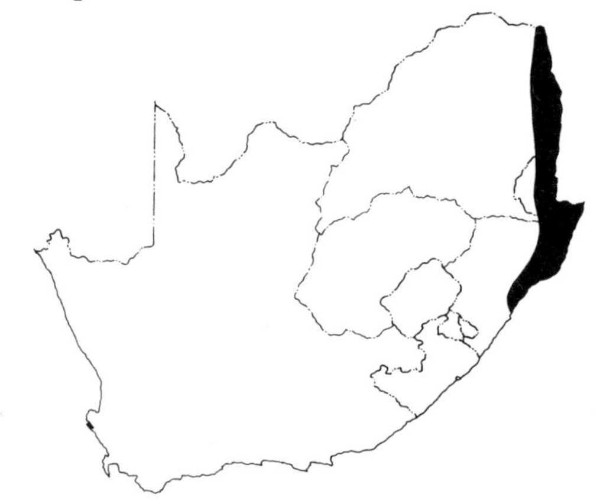

VOICE

A repetitive and incessant quacking. About one call per second.

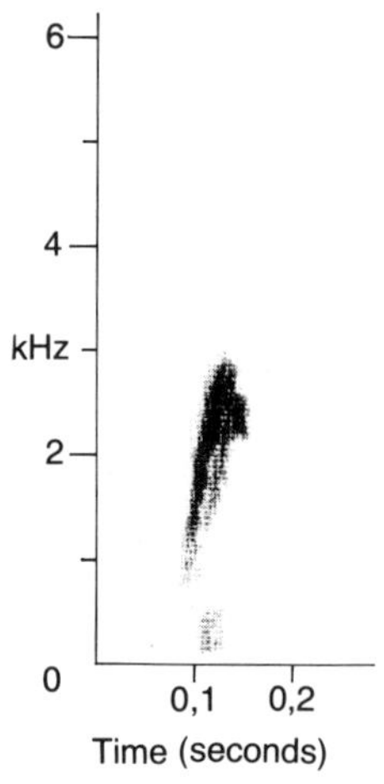

Kruger National Park, H. H. Braack

* The generic name *Hylambates* has been suppressed.

★ The dorsal pattern of large brown spots with pale outlines shows little variation.
★ Scarlet coloration is conspicuous on the inner thigh and axilla.

LIFE SIZE Tshaneni, Swaziland

★ The ventral surface is granular and white. In young animals it is interlaced with a dark network between the granules, but this appears to diminish with age. The gular disc in males is approximately oval, and deep yellow in colour. It partly conceals the dark membranous folds of the vocal sac.

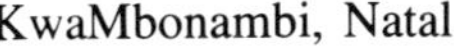

KwaMbonambi, Natal

★ Fingers and toes are terminally expanded into discs.

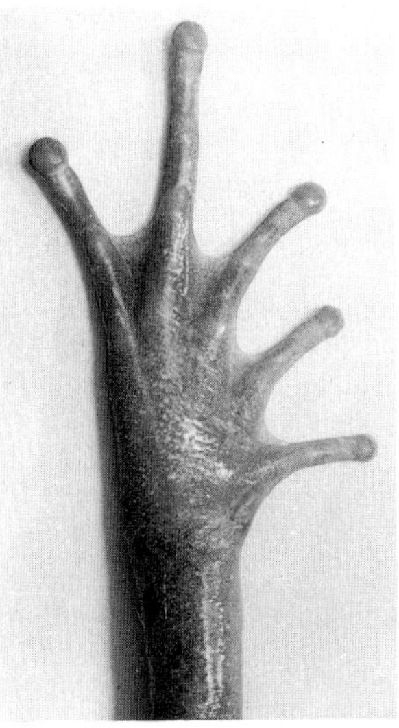

KwaMbonambi, Natal

BUBBLING KASSINA

Kassina senegalensis (Duméril and Bibron) 1841

Running Frog

BUBBLING KASSINA *Kassina senegalensis* Naboomspruit, Transvaal

BREEDING HABITAT

Grassland in the vicinity of vleis, pans or dams. Calling males generally occupy semi-concealed positions at the base of grass tufts.

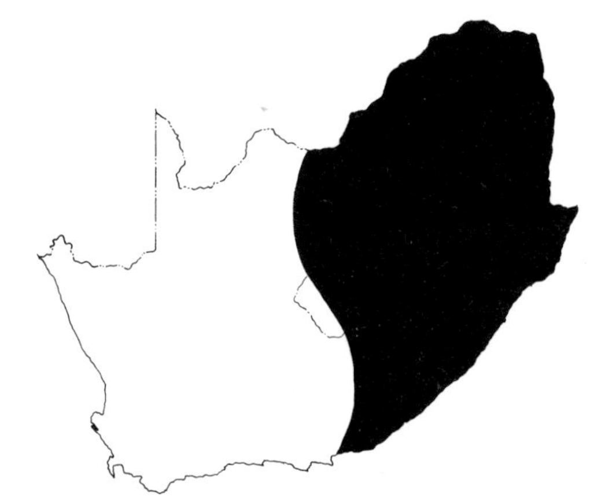

VOICE

A loud, clear 'quoip' uttered singly with long intervals between successive calls.

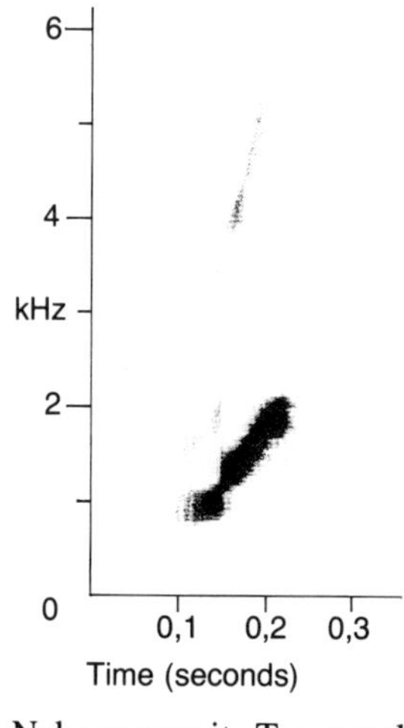

Naboomspruit, Transvaal

★ The dorsal pattern of bold dark stripes is characteristic. The ground colour may vary from silvery-beige to dark olive and the lateral stripes (never the vertebral stripe in South African material) may be broken.

LIFE SIZE Sandton, Transvaal

Mafuteni, Swaziland

★ The ventral surface is white. It is smooth anteriorly and granular posteriorly. A dark network is sometimes evident between the granulations. The gular disc ▲ in males is longitudinally oval and grey-brown in colour. The dark folds of the vocal sac are visible laterally.

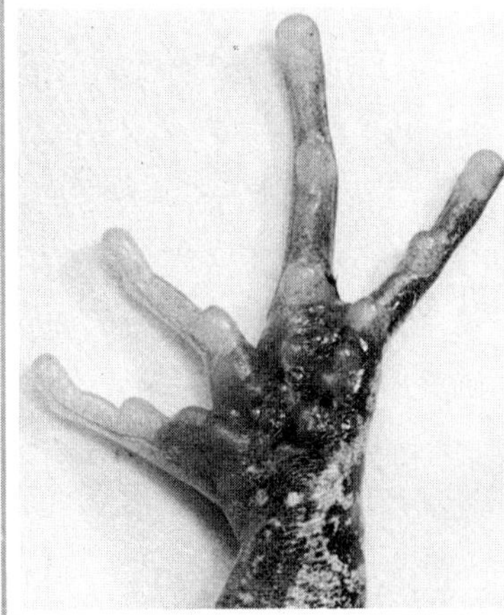

★ Hands and feet are whitish — cf. *K. wealii.*
★ Fingers and toes lack terminal discs — cf. *K. maculata.*
★ The toes, and to a greater extent the fingers, are shorter than those of *K. wealii.*

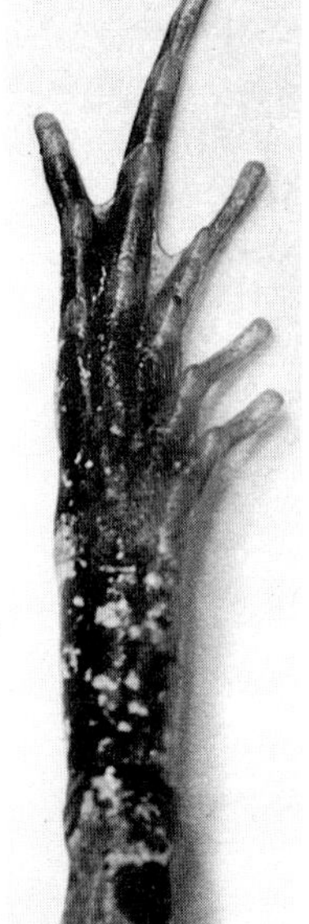

Tshaneni, Swaziland

RATTLING KASSINA *Kassina wealii* Boulenger 1882

Long-toed Running Frog, Weale's Frog

RATTLING KASSINA *Kassina wealii* Suikerbosrand Nature Reserve, Transvaal

BREEDING HABITAT

Well vegetated pans and pools in both subtropical and temperate regions. Males may call from elevated positions in the grass, or from exposed sites on the banks, or sometimes from well-concealed, partly submerged positions amongst the surface weed several metres out from the edge.

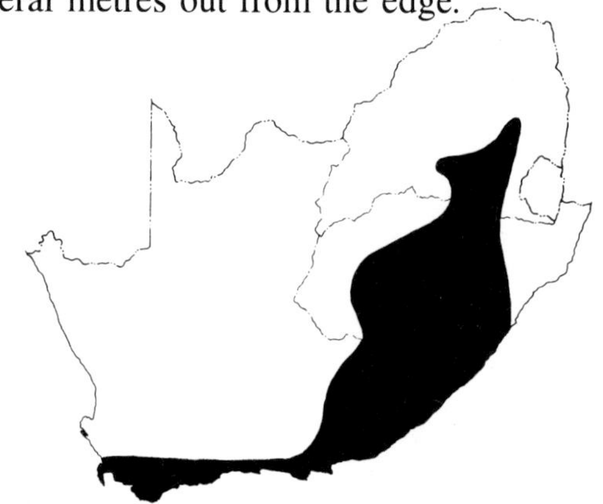

VOICE

A coarse, loud rattle, which lasts half a second. About one call every three to five seconds.

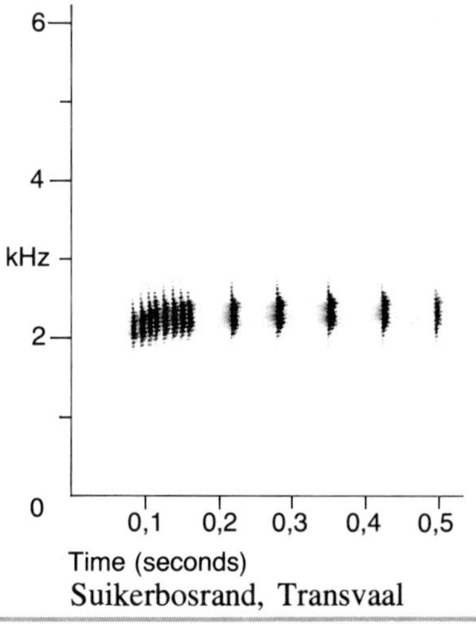

Suikerbosrand, Transvaal

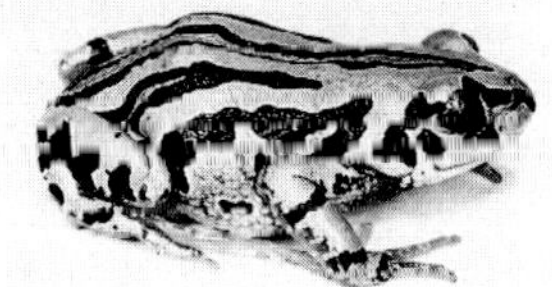

LIFE SIZE

★ The dorsal stripes are usually divided longitudinally, the dorso-lateral ones diverging posteriorly. They can be solid, however, and thus similar to those of *K. senegalensis.*

Richards Bay, Natal

Suikerbosrand Nature Reserve

★ The ventral surface is coarsely granular throughout — cf. *K. senegalensis*. A dark network is often evident between the granulations. The gular disc ▲ in the male is transversely oval and darkly pigmented.

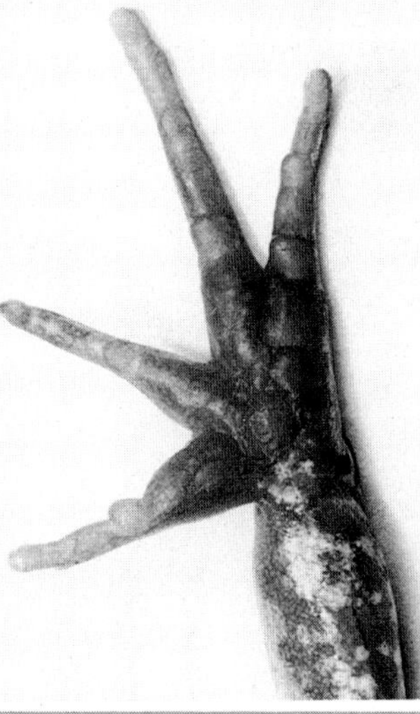

★ Hands and feet are yellow — cf. *K. senegalensis.*

★ Fingers and toes lack terminal discs — cf. *K. maculata.*

★ The toes, and to a greater extent the fingers, are longer than those of *K. senegalensis.*

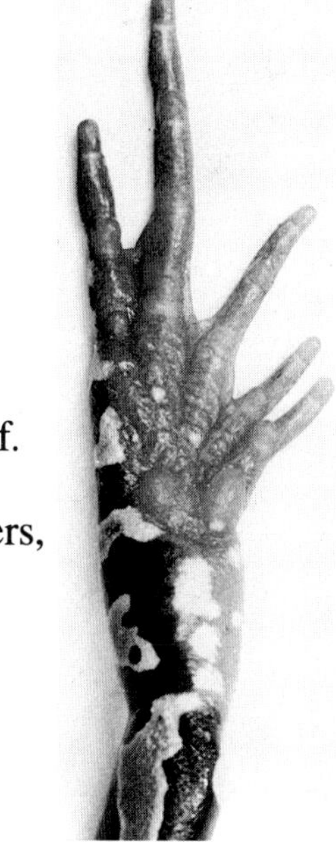

Suikerbosrand Nature Reserve

LEAF-FOLDING FROGS

Afrixalus Laurent

- ⋆ The tympanum is concealed — cf. *Leptopelis.*
- ⋆ The pupil is vertical — cf. *Hyperolius.*
- ⋆ The fingers and toes are webbed.
- ⋆ Fingers and toes bear terminal discs.

Three species occur in South Africa. The preferred habitats are pools, swamps and vleis. All species occur in sub-tropical areas at low altitudes.

The genus shows some over-all resemblance to the Reed Frogs, but can readily be distinguished by the vertical pupil. Two of the South African species are small (little more than 20 mm) whilst the third, *A. fornasinii*, is almost twice that size. The digits are webbed and terminally expanded into discs, and all species show climbing tendencies, utilizing the axils of leaves as retreats. *A. fornasinii* and *A. spinifrons* are also very aquatic in habit, seldom emerging more than a few centimetres from water. *A. brachycnemis*, on the other hand, is frequently found in daylight in exposed positions some distance from water. Small asperities are commonly present on the dorsal skin of all species, especially in the males.

Sexual Dimorphism

Males are distinguishable by the presence of the collapsed gular sac on the throat.

EGGS

The common name is derived from the unusual mode of oviposition. The eggs are unpigmented and laid in small numbers in leaf nests. A batch of eggs is deposited on a leaf, which is then folded, and its opposing faces are glued together by the very adhesive oviducal secretion. Such nests may be constructed either above or below the water level.

TADPOLES

The benthonic tadpoles emerge from the nests and larval development is continued in the water. The body is elongated and characteristically streamlined, with a terminal mouth.

DISTRIBUTION

The genus is comparativeley small and is distributed principally in tropical Africa.

GOLDEN LEAF-FOLDING FROG *Afrixalus brachycnemis* (Boulenger) 1896

Golden Spiny Reed Frog
Short-legged Banana Frog
Lesser Banana Frog

Subspecies
Afrixalus brachycnemis brachycnemis (Boulenger)
Afrixalus brachycnemis knysnae (Loveridge)
See page 260

A. b. knysnae Tsitsikamma National Park

A. b. brachycnemis Manzini, Swaziland

GOLDEN LEAF-FOLDING FROGS *Afrixalus brachycnemis*

BREEDING HABITAT

Sedge and other vegetation at the edges of pans and vleis. Males call from water-lily leaves or reeds.

VOICE

A short whizzing sound on a rising note.

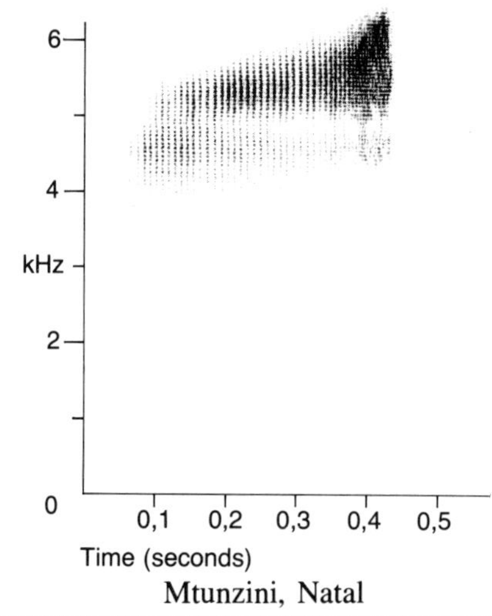

Mtunzini, Natal

LIFE SIZE

A. b. brachycnemis Mafuteni, Swaziland

- ★ The dorsal pattern is variable, but a golden-yellow ground colour and brown flanks are common.
- ★ The presence and extent of the dorsal spines are extremely variable. They are rarely found on specimens from Natal northwards (*A. b. brachycnemis*) and if so, they are confined to the upper eyelids. In southern material, (*A. b. knysnae*) they may be densely or sparsely distributed on the dorsum. They are not concentrated on the snout as in *A. spinifrons*.

A. b. knysnae Tsitsikamma National Park

Mafuteni, Swaziland

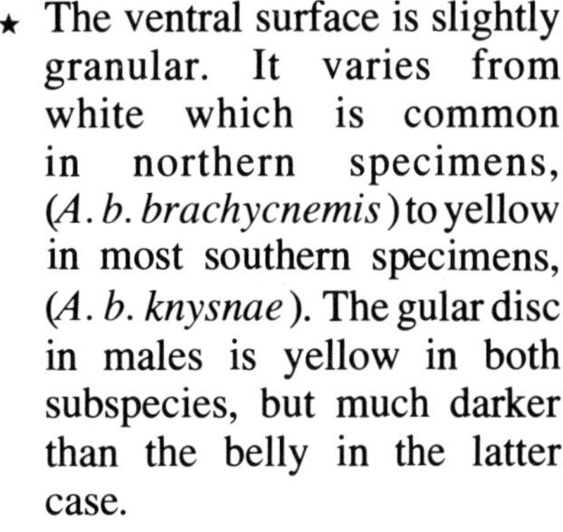

- ★ The ventral surface is slightly granular. It varies from white which is common in northern specimens, (*A. b. brachycnemis*) to yellow in most southern specimens, (*A. b. knysnae*). The gular disc in males is yellow in both subspecies, but much darker than the belly in the latter case.

- ★ Webbing between the fingers is visible but scanty — cf. *A. fornasinii*.

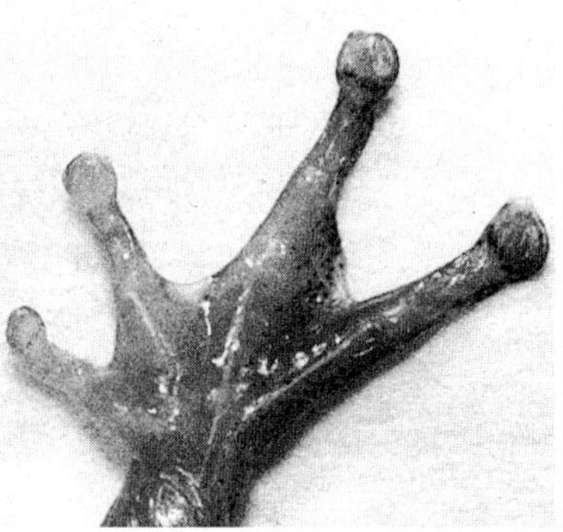

Mafuteni, Swaziland

NATAL LEAF-FOLDING FROG *Afrixalus spinifrons* (Cope) 1862

Golden Spiny Reed Frog

NATAL LEAF-FOLDING FROG *Afrixalus spinifrons* Eshowe, Natal

BREEDING HABITAT

Vleis and roadside pools in the coastal area of Natal. Males call from vegetation which emerges just above the surface.

VOICE

A sustained falsetto buzzing.

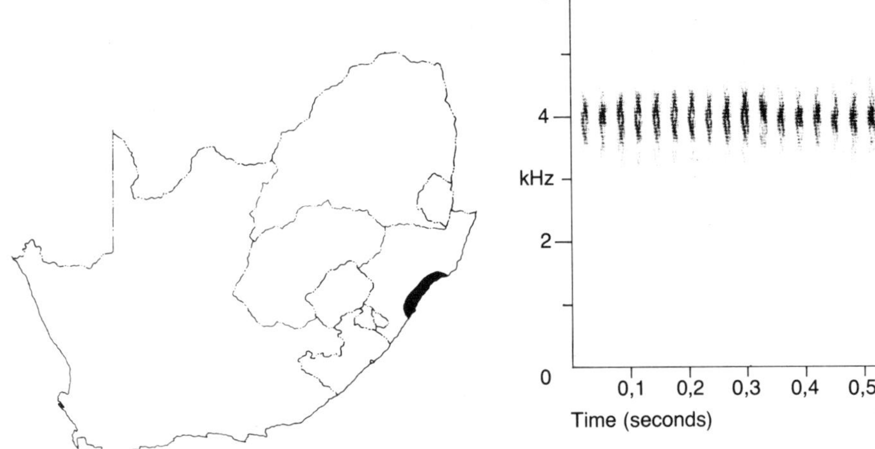

Eshowe, Natal

LIFE SIZE

Eshowe, Natal

- ★ The dorsal coloration of a broad, dark, median band on a golden ground colour is not very variable. Colour changes however, are extreme under differing lighting conditions, sometimes making the pattern obscure.
- ★ The snout is noticeably bulbous, with a concentration of black asperities ▲ which are sometimes scattered sparsely over the other parts of the dorsum — cf. *A. brachycnemis.*

Eshowe, Natal

- ★ The ventral surface is off-white with a yellow gular disc in males.

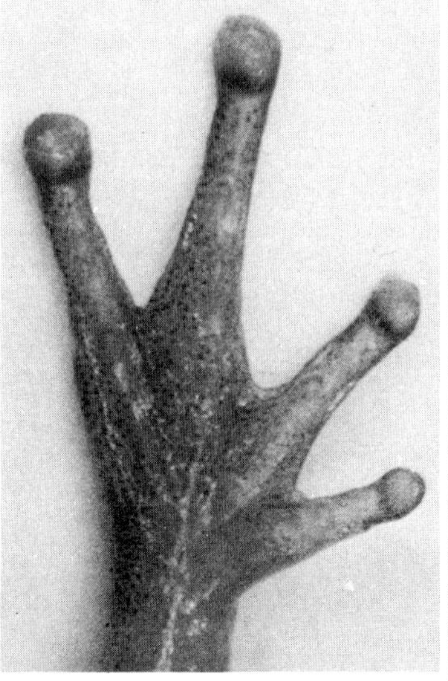

Eshowe, Natal

- ★ Webbing between the fingers is rudimentary — cf. *A. fornasinii.*

GREATER LEAF-FOLDING FROG *Afrixalus fornasinii* (Bianconi) 1850

Brown and White Spiny Reed Frog
Fornasini's Banana Frog

GREATER LEAF-FOLDING FROG *Afrixalus fornasinii* KwaMbonambi, Natal

BREEDING HABITAT

The peripheral areas of swamp and streams. Males call from positions on leaves and reed stems close to the surface of the water.

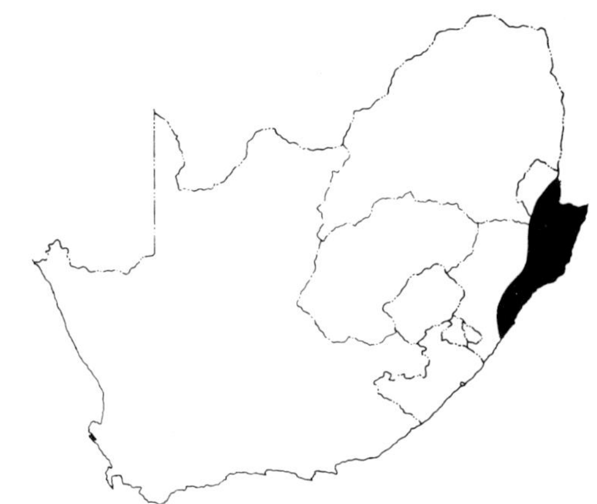

VOICE

A rapid series of loud and repetitive percussive notes. About twelve notes per second.

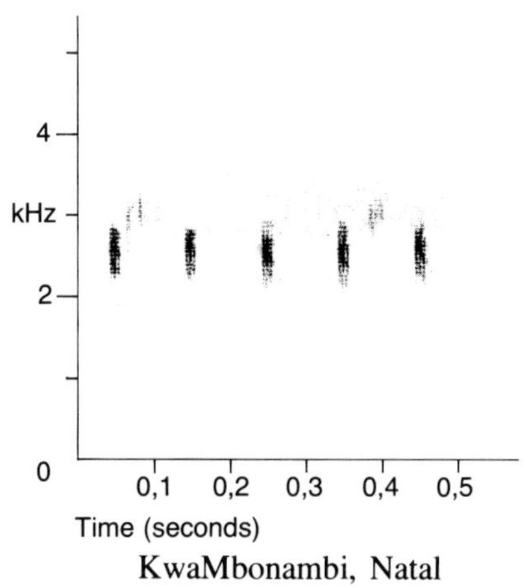

KwaMbonambi, Natal

- ★ The distinctive dorsal coloration consisting of an anteriorly pointed dark median band is not subject to much variation in South Africa. The ground colour, however, may vary from cream to grey-brown, sometimes becoming so dark that the vertebral band is indistinguishable.
- ★ The dorsum is covered with small asperities each within a white speck. They are not markedly concentrated on the snout as in *A. spinifrons*.

LIFE SIZE
KwaMbonambi, Natal

KwaMbonambi, Natal

- ★ The ventral surface is granular and creamy-white. The gular disc in the male is yellow.

- ★ The fingers are conspicuously webbed — cf. other species.

St Lucia, Natal

REED AND LILY FROGS

Hyperolius Rapp

- ★ The dorsal pattern is variable and usually very colourful.
- ★ The pupil is horizontal — cf. *Afrixalus* and *Leptopelis*.
- ★ Fingers and toes bear terminal discs.
- ★ The tympanum is concealed.

Seven species occur in South Africa. All species remain in fairly close proximity to water. Usual breeding sites are swamps, pans and dams, although they are also found in the vicinity of streams and rivers. Reed and Lily Frogs are absent from high-lying regions, but in coastal and more tropical parts of the country they are commonly encountered and usually abundant.

The description 'tree frog' is often used for *Hyperolius*, but this is not indicative of the preferred habitat of the South African species. Reed and Lily Frogs are slender, and small to moderate in size, with long hindlimbs. The digits are webbed and provided with expanded and flattened terminal discs. These afford purchase, even on very smooth surfaces, and contribute to the general agility and climbing ability of these animals. The horizontal pupil is distinctive. The majority of species are brilliantly and attractively coloured. Dorsal colour pattern has been used as a major systematic character, despite its often extensive intraspecific variation. Substantial powers of colour change are evident in many species, and good examples of colour pattern polymorphism can be found in the genus. Many species appear to utilize flash coloration, and the concealed surfaces of limbs are often brightly coloured. All species have large, subgular vocal sacs.

Sexual Dimorphism

In all species the deflated vocal sac, partly covered by a gular disc, is conspicuous in males.

Eggs

The eggs are pigmented, and in the case of most species they are laid in small clusters on submerged waterplants. Two species, however, have developed specialized methods of oviposition: *H. tuberilinguis* eggs are laid in a stiff jelly mass on vegetation just above the surface of the water. *H. pusillus* eggs are laid in small groups between overlapping leaves — usually water-lily leaves — which are then sealed by the oviducal secretion (Wager, 1965).

Tadpoles

The tadpoles of the South African species are similar, as they are in the genus as a whole. They are benthonic in habit and have long tails and well developed fins.

Distribution

This diversified genus, containing a wide variety of species, is distributed through most of sub-Saharan Africa.

ARUM LILY FROG *Hyperolius horstocki* (Schlegel) 1837

ARUM LILY FROG *Hyperolius horstocki* — Tsitsikamma National Park, Cape

BREEDING HABITAT

Pans in the southern and western Cape. Males call from elevated positions on the sedge, arums and shrubs at the perimeter.

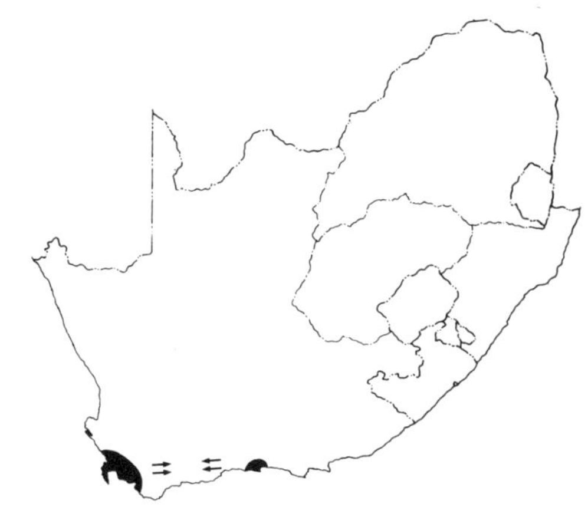

VOICE

A harsh, nasal bleat. About one call every two seconds.

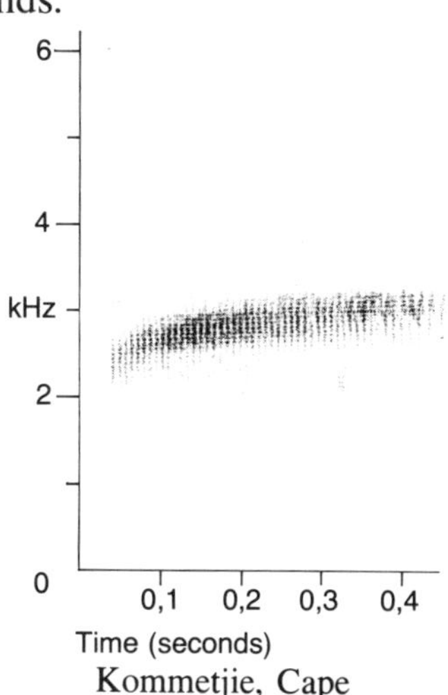

Kommetjie, Cape

★ The dorsum is plain and ranges in colour from cream to brown. A distinctive pale dorso-lateral line runs from the snout posteriorly along the flanks. The pale line is bordered ventrally by a dark brown lateral band. A fine dark line is usually present separating the pale line from the dark brown band — cf. juvenile pattern of *H. marmoratus*. Small black spots are sometimes present on the dorsum.

LIFE SIZE Ottery, Cape

Tsitsikamma National Park, Cape

★ The ventral surface is creamy-white and slightly granular. The gular disc in males is bright ochre.

★ The concealed surfaces of the limbs, the webbing and the digits are orange.

★ The webbing reaches the last tubercle ▲ of the longest toe on one side only — cf. *H. marmoratus* juvenile pattern.

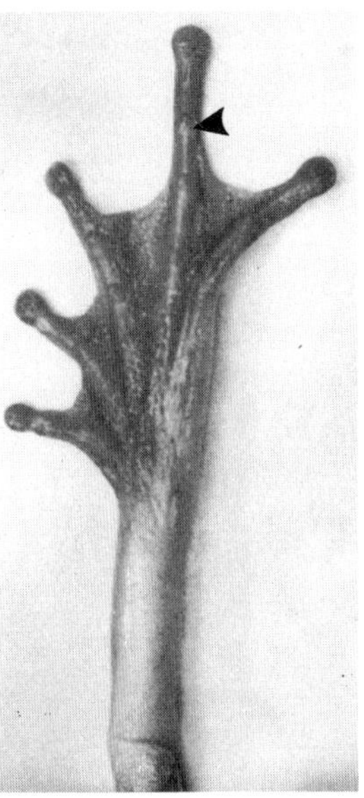

Ottery, Cape

YELLOW STRIPED REED FROG *Hyperolius semidiscus* Hewitt 1927

YELLOW STRIPED REED FROG *Hyperolius semidiscus* Mbabane, Swaziland

BREEDING HABITAT

Reedbeds at the edges of rivers. Males call from elevated sites near the tops of reeds.

VOICE

A harsh creak interspersed with a longer pulsatile croak.

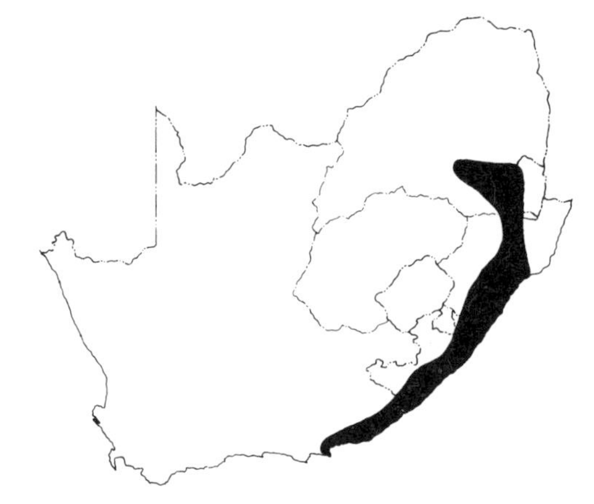

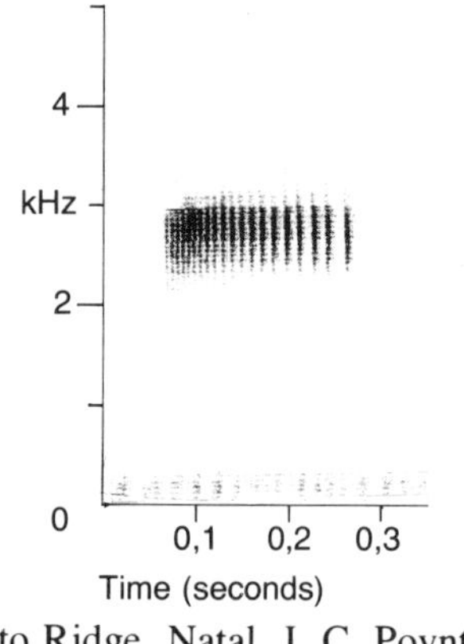

Cato Ridge, Natal, J. C. Poynton

★ The dorsal colour is usually green or brown. A yellow dorso-lateral line with well defined edges, and often a *thin* black outline, is distinctive. (It differs from that of *H. argus* where the black outline is thick.) The yellow line often extends from the flanks onto the snout, but it never appears on the snout alone, as in *H. argus*. In sub-adults it is occasionally absent.

LIFE SIZE
Mbabane, Swaziland

Mbabane, Swaziland

★ The ventral surface is cream or yellow and slightly granular. The gular disc in males is dark yellow.

★ The concealed surfaces of the limbs, the webbing and the digits are orange or yellow.

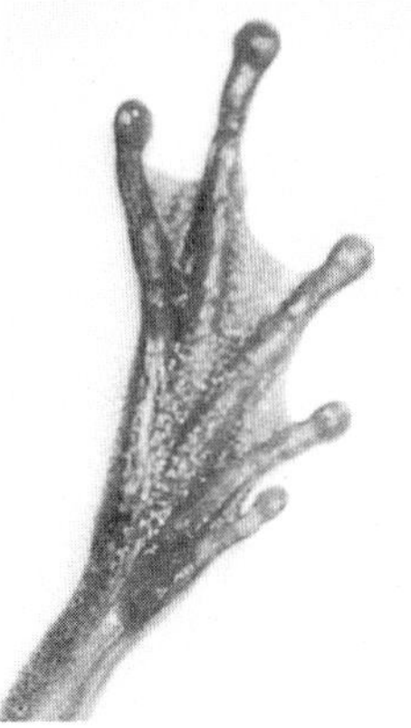

Mbabane, Swaziland

ARGUS REED FROG

*Hyperolius argus** Peters 1854

Yellow Spotted Reed Frog
Golden Sedge Frog

Syn: *Hyperolius p. puncticulatus* Poynton (non Pfeffer)

Mtunzini, Natal

ARGUS REED FROGS *Hyperolius argus* Richards Bay, Natal Richards Bay, Natal

BREEDING HABITAT

The dense vegetation on the perimeters of coastal pans. Calling males are often found on water-lily leaves.

VOICE

A low-pitched cluck, repeated rapidly and incessantly at a rate of about two to three per second.

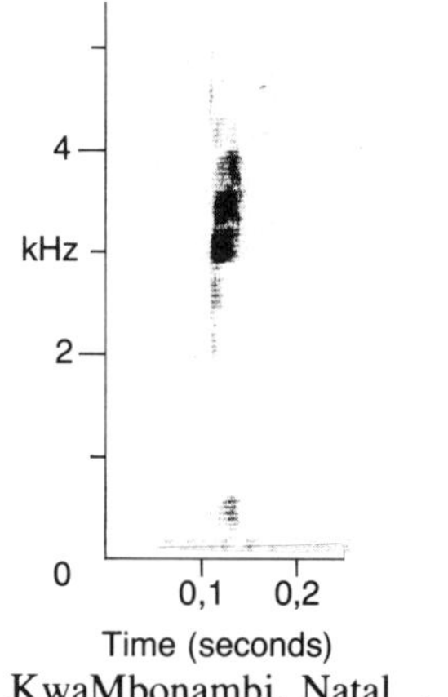

KwaMbonambi, Natal

*Poynton (personal communication) considers that all the Natal material previously referred by himself (Poynton, 1964) to *Hyperolius p. puncticulatus* is in fact *H. argus*.

★ The dorsal colour varies from light brown or green to nearly black. A yellow stripe passes from the snout to the eye. This is more prominent in females and encircles the eyes, giving a spectacled effect. The stripe usually continues onto the flank in males, but in females it is broken into yellow dots or is absent. The yellow lines or dots are outlined above and below by a broad border of dark stipples, the density of which is very variable — cf. *H. semidiscus*.

LIFE SIZE

KwaMbonambi, Natal

KwaMbonambi, Natal

★ The ventral skin is white or yellow. It is granular in males and the gular disc is yellow. The gular region in females is smooth and the belly is semi-transparent.

★ Flash coloration on the concealed surfaces of the limbs is less conspicuous than in most other species and varies from orange to brown.

KwaMbonambi, Natal

TINKER REED FROG *Hyperolius tuberilinguis* Smith 1849

Yellow-green Reed Frog
Green Reed Frog

TINKER REED FROG *Hyperolius tuberilinguis* Tshaneni, Swaziland

BREEDING HABITAT

Lowveld pans and swamps, especially those where vegetation is abundant. Males take up elevated or semi-concealed call sites in the vegetation.

VOICE

A loud staccato tap, repeated once or twice quickly, with long intervening pauses.

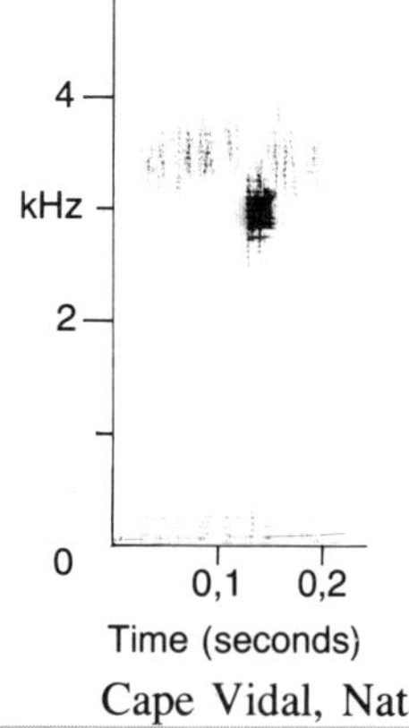

Cape Vidal, Natal

★ In adults the dorsum is generally without any pattern. The dorsal coloration is often bright green, but sometimes yellow or brown. Juveniles have a brown or mottled green dorsum, with a geometric pattern.

LIFE SIZE Eshowe, Natal

★ The ventral surface is cream and granular. The gular disc is yellow in males.

KwaMbonambi, Natal

★ The concealed surfaces of the limbs, the webbing and the digits are yellow or orange.

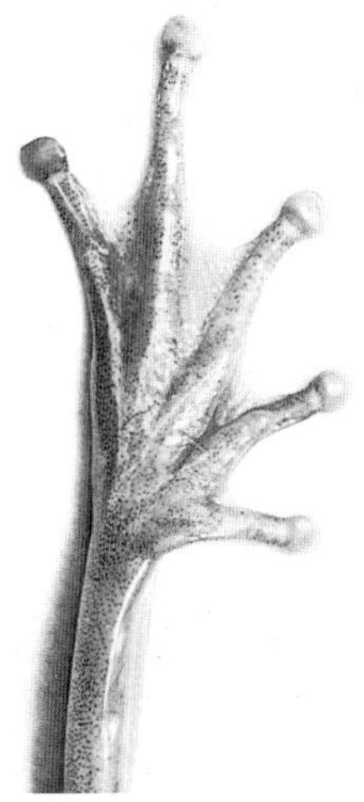

KwaMbonambi, Natal

WATER LILY FROG

Hyperolius pusillus (Cope) 1862

Translucent Tree Frog

WATER LILY FROGS *Hyperolius pusillus*

KwaMbonambi, Natal

BREEDING HABITAT

Pans and vleis in the warmer lowveld and coastal regions, especially where there are water lilies or other floating plants. Males call from exposed positions on vegetation close to the surface of the water.

VOICE

A blurred tick. About three every two seconds.

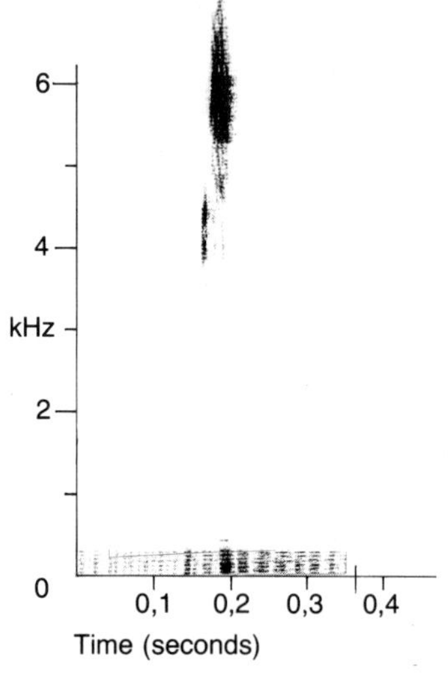

KwaMbonambi, Natal

LIFE SIZE

- ★ The dorsum is translucent green. There is no marked variation except for the presence of faint dorsal stripes and small dark spots in some specimens.
- ★ The snout is blunt and broad without a particularly protruding upper jaw — cf. *H. nasutus*.

KwaMbonambi, Natal

Tshaneni, Swaziland

- ★ The ventral surface is smooth and either white or transparent. The gular disc is bright yellow in males.

- ★ The concealed surfaces of the limbs are translucent lime-green.
- ★ The webbing and the digits are yellow.

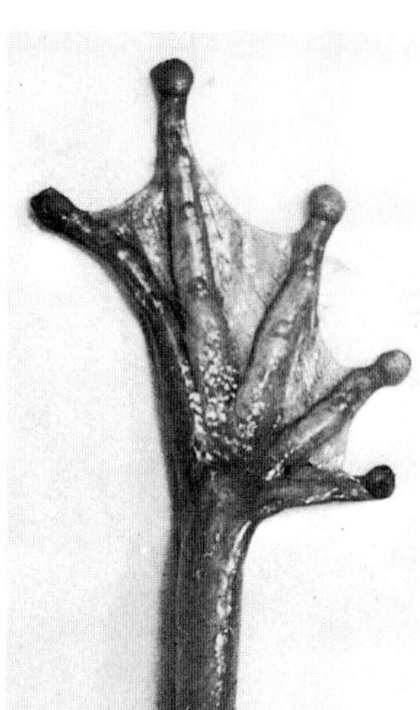

KwaMbonambi, Natal

LONG REED FROG

Hyperolius nasutus Günther 1864

Sharp-nosed Reed Frog

Subspecies
The form in South Africa is *Hyperolius nasutus nasutus* Günther. Other subspecies are recognized elsewhere in Africa.

Eshowe, Natal

Richards Bay, Natal

LONG REED FROGS *Hyperolius nasutus*

BREEDING HABITAT

Swamp grass or sedge associated with shallow pans and vleis along the Natal coastal belt. Males call from elevated positions on reeds or grass stems.

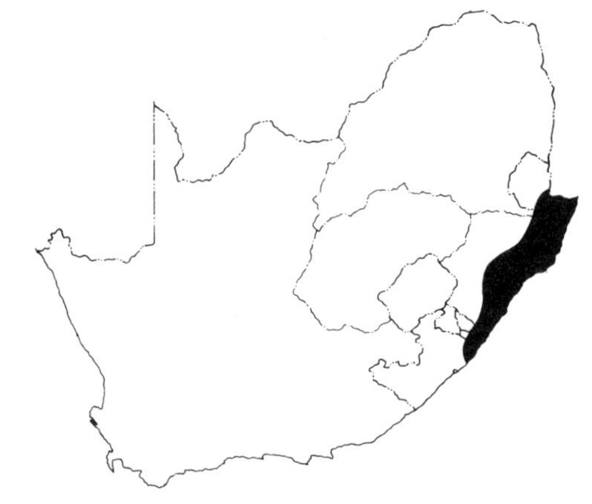

VOICE

A harsh and acute chirp. About one per second.

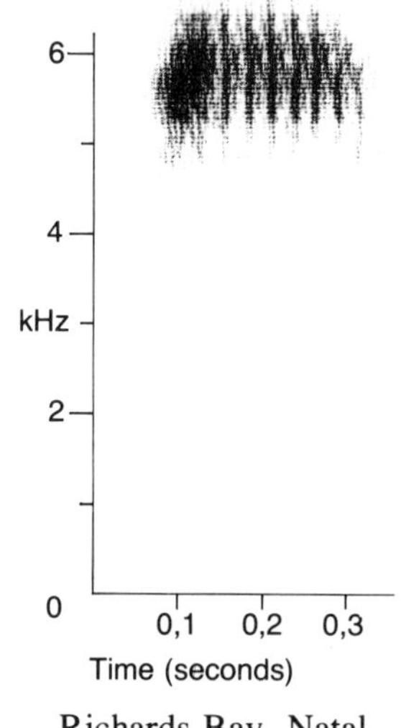

Richards Bay, Natal

LIFE SIZE

Eshowe, Natal

- ★ The body is characteristically elongated.
- ★ The dorsal colour varies from green to brown and there are frequently two bright white dorso-lateral stripes. Other variations include lines of small dots dorsally or an over-all stippling of dark specks. In some instances, distinction between this species and *H. pusillus* is difficult if based on dorsal colour alone.
- ★ The snout is acutely pointed with a strongly projecting upper jaw — cf. *H. pusillus*.

Eshowe, Natal

- ★ The ventral surface is silvery-white and smooth. Males have a yellow gular disc.

- ★ The concealed surfaces of the limbs are translucent green.
- ★ The webbing and the digits are green or yellow.

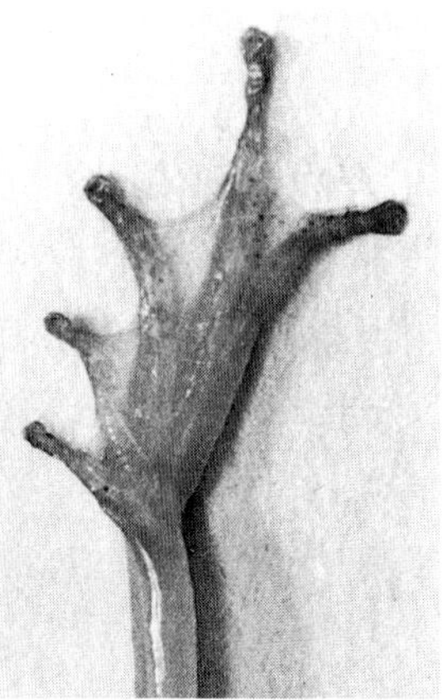

Eshowe, Natal

PAINTED REED FROG

*Hyperolius marmoratus** Rapp 1842

Marbled Bush Frog, Spotted Tree Frog

Syn: *Hyperolius viridiflavus* (Duméril and Bibron)

Subspecies
Hyperolius marmoratus verrucosus Smith
Hyperolius marmoratus marmoratus Rapp
Hyperolius marmoratus taeniatus Peters
See page 261
Other subspecies occur elsewhere in Africa.

H. m. taeniatus Barberton

H. m. marmoratus KwaMbonambi

JUVENILE PATTERN Sordwana Bay

H. m. verrucosus Tsitsikamma

H. m. marmoratus Richards Bay

PAINTED REED FROGS *Hyperolius marmoratus*

VOICE

A short, and very loud, piercing whistle commonly heard in large choruses. About two every three seconds.

BREEDING HABITAT

Sedgefields or other erect water plants growing around almost any permanent body of water in the lowveld and coastal regions. Calling is from elevated positions on reed stems or other suitable vegetation.

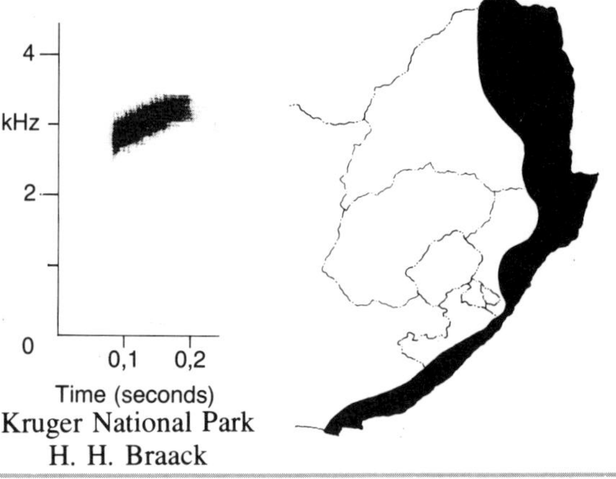

Kruger National Park
H. H. Braack

*On the advice of Poynton (personal communication) *marmoratus* has been retained in favour of *viridiflavus* (see further Laurent, 1976).

★ Dorsal colours and pattern show extreme variation. Over-all patterns, however, correlate to some extent with geographic distribution — hence the subspecific divisions. Populations from the southern limit of the range — Tsitsikamma to Transkei — tend to be spotted, (*H. m. verrucosus*). From Transkei to about St Lucia, a variety of mottled patterns are found, (*H. m. marmoratus*). From St Lucia to the north, specimens are typically striped in black, red, white and yellow, (*H. m. taeniatus*).
Within these broad groups of patterns there is considerable variation and throughout the range a brown and tan pattern is common in juveniles and young mature males.

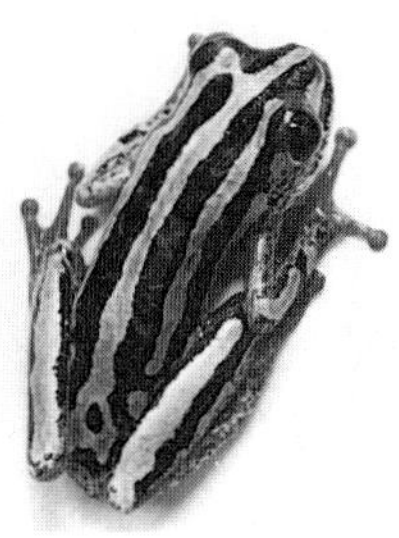

LIFE SIZE
KwaMbonambi, Natal

Manzini, Swaziland

Manzini, Swaziland

★ The ventral surface is granular and white or pink, tending to become dark pink towards the limbs. The male gular disc is grey, sometimes with orange spots.

★ The concealed surfaces of the limbs, the webbing and the digits are red.
★ The webbing reaches the last tubercle ▲ of the longest toe on both sides — cf. *H. horstocki*.

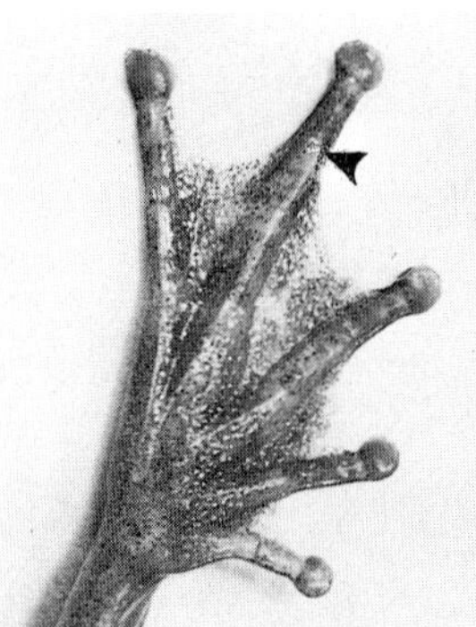

Tsitsikamma National Park, Cape

APPENDIX

SUMMARIES OF DISTRIBUTION AND CHARACTERS USED TO DISTINGUISH THE SUBSPECIES

The validity of many of the presently recognized subspecies in South Africa is doubtful and requires investigation. As an aid and stimulant to such work, the morphological characters which have been used to distinguish the subspecies which occur in South Africa are tabulated below. The information is summarized from Poynton (1964).

Heleophryne purcelli
Four subspecies have been recognized, although examination of material from intermediate areas may show that they are inseparable.

	H. p. purcelli	*H. p. depressa*	*H. p. orientalis*	*H. p. regis*
Distribution	Hottentots Holland to Du Toit's Mountains	Hex River Mountains and Kwadouwsberge	middle Langeberge	eastern Langeberge
Tibiotarsal articulation	not, or only slightly extending beyond the eye	reaching from eye to nostril	reaching from eye to slightly beyond nostril	reaching from eye to beyond nostril
Webbing: 4th toe	2 phalanges free	2 phalanges free but fringed	2 phalanges free	2½ to 3 phalanges free
5th toe	reaching almost to tip; deeply incised between 4th and 5th toes	reaching almost to the tip; not incised	reaching half-way along last phalanx	last phalanx free to nearly free

Bufo gariepensis
Three subspecies have been recognized, two of which fall within the scope of this book. The ranges of these two forms are separated in terms of altitude, *B. g. nubicolus* being confined to the summit areas of the Drakensberg, alt. 3 000 m. Poynton found evidence of merging between the two forms in Lesotho, and the present authors have examined Swaziland specimens (alt. approx. 1 000 m), which exhibit most of the morphological characteristics of *nubicolus*.

	B.g. gariepensis	*B.g. nubicolus*
Distribution	Cape Province, Orange Free State, southern Transvaal	summit areas of the Drakensberg
Tarsal fold	massive and glandular	ridged to flattened
Ratio of length of metatarsal tubercles	outer more than half inner	outer less than half inner
Dorsal pupillary umbraculum	poorly developed to absent	usually well developed
Parotid glands	massive	flattened and inconspicuous
Dorsal markings	separate irregular dark patches	sparse light reticulations on a dark background

Bufo vertebralis

Six subspecies have been recognized, two of which fall within the scope of this book. With reference to these two, Poynton states that "it is probable that intergradation takes place in the Mafeking area". Tandy on the other hand regards these as separate species (personal communication).

	B.v. vertebralis	*B.v. fenoulheti*
Distribution	north-east Cape and Orange Free State	Transvaal and northern Natal
Skin on snout	smooth	granular
Skin on throat	smooth or slightly granular	wrinkled
Webbing: 3rd toe	2 phalanges free	2½ phalanges free
Venter	white with distinct dark blotches	immaculate white, rarely with a few spots

Breviceps verrucosus

Two subspecies have been recognized, and "variation in the markings of *tympanifer* suggests that it will be found to intergrade with *verrucosus* in these features" (Poynton, 1964). We consider *B. maculatus* FitzSimons to be conspecific with this form (see p. 84), and this species has, for convenience, been included in the table.

	B.v. verrucosus	*B.v. tympanifer*	*B. maculatus*
Distribution	lower eastern plateaux slopes from Transkei to Sabie	south-eastern Cape hinterland	Drakensberg and Lesotho
Dorsum	colour uniform; one or more pairs of dorsal ridges	colour uniform sometimes with intermingling of yellow; light dorsal band usual; light line from heel to heel	broadly serrated light median band, or paired series of black dots, or without clear markings; light, more or less vertical lateral bands
Venter	uniform off-white with brown mottle on yellow	off-white, rarely faintly speckled	mottled brown on yellow white

Breviceps sylvestris

In the case of these two subspecies, the habitats are geographically separated.

	B.s. sylvestris	*B.s. taeniatus*
Distribution	Woodbush area	Soutpansberg
Outer toe	reaching basal tubercle of 4th toe, falling short of 2nd toe	reaching basal tubercle of 4th toe, reaching 2nd toe
Paravertebral dorsal ridges	converging between eye and scapular region, parallel in sacral region	not converging markedly from eye to sacral region
Pattern between ridges	paired light patches or generally light	paired dark transverse lines pointing obliquely backwards

Breviceps rosei

Two subspecies, differing only in dorsal coloration, have been recognized. Craye (personal communication) reports finding a population at Melkbosstrand where individuals exhibited a range of markings which included both dorsal patterns.

	B.r. rosei	*B.r. vansoni*
Distribution	south western Cape coastal sandveld west of Hangklip	south western Cape coastal sandveld east of Hangklip
Dorsum	thin lines absent	thin vertebral line bisects a similar line running from heel to heel

Breviceps adspersus.

B. a. adspersus and *B. a. pentheri* were regarded by Poynton (1964) as subspecies. However, in the limited sample examined by us, strong differences were evident in the mating calls of these forms. Further investigation will probably reinstate their distinction at the specific level.

	B.a. adspersus	*B.a. pentheri*
Distribution	South West Africa/ Namibia, Botswana, Rhodesia, northern and eastern Transvaal, Swaziland and Natal below 1 200 m	Natal eastern plateau and south-eastern Cape
Dorsum	variable light patches always present, some in paravertebral pairs	generally darker and more warty; light median band with deeply serrated edges, or pairs of paravertebral patches, or uniform
Venter	immaculate white to cream	chest and belly with dark flecks

Cacosternum nanum

Two subspecies have been recognized.

	C.n. nanum	*C.n. parvum*
Distribution	southern and eastern Cape, Natal (below about 1 200 m) and the eastern Transvaal midlands	Natal north of 30°S and above 1 200 m and the eastern Transvaal escarpment
Metasternum	not shorter than the ventral symphysis of the coracoids	shorter than the ventral symphysis of the coracoids
Throat	heavily mottled with grey, sometimes leaving only a whitish network	grey all over but with a faint lighter network visible; very dark in males
Inter-orbital distance	greater than width of the upper eyelid	less than width of upper eyelid

Afrixalus brachycnemis

Two subspecies have been recognized. With reference to *A.b. knysnae*, Poynton (1964) states that "it appears to intergrade with *brachycnemis* via the Natal midlands".

	A.b. brachycnemis	*A.b. knysnae*
Distribution	eastern Transvaal lowveld and Natal lowveld	south-eastern seaboard from Knysna north through Transkei inland to the Natal midlands
Subarticular tubercle of 2 outer fingers	double	entire
Dorsal asperities	absent or confined to eyelids	scattered over dorsum

Hyperolius marmoratus

This is a large and extremely complex taxon found throughout tropical and sub-tropical Africa. More than fifty subspecies might be recognized, three of which occur in South Africa. Precise delimitation of their ranges is not possible and intergrading almost certainly occurs at their boundaries. Schiøtz (1971) noted that "subspecies in this group is a taxonomic tool, not a systematical necessity".

	H.m. taeniatus	*H.m. marmoratus*	*H.m. verrucosus*
Distribution	from St Lucia through northern Natal and eastern Transvaal	Natal seaboard from Umkomaas to St Lucia	south-eastern seaboard from Tsitsikamma through Transkei to Umkomaas
Dorsal pattern	dark with 5 light longitudinal stripes, the 3 median ones very regular	variable marbling with a tendency towards longitudinal striping	brown with small light, black-edged spots

GLOSSARY

Aggregate. A group of individuals of the same species, gathered together in the same place.

Allopatric. Referring to organisms (populations or species) that inhabit mutually exclusive geographic ranges.

Antiphonal. Referring to the ordered pattern of vocal responses produced by two individuals stationed apart.

Anura. An order of the class Amphibia, containing the frogs and toads.

Axilla. Armpit.

Asperities. Small, hard and often spiny, projections in the skin.

Benthonic. Referring to aquatic organisms that inhabit the bottom regions of lakes, oceans and other bodies of water.

Chromatophore. Cell in the skin, containing pigment.

Cline. A gradual and continuous change in a character through a series of contiguous populations, generally along an environmental gradient.

Conspecific. Referring to individuals and populations of the same species.

Cryptic coloration. Camouflaging coloration which allows the animal to blend with the background.

Cryptic species. A species which is difficult to identify because its diagnostic characters are not easily perceived.

Digit. Finger or toe.

Disc (digital). An expanded pad-like structure located on the tips of the digits.

Dimorphism. Occurrence of two distinct forms in a single population.

Dorsum. The upper surface of the body.

Ectothermic. Referring to an animal whose body heat is derived largely from the surrounding environment.

Fecundity. Reproductive potential, as measured by the quantity of sex cells produced.

Frequency modulation. Variation in pitch over a period of time.

Gastrulation. The process in which the embryo acquires three layers (germinal layers) of cells.

Gene. A unit of inheritance, carried in the chromosome, transmitted from generation to generation by the gametes, and controlling the development and characteristics of an individual. **Gene flow**: the exchange of genes between populations. **Gene pool**: the totality of the genes of a given population existing at a given time.

Gular. Referring to, or situated in, the gula or throat region. **Gular fold**: an external fold in the skin in the gular region. **Gular disc**: an area of thickened or unmodified skin, often ovoid or circular in shape, located in the gular region. **Gular slit**: small slits, usually paired and located laterally on the throat, and allowing for the extrusion of the vocal sacs.

Inguinal region. The groin.

Lateral line sense organ. Small sense organs, located in pores or canals arranged in a line down each side of the body, and in patterns of lines on the head. Sensitive to pressure changes in the water.

Lentic. Referring to still waters, such as lakes and ponds.

Metamorphosis. An abrupt post-embryonic transition from one developmental stage to another. In the Anura it refers to the rapid transition from tadpole to adult.

Metatarsus. The part of the hind foot located between the tarsus (ankle) and the phalanges (toes).

Mimicry. Assumption of colour, form or behaviour patterns by one species of another species, usually for camouflage or protection.

Morph. A particular form.

Morphology. The physical form of an animal.

Nares. Nostrils.

Nektonic. Referring to aquatic organisms that swim freely in open water.

Nuptial pads. Roughened, elevated and sometimes spinose areas on the skin of male frogs. Usually well developed in the breeding season on the first digit of the hand, but sometimes located on other digits, on the arm, in the axilla, or on several of these areas.

Occipital region. The region at the base of the head.

Organogenisis. The process of organ formation in an embryo.

Papilla. A small nipple-like protrusion.

Paravertebral. Referring to structures such as stripes, located alongside of the vertebral column.

Parotid gland. A compact mass of poison glands located on the back of the neck which exude a viscous toxin.

Phalanx. One of the bones of the fingers or toes.

Polymorphism. The occurrence of several different forms of individuals in a single species.

Phenotype. The observable characters of an organism.

Sacral region. The extreme lower back, in the vicinity of those vertebrae which articulate with the pelvic girdle.

Scapular region. The region of the dorsum, just posterior to the neck, which corresponds with the position of the dorsal part of the pectoral girdle.

Shank. The lower leg.

Sibling species. Morphologically similar or identical populations that do not interbreed in nature.

Subarticular tubercle. A small projection on the ventral surface of a digit, at the point of junction of two phalanges.

Sympatric. Referring to the occurrence of two or more populations at the same locality.

Tarsus. Ankle.

Tarsal fold. A longitudinal skin elevation in the ankle region.

Tubercle. A small, knob-like prominence.

Tympanum. The ear drum or tympanic membrane separating the outer from the middle ear.

Umbraculum. A translucent structure in the cornea of the eye.

Uricotelic. Referring to animals that excrete uric acid rather than urea. Characteristic of many terrestrial animals and important in water conservation. Rare in frogs.

Urostyle. Several fused vertebrae which form the posterior part of the vertebral column.

Vent. The external opening of the cloaca.

Venter. The lower surface of the body.

Vermiculation. Irregular worm-like markings.

Vertebral. Referring to the vertebral column which runs along the dorsal side of the vertebrate body.

Vocal sac. Sac-like outpouchings of the mouth cavity in male frogs, that extend ventrally and laterally under the skin and muscles of the throat.

Zygote. A fertilized egg that results from the fusion of a spermatozoon with an ovum.

SELECTED BIBLIOGRAPHY

The following sources were consulted in the preparation of this work. They will serve also as a basis for further reading.

BAGNARA, J. T. (1976). Colour change. In *Physiology of the Amphibia* (B. Lofts ed.), Vol. III, pp. 1-44. New York, Academic Press.

BALINSKY, B. I. (1969). The reproductive ecology of amphibians of the Transvaal highveld. *Zool. Afr.* 4, 37-93.

BALINSKY, B. I. (1970). *An Introduction to Embryology*; 3 ed. Philadelphia, Saunders.

BLACKITH, R. M. and SPEIGHT, M. C. D. (1974). Food and feeding habits of the frog *Rana temporaria* in bogland habitats in the west of Ireland. *J. Zool., (Lond.)* 172, 67-79.

BLAIR, W. F. (1958). Mating call and speciation of anuran amphibians. *Am. Nat.* 92, 27-51.

BLAIR, W. F. (1972). Evidence from hybridization. In *Evolution of the Genus* Bufo (W. F. Blair ed.), pp. 196-232. Austin, University of Texas Press.

BOGERT, C. M. (1960). The influence of sound on the behaviour of amphibians and reptiles. In *Animal Sounds and Communication. Am. Inst. Biol. Sci. Publ.* 7, pp. 137-320.

BROADLEY, D. G. (1965). The *Hyperolius marmoratus* superspecies — distribution of the central and southern African forms. *J. Herpetol. Assoc. Afr.* 1, 23-26.

BROADLEY, D. G. (1973). Provisional list of vernacular names for Rhodesian reptiles and amphibians. *J. Herpetol. Assoc. Afr.* 10, 17-24.

BROADLEY, D. G. (1974). Vernacular names for Rhodesian reptiles and amphibians. *J. Herpetol. Assoc. Afr.* 12, 31.

BRODE, W. E. (1959). Territoriality in *Rana clamitans. Herpetologica* 15, 140.

BUNNELL, P. (1973). Vocalizations in the territorial behaviour of the frog *Dendrobates pumilio. Copeia* 227-284.

CAPRANICA, R. R. (1965). *The Evoked Vocal Response of the Bullfrog: A Study of Communication by Sound*. Cambridge Mass., M.I.T. Press. M.I.T. Research Monograph No. 33.

CARRUTHERS, V. C. (1976). *A Guide to the Identification of the Frogs of the Witwatersrand.* Johannesburg, Conservation Press.

CHANNING, A. (1976a). Premating isolation in the genus *Kassina* (Amphibia, Anura, Rhacophoridae) in southern Africa. *J. Herpetol*. 10, 19-23.

CHANNING, A. (1976b). Life histories of frogs in the Namib Desert. *Zool. Afr.* 11, 299-312.

CHANNING, A. and VAN DIJK, D. E. (1976). *A Guide to the Frogs of South West Africa.* Durban, University of Durban-Westville Press.

COCHRAN, D. M. (1967). *Living Amphibians of the World*. New York, Doubleday.

COTT, H. B. (1940). *Adaptive Colouration in Animals*. London, Methuen.

CRUMP, M. L. (1972). Territoriality and mating behaviour in *Dendrobates granuliferus* (Anura; Dendrobatidae). *Herpetologica* 28, 195-198.

CRUMP, M. L. (1974). Reproductive strategies in a tropical anuran community. *Univ. Kans. Publs. Mus. nat. Hist.* No. 61, 1-68.

DUELLMAN, W. E. Social organization in the mating calls of some neotropical anurans. *Am. Midl. Nat.* 77, 156-163.

DU TOIT, C. A. (1971). Amphibians. In *Animal Life in Southern Africa* (D. J. Potgieter, P. C. du Plessis, & S. H. Skaife, compilers), pp. 262-268. Cape Town, Nasou.

EMLEN, S. T. (1968). Territoriality in the bullfrog, *Rana catesbiana. Copeia* 240-243.

Feng, A. S., Gerhardt, H. C. and Capranica, R. R. (1976). Sound localization behaviour of the Green Treefrog (*Hyla cinerea*) and the Barking Treefrog (*H. gratiosa*). *J. Comp. Physiol.* 107, 341-352.

Frazer, J. F. D. (1973). *Amphibians*. London, Wykeham Publications.

Gerhardt, H. C. (1974). The significance of some spectral features in mating call recognition in the Green Treefrog (*Hyla cinerea*). *J. exp. Biol.* 61, 229-241.

Goin, C. J. (1949). The peep order in peepers; a swamp water serenade. *Q. Jl Fla Acad. Sci.* 11, 59-61.

Goin, C. J. and Goin, O. B. (1971). *Introduction to Herpetology*. San Francisco, Freeman.

Hewitt, J. (1937). *A Guide to the Vertebrate Fauna of the Eastern Cape Province, South Africa.* Part II, Reptiles, Amphibians and Freshwater Fishes. Grahamstown, Albany Museum.

Heyer, W. R. (1976). Studies in larval amphibian habitat partitioning. *Smithson. Contrib. Zool.* No. 242, 1-27.

Hödl, W. (1977). Call differences and calling site segregration in anuran species from central Amazonian floating meadows. *Oecologia* 28, 351-363.

Kenneth, J. H. (1967). *Henderson's Dictionary of Biological Terms*; 8 ed. Edinburgh, Oliver & Boyd.

Lambiris, A. J. L. (1974). Some comments on the genus *Kassina* Girard in the eastern Cape province of South Africa. *J. Herpetol. Assoc. Afr.* 12, 17-18.

Laurent, R. F. (1976). Nouveaux commentaires sur la superespèce *Hyperolius viridiflavus* (Anura). *Ann. Mus. Roy. Afr. Centr., Sci. zool.* 213, 69-114.

Littlejohn, M. J. (1965). Vocal communication in frogs. *Aust. nat. Hist.* 15, 52-55.

Littlejohn, M. J. (1968). Frog calls and the species problem. *Aust. Zool.* 14, 259-264.

Littlejohn, M. J. and Martin, A. A. (1969). Acoustic interaction between two species of Leptodactylid frogs. *Anim. Behav.* 17, 785-791.

Loftus-Hills, J. J. (1975). The evidence for reproductive character displacement between the toads *Bufo americanus* and *B. woodhousii fowleri*. *Evolution* 29, 368-369.

Lombard, E. R. and Straughan, I. R. (1974). Functional aspects of anuran middle ear structures. *J. exp. Biol.* 61, 71-93.

Main, A. R. (1968). Ecology systematics and evolution of Australian frogs. *Adv. ecol. Res.* 5, 37-86.

Martof, B. S. (1953). Territoriality in the Green Frog *Rana clamitans*. *Ecology* 34, 165-174.

Mayr, E. (1970). *Populations, Species and Evolution.* London, Oxford University Press.

Mertens, R. (1971). Die Herpetofauna Südwest-Afrikas. *Abh. Senckenb. naturforsch. Ges.* 529, 1-110.

Morton, E. S. (1975). Ecological sources of selection on avian sounds. *Am. Nat.* 109, 17-34.

Narins, P. M. and Capranica, R. R. (1976). Sexual differences in the auditory system of the Tree Frog *Eleutherodactylus coqui*. *Science* 192, 378-380.

Noble, R. G. (1974). An evaluation of the conservation status of aquatic biotopes. *Koedoe* 17, 71-83.

Oldham, R. S. and Gerhardt, H. C. (1975). Behavioural isolating mechanisms of the Tree Frogs *Hyla cinerea* and *H. gratiosa*. *Copeia* 223-231.

Passmore, N. I. (1972). Intergrading between members of the '*regularis* group' of toads in South Africa. *J. Zool., (Lond.)* 167, 143-151.

Passmore, N. I. (1976). Vocalizations and breeding behaviour of *Ptychadena taenioscelis* (Anura; Ranidae). *Zool. Afr.* 11, 339-347.

Passmore, N. I. (1977). Mating calls and other vocalizations of five species of *Ptychadena* (Anura; Ranidae). *S. Afr. J. Sci.* 73, 212-214.

Passmore, N. I. and Carruthers, V. C. (1975). A new species of *Tomopterna* (Anura; Ranidae) from the Kruger National Park, with notes on related species. *Koedoe* 18, 31-50.

Paterson, H. E. H. (1978). Problems with the Concept of Isolating Mechanisms. Unpublished lecture delivered at the British Museum (Natural History) on 17 January, 1978.

Perret, J-L. (1976). Revision des amphibiens africains et principalement des types, conservés au Musée Bocage de Lisbonne. *Arq. Mus. Boc.* 6, 15-34.

Pickersgill, M. (1975). Some surprises in the ecology of *Breviceps v. verrucosus* Rapp. *J. Herpetol. Assoc. Afr.* 14, 23-27.

PIENAAR, U. de V., PASSMORE, N. I. and CARRUTHERS, V. C. (1976). *The Frogs of the Kruger National Park*. Pretoria, National Parks Board.

PORTER, K. R. (1972). *Herpetology*. Philadelphia, Saunders.

POYNTON, J. C. (1964). *The Amphibia of Southern Africa: A Faunal Study*. *Ann. Natal Mus.* 17, 1-334.

POYNTON, J. C. (1966). Amphibia of northern Mozambique. *Mems. Inst. Invest. cient. Moçamb.* 8, 13-34.

POYNTON, J. C. (1970). Guide to the *Ptychadena* of the southern third of Africa. *Ann. Natal Mus.* 20, 356-375.

POYNTON, J. C. and PRITCHARD, S. (1976). Notes on the biology of *Breviceps* (Anura: Microhylidae). *Zool. Afr.* 11, 313-318.

ROSE, W. (1962). *The Reptiles and Amphibians of Southern Africa.* Cape Town, Maskew Miller.

ROSEN, M. and LEMON, R. E. (1974). The vocal behaviour of Spring Peepers, *Hyla crucifer*. *Copeia* 940-950.

SALTHE, S. N. and MECHAM, J. S. (1974). Reproductive and courtship patterns. In *Physiology of the Amphibia* (B. Lofts ed.), Vol. II, pp. 309-521. New York, Academic Press.

SCHIØTZ, A. (1964). The voices of some west African amphibians. *Vidensk. Meddr fra dansk naturh. Foren.* 127, 35-83.

SCHIØTZ, A. (1967). The Treefrogs (Rhacophoridae) of West Africa. *Spolia zool. Mus. haun.* 25, 1-346.

SCHIØTZ, A. (1971). The superspecies *Hyperolius viridiflavus* (Anura). *Vidensk. Meddr fra dansk naturh. Foren.* 134, 21-76.

SCHIØTZ, A. (1973). Evolution of anuran mating calls: ecological aspects. In *Evolutionary Biology of the Anurans* (J. L. Vial ed.), pp. 311-319. Columbia, University of Missouri Press.

SCHIØTZ, A. (1974). Revision of the genus *Afrixalus* (Anura) in eastern Africa. *Vidensk. Meddr fra dansk naturh. Foren.* 137, 9-18.

SCHIØTZ, A. (1975). *The Treefrogs of Eastern Africa*. Copenhagen, Steenstrupia.

STEVENS, R. A. (1974). An annotated checklist of the amphibians and reptiles known to occur in south-eastern Malawi. *Arnoldia Rhod.* 6 (30) 1-22.

STEWART, M. M. (1967). *Amphibians of Malawi*. State University of New York Press.

STEWART, M. M. (1974a). Parallel pattern polymorphism in the genus *Phrynobatrachus* (Amphibia: Ranidae). *Copeia* 823-832.

STEWART, M. M. (1974b). Polymorphism in Cricket Frogs: an hypothesis. *Evolution* 28, 489-491.

STEWART, M. M. and SANDISON, P. (1972). Comparative food habits of sympatric mink frogs, bullfrogs and green frogs. *J. Herpetol.* 6, 241-244.

TANDY, M. (1972). The Evolution of African *Bufo*. Unpublished Ph.D. thesis, University of Texas at Austin, Texas.

TANDY, M. and KEITH, R. (1972). *Bufo* of Africa. In *Evolution of the Genus* Bufo (W. F. Blair ed.), pp. 119-170. Austin, University of Texas Press.

TAYLOR, P. (1971a). Observations on the breeding habits of *Chiromantis xerampelina* Peters. *J. Herpetol. Assoc. Afr.* 8, 7.

TAYLOR, P. (1971b). Observations on the egg masses of *Chiromantis xerampelina*. *J. Herpetol. Assoc. Afr.* 7, 14-18.

THORNLEY, A. L. (1971). Keratinization in the frog epidermis. Unpublished Ph.D. thesis, University of the Witwatersrand, Johannesburg.

VAN DIJK, D. E. Anuran ecology in relation particularly to oviposition and development out of water. *Zool. Afr.* 6, 119-132.

VISSER, J. (1971). Hunting the eggs of the Ghost Frog. *Afr. wild Life* 25, 22-24.

WAGER, V. A. (1965). *The Frogs of South Africa*. Cape Town, Purnell.

WAGER, V. A. (n.d.) *The Frogs that Inhabit the Wildlife Sanctuaries of Natal*. Natal Society for the Preservation of Wild Life.

WELLS, K. D. (1977). The social behaviour of anuran amphibians. *Anim. Behav.* 25, 666-693.

WHITNEY, C. L. and KREBS, J. R. (1975). Mate selection in Pacific Tree Frogs. *Nature, (Lond.)* 255, 325-326.

WILSON, E. O. (1975). *Sociobiology: The New Synthesis.* Cambridge, Harvard University Press.

INDEX

Bold type denotes pages on which full treatment of genera and species occurs.